DISCRIMINATING AGAINST DISCRIMINATION

DISCRIMINATING AGAINST DISCRIMINATION

Preferential Admissions and the *DeFunis* Case

ROBERT M. O'NEIL

INDIANA UNIVERSITY PRESS

BLOOMINGTON   LONDON

Library of Congress Cataloging in Publication Data
O'Neil, Robert M
Discriminating against discrimination.
Bibliography
Includes index.
1. Universities and colleges—United States—
Admission. 2. Discrimination in education—Law and
legislation—United States. 3. DeFunis, Marco.
4. Odegaard, Charles Edwin, 1911– I. Title.
KF4155.O5   344'.73'0798   75-3888
ISBN 0-253-31800-9   1 2 3 4 5 80 79 78 77 76

To Miriam and Alex Elson

CONTENTS

PREFACE

The origin of this book long predates the filing of the lawsuit which is its subject. As early as 1968, and surely by the spring of 1970, it was clear that the question of preferential admissions would soon reach the courts, even though no cases were yet pending. The clearest indication of that prospect was the comment of then Vice President Spiro Agnew when he read of the University of Michigan's agreement to increase its black enrollment to ten percent. The commitment clearly implied that Michigan would give preference to black applicants in order to reach its goal. That, said Agnew, is "some strange madness." In order to meet the goal—which he called a quota— "some better prepared student is denied entrance." Even though there may have been discrimination in the past, Agnew charged, "it just does not make sense to atone by discriminating against and depriving someone else."

In this sector of public life (if not in others) Agnew's comments were prophetic. During the next year several lawsuits were filed by white applicants who felt they had been rejected, despite better qualifications, by institutions that gave preference to minority group members. Clearly this issue would eventually reach the United States Supreme Court; the only question was which case would provide the initial testing ground. The lucky plaintiff turned out to be Marco DeFunis, Jr., about whom we will learn more in the early chapters. While his case was working its way up through the courts, and after the Supreme Court declined to decide it, other suits were filed and many are now pending throughout the country. Obviously there will have to be a clear, definitive decision on the constitutionality of preferential admissions before very long. Colleges and universities are trying to do the best they can in the current limbo, but guidance from the courts is badly needed and will continue to be sought.

Preferential admissions has been a deeply divisive issue within the academic community as well as in the courts. Also, no other public policy question has so seriously perplexed the liberal Jewish scholarly and professional community. Few persons of conscience question the past deprivation of minority groups, or their exclusion from the benefits of higher education; the controversy relates to the fairness and lawfulness of remedies for that condition. Everyone wishes it were possible to help one group, and ameliorate the injustices of the past, without disadvantaging other groups and creating new injustices. The critical issue—one of both law and public policy—is whether preferential admission meets that objective.

This book is not simply an abstract essay about a fascinating legal controversy. While it does not always so indicate, it is written from the perspective of a participant. During the later phases of the *DeFunis* litigation, I was Chairman of the Council on Legal Education Opportunity, the major national organization formed to enhance opportunities for minority persons to study and practice law. The dramatic expansion in minority law school enrollments in the late 1960s and early 70s had been partly the result of preferential admission policies, so CLEO had a direct and substantial interest in the *DeFunis* case. Both in the Washington Supreme Court and the United States Supreme Court I wrote and filed a brief for CLEO as amicus curiae. As a member of the CLEO Council I spent many hours discussing both the philosophical and practical implications of preferential admissions and the litigation over its constitutionality. From this brief account, my own bias on the policy question should be apparent— though I trust it has not impaired the discussion of the legal and constitutional issues.

My understanding of these matters has been greatly enhanced by close association with two executive directors of CLEO. Dr. Melvin D. Kennedy, formerly head of the History Department at Morehouse College, was the first director and in all ways the founder of CLEO. From him I learned a very great deal about the educational needs and opportunities of minority students, and the critical importance of such a program. His successor, Professor Michael J. Moorhead of the Howard University law faculty, has continued this educational process in later years. Discussions with both these colleagues have played a major part in forming the views set forth in this book.

This volume would not have seen the light of day had it not been for the patient and perceptive hand of Mrs. Barbara Holub, who not only typed the manuscript but read it carefully as she went and offered many helpful comments and suggestions. Her capacity to concentrate on this project, despite the cares and pressures of a busy administrative office, were ensured by my assistant, Mrs. Marie Ludeke, who somehow managed to keep matters on an even keel.

Most important, my wife (and sometime co-author) Karen Elson O'Neil, made countless contributions to this book. She read every word of it at least once very carefully, and much of it more than once. Where she did not like the original version or felt it could be improved, she pressed for change—always successfully. Beyond this ongoing involvement in the editorial process, she continued to believe that what was being said was important and sound. Her convictions about justice and equality have strengthened and enriched my own. In this sense it is a joint work, although it bears only one name.

Cincinnati, Ohio   ROBERT M. O'NEIL
July 1975

DISCRIMINATING AGAINST DISCRIMINATION

CHAPTER ONE
MARCO DE FUNIS
GOES TO COURT

In late September 1971, a trial judge ordered the University of Washington to admit an applicant who had been rejected earlier in the year. The student, Marco DeFunis, Jr., had made a respectable academic record as an undergraduate at the university. He and his parents had been lifelong residents of the state of Washington. Although he was accepted by four other law schools in neighboring states (including the University of Oregon), he preferred to remain in Seattle for his legal education. He had applied to the University of Washington Law School the year before, but was turned down. In order to improve his chances the next year, he took some graduate courses in political science. When he was rejected the second time around, despite A's in these courses, DeFunis sued the university to gain admission. This time he succeeded.

The national press does not typically report decisions of state trial courts. In the aftermath of the turbulent period of campus disorder that was just coming to a close in 1971, suits by students against colleges were hardly unusual. But the case of Mr. DeFunis was clearly newsworthy for quite different reasons. It represented the first court decision on the legality of preferential admission of minority group students (some called it "reverse discrimination"). Such a test case had been expected for some time—indeed was already overdue.

Admissions officers began to be concerned about the severe underrepresentation of black, Spanish-speaking, and American Indian students on their campuses in the mid-1960s. The death of Martin Luther King sharply intensified the pressure to admit more minority

3

students. Many colleges and universities developed special recruitment programs, scholarships, and supplemental courses to attract blacks and chicanos to traditionally white-Anglo campuses. Since many of these students were poorly prepared and scored less well on standardized entrance tests than did middle class whites, their admission often required special consideration—by changing the mix of factors in the admission decision, or by creating a special "track" with lower requirements.

While the precise extent of preferential admissions was never known, it was clear that more minority applicants were getting into college and graduate schools than ever before. Nonwhite students were suddenly more visible—sometimes (as in the 1969 *Life* magazine cover picture of militant armed blacks occupying the student union at Cornell) in ways that frightened or offended white parents and students. At the same time, the overall demand for higher education pushed up regular admission standards quite rapidly in the late 1960s. For reasons quite unrelated to preferential minority programs, white-Anglo students found it harder and harder to get into selective universities and particularly into such high-demand professional programs as law and medicine.

By 1970 preferential minority programs had become a target of both educational and political controversy. Vice President Spiro Agnew gave a major speech on this theme in April 1970—just after he learned about the University of Michigan's agreement to work toward ten percent black enrollment. Agnew called preferential policies "some strange madness" which colleges and universities should renounce by resisting the demands of minority students:

> For each youth unprepared for college curriculum who is brought
> in under a quota system, some better-prepared student is denied
> entrance. Admitting the obligation to compensate for past
> deprivation and discrimination, it just does not make sense to atone
> by discriminating against and depriving someone else.

Agnew was not alone in perceiving the political potential of this issue. A Polish-American congressman from Chicago, representing a white constituency that was also underrepresented in higher education, charged that "many who are now in the forefront of leading the rioting and the unrest in our universities are the very people that have been admitted into these universities at lower standards." There were other less strident but consonant voices as the white-Anglo community began to feel that preference for minorities might somehow jeopardize their own educational aspirations.

When an issue becomes this divisive and potentially explosive, it is almost certain to end up in court. (Alexis de Tocqueville, the French critic who wrote about the United States in the 1840s, remarked that Americans even then had a unique penchant for taking political conflicts and issues into the courts.) Indeed, several suits had been brought to test the legality of racial and ethnic preferences before the University of Washington rejected Mr. DeFunis. But the other cases had become bogged down in procedural details. As of the late summer of 1971, there still was no court decision resolving the constitutionality of a practice that had already become extensive enough to draw the Vice President's barbs and the concerns of several white ethnic organizations. Thus the time was ripe for a new test case at just the moment Marco DeFunis received his second rejection notice.

It is ironic that DeFunis' case was to be the first substantial review of preferential admissions. Like many plaintiffs in major test cases, his personal goal was much narrower than the setting of a new constitutional precedent. Quite simply, he wanted to get into law school, and he believed that he had been wrongfully rejected for reasons that had little or nothing to do with the minority program. When he had exhausted all other channels, including several appeals to University of Washington officials, he took his case to the courts as a last resort. Had it been possible for him to be admitted without the massive publicity that has given him national notoriety, Marco DeFunis would undoubtedly have preferred that route. But because his case was the first occasion to explore major constitutional issues, there was simply no way to avoid the publicity or the controversy that ensued.

Had a student with DeFunis' record—a high B average and

election to Phi Beta Kappa—applied to the University of Washington Law School in the early or even mid-1960s, his acceptance would have been nearly automatic. But a great many bright and able students had now found doors to graduate professional programs closing as a result of the sheer increase in the demand for admission. The number of applications to the Washington law school more than doubled from 1968 to 1971, and in the last of those three years rose from about 1,000 to over 1,600. Only about 20% of all who applied could be accepted. The other four fifths—the vast majority of whom were quite competent to do law school work and would make respectable attorneys— were rejected. (Actually the size of the entering class would be only about 10% of the number of 1971 applicants. Admissions officers know from experience that many who are admitted will choose to go elsewhere, so they generally admit about twice the number they need to make up a freshman class.)

Even these figures do not reveal the full impact of the rising odds. During this period the University of Washington had become increasingly a national institution, and was now attracting to its professional schools top students from all over the country. For decades (except on the athletic field) the University of Washington was overshadowed by its illustrious Pacific coast sisters, Berkeley, Stanford, and UCLA. Even Oregon and Southern Cal were better known in eastern educational circles. Humanists and historians knew about Vernon L. Parrington, the eminent literary critic of the 1920s and 1930s, but did not readily connect him with Washington or its university. Outside the discipline, few people knew that the first institute for Oriental studies was founded in Seattle during World War I. Even today, most people do not know that the University of Washington now ranks second (behind MIT) in receipt of federal research and development funds. The university has been, in short, a sleeping giant of higher education—its professional programs were on the verge of national eminence until just about the time Marco DeFunis received his baccalaureate degree from a still predominantly regional undergraduate division. As the law and medical schools increasingly drew a national clientele, the admission prospects for average—even outstanding—Washingtonians diminished faster than the bare numbers would suggest. (Californians and to some extent Oregonians, like Coloradans and Vermonters, long ago perceived the attractiveness of their state universities to out-of-state students. Washington was "discovered" somewhat later, and had not yet taken comparable steps to restrict nonresident access.)

The law school application boom at the University of Washington was a microcosm of the national pattern. Between the late 1950s and the early 1970s, the number of persons taking the Law School Admission Test increased nearly tenfold. Meanwhile the actual number of freshman slots in approved schools barely doubled during the 1960s. Even though not all persons who took the law test applied for admission, it was clear that the number of students anxious to study law far exceeded the number of places available to them. Modest expansion of established law schools and the opening of a number of new schools—including some marginal, unaccredited institutions of a dubious character—did not approach the demand. Many applicants were thus, like DeFunis, turned away at the gates. (By the late 1960s, the University of California at Berkeley was rejecting for law study more Harvard magna cum laude graduates than it could accept.)

Why the sudden surge of interest in law and law schools? In part the rising demand for legal education resulted simply from the sharp increase in the number of graduating seniors; this, after all, was the final phase of the post–World War II baby boom, and swelled all graduate schools to some degree, as it had impacted undergraduate institutions several years earlier. But there were special forces pulling applicants to law school. A generation of students who were more idealistic and more activist than their predecessors perceived the law as a way to effect social change, and to bring greater justice to a governmental system that seemed fraught with injustice. Especially for students who had had some personal contact with perceived injustice—at the end of a policeman's club during a campus sit-in or on a civil rights march—the call of law practice was especially compelling. Meanwhile, the new opportunities for "relevant" community law practice created by the Office of Economic Opportunity and by major foundation support promised career outlets for the activists of the late 1960s. As the legal education consultant to the American Bar Association observed after reviewing the reasons for the dramatic increase in law school applications:

> Many young people have come to believe that law is where the action is; they want to express in their practice of their profession their social concern. They want to work within the system for orderly change.

Other factors reinforced this general trend. Law was becoming increasingly attractive to women, who were either totally excluded (as at the Harvard Law School until 1948) or at least discouraged from pursuing legal education. In 1963, there had been a token 1,883 women (out of nearly 50,000 students) in accredited law schools. A decade later that figure had risen to 16,760, and women constituted nearly one sixth of all law students.

Many students turned to law school during this period as much for negative as positive reasons. Traditionally parallel or alternative career paths looked less attractive at just about the time the pull of the law intensified. The fields of engineering and public school teaching were already glutted. Opportunities for college teaching and research were also drying up—not only in the natural and physical sciences, which had been overbuilt in the post-Sputnik area through federal support, but also in the social sciences and humanities. Across all fields, the need for college professors was leveling off for precisely the reason that demand for graduate school increased: the products of the "baby boom" were finishing college, and the number of regular full-time undergraduates was starting to decline. Many who might have become college professors in earlier times now turned to law, not only because they wanted to change institutions rather than studying them, but also because academic careers were simply no longer available as they had been earlier. For a variety of reasons—all converging at about the same time—the number of college seniors applying to law school grew in almost frightening proportions.

Marco DeFunis' experience as a law school applicant may be

easier to understand in this context. Since he had made Phi Beta Kappa—the coveted top ten percent of his undergraduate class—he quite naturally assumed that a place would await him at the School of Law. He had not counted on the dramatic rise in the volume of applications—nearly tripled during the time he was in college—or the growing attractiveness of his university to the very top students from other states. There was, however, another complication. Standardized examinations were apparently not Mr. DeFunis' forte. When he first took the Law School Admission Test, he received a mediocre 512. This score placed him around the middle of all those taking the test, and far below where one would expect a Washington Phi Beta Kappa to rank. Two months later he took the test again, and this time scored 566—better but still well below the top bracket. About this time (the middle of his senior year in college) he was advised by the Associate Dean of the Law School that his chances might improve if he waited a year. Thus he decided to enroll in the graduate program in political science, his undergraduate major. During the next year he did A work in all but one of his courses (where he took an incomplete), worked at an off campus job between twenty and forty hours a week, listened to classical music, taught Sunday School, and waited for the next law school application cycle.

In the fall of 1970 DeFunis again took the Law School Admission Test, and this time earned a 668, a score which would place him in the top 7% of all persons taking the test. He did not, however, get full credit for this much improved score. What law schools do in such a case is to average the results of all testings, on the theory that simple familiarity with the test format is bound to improve an individual's performance. The composite LSAT score was then worked in with DeFunis' undergraduate grades, according to a rather complex formula, to project a probable first year grade point average (PFYA). (The formula for each law school's PFYA is actually developed by the Educational Testing Service on the basis of information supplied by the school, and thus reflects a stylized mix of ingredients. The applicants' PFYA's are then reported back to the law school, which uses them in making admissions decisions.)

DeFunis' projected or predicted first year average was 76.23—a figure which left no doubt that he should do reasonably well if admitted, but which was well below the top of the applicant group. A Law School Admissions Committee of five faculty members and two students reviewed applications with PFYA's above 77 as they came in, and early favorable decisions were reached in most such cases. At the other end of the scale, applicants whose predicted averages were below 74.5 were either rejected outright by the chairman of the admission committee, or (if the person showed special promise) placed in a group for later review by the full committee. There were two exceptions to this procedure at the lower end of the scale. Students who had been previously admitted but were unable to enter or were forced to withdraw because of military service, were allowed to reenroll immediately after completion of their tour of duty—even though the intervening change in admission standards would otherwise have closed them out. The second exception related to members of minority groups—blacks, chicanos or Mexican-Americans, American Indians, and Philippine Americans. Applicants from these ethnic groups were considered by the full committee, after being individually reviewed through a special procedure. In appraising these files, less weight was given to the PFYA than for regular applicants. The potential of minority students was judged on the basis of broader and more flexible criteria. The law school had set as a goal a reasonable representation of qualified minority students, and thus determined to accept some nonwhites who would not have been admitted if judged solely on the basis of their paper records. (In fact, of all minority applicants for the class entering in the fall of 1971, only one would have been admitted on a strictly numerical basis.) Essentially, the process compared minority applicants to one another, rather than to white-Anglo applicants. On this basis, some were admitted and others were placed on the waiting list for possible future consideration.

Most of the applicants, obviously, were not members of minority groups. The largest group had PFYA's between 74.5 and 76.99; their applications were accumulated and held until the deadline had passed. DeFunis, with a 76.23, was among this group. The committee's review of these "close cases" in the middle range involved a variety of factors, going well beyond test scores and undergraduate grades. The process was described in the "Guide for Applicants" as follows:

> We gauged the potential for outstanding performance in law school not only from the existence of high test scores and grade point averages, but also from careful analysis of recommendations, the quality of work in difficult analytical seminars, courses, and writing programs, the academic standards of the school attended by the applicant, the applicant's graduate work (if any), and the nature of the applicant's employment (if any), since graduation.
>
> An applicant's ability to make significant contributions to law school classes and the community at large was assessed from such factors as his extracurricular and community activities, employment, and general background.
>
> We gave no preference to, but did not discriminate against, either Washington residents or women in making our determinations. An applicant's racial or ethnic background was considered as one factor in our general attempt to convert formal credentials into realistic predictions.*

As a result of this process, admission letters were initially sent to some 200 applicants, from whom a class of about 150 was anticipated. Against the possibility of unusually high attrition, the committee placed approximately 155 additional applicants on a waiting list, divided into four quartiles. The balance of the applicants were then notified that they had been rejected. While DeFunis was not among those initially admitted in May, neither was he rejected. He was placed on the waiting list, in the fourth or lowest quartile.

Around this time DeFunis made contact with Josef Diamond, a Seattle attorney, through a junior member of Diamond's law firm who had been a friend and fraternity brother. Early in June, Diamond formally requested the law school to reconsider his client's status, and supported the request with a letter from a physician which offered a medical explanation for DeFunis' poor performance on the first

*Brief of Respondents, *DeFunis* v. *Odegaard*, 416 U.S. 312 (1974).

LSAT. The admissions committee met on this request several days later but made no change in DeFunis' ranking. On July 21 the committee met again and decided to admit an additional group from the first quarter of the waiting list. Since it now seemed certain that the bottom part of the waiting list need not be reached, DeFunis and others were notified of their rejection. This information reached the unsuccessful applicants on August 2, by letter from the Associate Dean.

In all, 275 persons had been offered admission to the first year class. Of these, 74 had lower PFYA's than DeFunis—36 minority students, 22 returning veterans, and 16 others judged by the committee as meritorious on other grounds. Twenty-nine applicants with predicted first year averages higher than DeFunis' had been rejected. The geographical distribution of the successful applicants was noteworthy: of the 275 persons offered admission, 127 were residents of other states. Eventually, however, only 32 nonresidents (21.6% of the entering class) actually enrolled. Only half the minority applicants admitted (18 out of 36) accepted the offer. Thus the rate of declination for nonresidents was substantially higher, and for minority students somewhat higher, than for the white-Anglo Washingtonians who made up the bulk of the applicants and of the eventual students.

Barely two weeks after the final rejection notices were sent, Diamond brought suit in the Superior Court of King County, asking that DeFunis be admitted to the law school and that he be awarded damages in the amount of $50,000. (The damage claim was dropped early in the proceedings.) By this time DeFunis had been admitted to no fewer than four other law schools—Gonzaga, Willamette, and the Universities of Oregon and Idaho. He could have attended either of the two neighboring state universities for the same tuition fees he would pay at home, as a result of an interstate compact designed to increase student mobility. The financial problem, however, was more complex. DeFunis was married, and his wife had a good job as a dental technician; the family had counted on her earnings to support the husband's legal education. Since there was no assurance of a comparable employment in such smaller communities as Moscow, Salem, Spokane, or Eugene, they did not consider educationally comparable options to be financially acceptable. DeFunis' father, a furniture salesman, apparently could offer only meager assistance; the son had, in fact, worked regularly all through undergraduate school even though he lived at home and paid relatively low tuition. Thus the suit seemed to provide DeFunis' last chance to attend law school: either he would stay in Seattle and study at home or he would not study law at all.

When the suit was filed, attorney Diamond had little if any information about the admissions process we have already reviewed. His complaint, in fact, barely mentioned minority students or programs. At one point it did allege that among the applicants chosen for the class of 1971 were "many candidates whose qualifications and credentials are much below the credentials and qualifications of the plaintiff. . . ." The full story about the nature and extent of the minority preferential program came out in response to a set of pretrial questions which Diamond sent to the attorneys for the University of Washington shortly after the suit was filed. One of the questions asked for a list of all persons admitted to and on the waiting list for the 1971 entering class, including an indication whether the person was a minority group member. The university supplied all the requested information. Its answers revealed that most of the minority applicants who were eventually admitted would have been turned down on the basis of strict numerical ranking by PFYA, and thus had received special consideration.

The focus of DeFunis' complaint was not *race* but *geography*. The principal contention was that the plaintiff was entitled to special consideration as a resident of the state of Washington. The argument ran as follows: A state university is supported by the taxpayers of the state. While such an institution may reasonably admit some residents of other states, it has a special duty to make room for all qualified local applicants, even if there are higher ranking or better qualified nonresidents seeking admission. There is, of course, a special irony to this argument in the present case. DeFunis, who has emerged as the most visible critic of preferential admission policies, began by seeking for himself precisely such a preference—albeit on the basis of residence rather than race. To give legal force to this plea for special treatment, Diamond cited Washington state laws and constitutional provisions which allegedly required the university to give first consideration to native sons and daughters.

The very day the complaint was filed, a Superior Court judge entered a temporary restraining order. This decree prevented the University of Washington from "selecting students for admission to the Law School . . . during the pendency of this action" and set a time for a full hearing on the allegations. Clearly this was a rather drastic measure, since it virtually froze the law school admission process until the case had been heard on the merits. (Since the selection of the entering class had been nearly completed by late August, the practical consequence was limited. If, however, the case had arisen earlier in the summer, such a court order could have crippled the internal operation of the university.) The intrusion was the more drastic because a temporary restraining order is issued against a defendant without notice to the party; the first news the university had about the decree came after the judge had made his preliminary decision. A court will use so extreme a measure only when it believes that legal interests or rights of the plaintiff require immediate preservation of the status quo—in this case, that no more applicants be admitted to the law school.

The hearing on the merits was originally scheduled for August 25, but the university needed additional time to gather the extensive material requested in Diamond's interrogatories. The university's response was submitted on September 13—less than two weeks after the receipt of the request, with the Labor Day weekend intervening. Nine days later the case came on for hearing before Judge Lloyd Shorett, a colleague of the judge who issued the restraining order. By this time the record was somewhat fuller; in addition to the university's response to the interrogatories and its answer to the complaint, there were depositions (sworn statements) from the Dean of the Law School and the faculty chairman of the admissions committee.

For Judge Shorett, the task of deciding the central issue of this case was an awesome and novel prospect. There was no constitutional precedent that offered much guidance; while the United States Supreme Court and many lower courts had decided hundreds of cases barring racial segregation in public schools, the issue here was the use of race in favor of, rather than against, minority groups. The case was either very simple or very hard—one could say either that the constitution was color blind and forbade all racial classification, or one could try to differentiate subtly between classifications that hurt and those that helped minorities. Judge Shorett took the easy road:

> It seems to me that the law school here wished to achieve greater minority representation and in accomplishing this gave preference to the members of some races. . . . Since no more than 150 applicants were to be admitted the admission of less qualified resulted in a denial of places to those otherwise qualified. The plaintiff and others in this group, have not in my opinion, been accorded the equal protection of the law guaranteed by the Fourteenth Amendment. . . . Policies of discrimination will inevitably lead to reprisals. In my opinion the only safe rule is to treat all races alike and I feel that is what is required under the equal protection clause.

The judge clearly recognized the vast implications of the case. "Counsel," he prefaced his judgment, "we all know that this case is of a type that will, and indeed should be, reviewed very quickly by the Supreme Court of the State. . . ." Indeed, it was widely rumored that Judge Shorett's personal sympathies lay on the other side, but that he decided as he did because had the case gone against DeFunis it might not have been appealed and the opportunity for a major constitutional decision would thus have been lost. Such speculation is, of course, impossible to verify. It seems highly questionable on several grounds, chiefly because a judge's oath of office compels him to decide cases in accordance with the law rather than because he hopes to get the issue before a higher court. Moreover, Diamond and his colleagues were by this time totally immersed in the case and committed to pressing the issue. One of Diamond's partners later told a reporter that they had been contacted by a number of other potential plaintiffs with similar claims, but "we discouraged them" awaiting the outcome of *DeFunis*.

With this investment in the case, it seems almost certain that Diamond would have carried the case to the state supreme court if he had lost the first round.

Two other facets of the trial court ruling deserve special comment. Judge Shorett was not impressed by the claim that DeFunis was entitled to special admission preference as a Washington resident and taxpayer. Nothing in state law limited out-of-state enrollment; in fact, the nonresident percentage had declined from 30% the previous year to 21.6% in 1971, largely as a result of increased nonresident tuition. Moreover, the court said, "many Washington students attend law schools in other states thus equalizing the load between the states." What might have been the situation if nonresidents had actually been *favored*—as is the case in many private colleges and a few public institutions seeking to attract a more diverse student body—that issue was not before the court.

The other feature of the trial court decision is more problematic. Recall that DeFunis was well down on the waiting list—in the fourth quartile, in fact. When the class was completed in early August, most applicants below the first quartile were told they would not be admitted. In short, there were many other nonminority applicants who had been ranked higher than DeFunis who might now like to take advantage of his suit. In theory Judge Shorett's decision applied to all of these other applicants—at least all white-Anglo applicants with PFYA's equal to or higher than that of the lowest-ranking preferentially admitted minority candidate. This would include nearly the entire applicant pool—perhaps as many as 1,200 additional persons. If even a fraction of that group could take advantage of the *DeFunis* ruling, the problems for the law school would quickly become unmanageable. Judge Shorett foreclosed such a prospect by holding that all the others had "slept on their rights" and were thus barred by the equitable doctrine of "laches" from taking advantage of DeFunis' triumph. Since none of the other rejected applicants had brought a similar suit, and since DeFunis had not sued for a "class" of persons, it was proper to confine relief to the single plaintiff.

Several weeks later, formal findings and conclusions of law were entered on the record. The university promptly appealed the decision to the Supreme Court of Washington. (In ordinary civil cases, one would usually go first to an intermediate court of appeals, but when a constitutional claim surfaces in the trial court a direct appeal to the state's highest court is permissible.) By this time, Marco DeFunis was well into his first month of law school, having been treated like a regular matriculant after Judge Shorett's oral decision.

The potential implications of the case were widely recognized by now. Not only had it been noted in the national press, but many organizations had sought to express their views to the Washington Supreme Court. A number of local and national groups and individuals submitted briefs as "amici curiae" or "friends of the court" in support of the university's position. Among these were the American Bar Association, the National Bar Association, the Association of American Law Schools, the Law School Admission Council (which administers the Law School Admission Test), the city of Seattle, the Washington State Bar, the American Civil Liberties Union, and several law student groups. Technically, none of these groups could appear directly in the case; the Washington Supreme Court had a quaint and curious rule that only lawyers admitted to practice in that court could appear as "friends of the court." This rule initially created some problems for national groups. It so happened that the treasurer of the American Bar Association was a practitioner in Chehalis, Washington, and was eager to speak for various legal organizations. Eventually he and the Washington state member of the ABA's House of Delegates filed a comprehensive brief—formally on behalf of two individual lawyers, but actually as spokesmen for national groups with hundreds of thousands of members. (Despite its full compliance with the court's rules, even this brief was not filed without opposition. Josef Diamond moved to strike this and many other briefs which reflected views of national organizations through Washington attorneys. He claimed that, while following the letter of the rule, these briefs violated its spirit by using local lawyers as "mouthpieces" for the forbidden views of out-of-state groups. The Washington justices, sensing the national import of the case, rejected this claim and ruled valid all amicus briefs that formally complied with its strictures.)

The case was set down for hearing on May 15, 1972. Battle lines were clearly drawn in the briefs and in the oral argument. The university, now the appellant, offered several lines of argument: First, it claimed that consideration of race for the purpose of benefiting rather than discriminating against minority groups was compatible with the equal protection clause of the Fourteenth Amendment. While the U.S. Supreme Court had forbidden many uses of race—for example, in the context of school segregation, and in one case involving the exclusion of black applicants from a state university law school—the Court had never held that the constitution is "color blind" for all purposes. Recently, in fact, there had been indications that race conscious remedies might be permitted and even required to overcome the effects of past discrimination and racial exclusion. Since the University of Washington was seeking to overcome an imbalance or underrepresentation of minority groups, its preferential policy fell squarely within this exception. Second, the university argued that the use of race in the law school admissions process was in no sense invidious discrimination, but was rather an attempt to meet in the only effective way a critical national problem—the shortage of minority group attorneys.

The brief and argument supporting DeFunis addressed two dimensions of preference, the one racial and the other residential. Since the Superior Court decision rested entirely on the racial issue, the brief sought to sustain the judgment by invoking a strict "color blindness" standard. Under this test, as the trial judge had held, *any* racial classification was a per se violation of the equal protection clause regardless of a benign purpose or effect. In the present case, moreover, a white-Anglo applicant was said to have been excluded on the basis of race; had he been a member of a preferred minority group he would not only have received special consideration but would almost certainly have been admitted. The *DeFunis* brief went on to argue that the university's admissions policies were unconstitutional because they lacked adequate standards and thus resulted in arbitrary and capricious judgments among applicants.

The case was under consideration for nearly a year after the oral argument. DeFunis, now in his second year and doing quite acceptable academic work despite having become something of a celebrity, was probably less concerned about the outcome than were educators and admissions officers around the country. Foundation officials and governmental agencies also became increasingly uneasy about the case. It was widely believed that some grants for minority students were delayed because of uncertainty about the legality of preferential programs. While a Washington state court decision would be final and binding only within that state, other states courts looked increasingly to Washington for guidance in this area. Olympia was not Olympus, to be sure, but it was fast becoming the center of national attention. Lawyers close to the scene tried to warn colleagues from other states that the Washington Supreme Court works slowly in constitutional cases. But few observers imagined it would take a whole year. The United States Supreme Court, by contrast, either decides a case within the term at which it is argued—October through June—or in rare instances sets the case down for reargument the following year.

When the decision in the university's favor actually did come down on March 8, 1973, it surprised observers on both sides. Even the university and its supporters had not expected either that the vote would be so clear (6–2) or that the support for the preferential admissions program would be so unequivocal. The opinion began by setting a constitutional standard that would be difficult for proponents of preference to meet: any racial classification (whether harmful or helpful to minorities) was constitutionally permissible only if it could be proven to serve a "compelling state interest." The court then went on to find that the university had in fact met this burden of proof. The court summarily rejected the trial court's "color blind" view of racial classifications after reviewing the U.S. Supreme Court's decisions on school segregation and employment. These cases had been concerned only with practices that harmed and not with preferences designed to help them. The university's admission policy designed to enhance minority group opportunities presented a totally different situation.

In order to find the requisite "compelling interest" the court took what is called "judicial notice" of the need for more blacks, chicanos, and Indians in the legal profession. Three elements gave the state interest its "compelling" quality: First, the university might properly seek to overcome the past effects of racial discrimination, even though no minority applicant had ever been barred in Washington (as in the South) by any exclusionary policy. "We see no reason," said the court, "why the state interest in eradicating the continuing effects of past discrimination is less merely because the law school itself may have previously been neutral in the matter." Second, "the state also has an overriding interest in providing all law students with a legal education that will adequately prepare them to deal with societal problems which will confront them upon graduation." This interest was heightened by the pivotal role of the legal profession in governmental and business decision-making.' Finally, the current shortage of minority lawyers and judges was itself a compelling reason for pursuing race conscious ameliorative steps—"If minorities are to live within the rule of law, they must enjoy equal representation within our legal system."

The court then touched lightly upon a further and potentially troublesome issue—whether race conscious admissions policies were essential to achieve these compelling interests or whether nonracial alternatives might suffice. The court simply declared, without elaboration, that racial imbalance in legal education "can only be corrected by providing legal education to those minority groups which have been previously deprived." There was theoretically a range of nonracial alternatives. In practice, however, they were unlikely to remedy the racial imbalance: "If the law school is forbidden from taking affirmative action, this underrepresentation may be perpetuated indefinitely"—apparently because mere "nondiscrimination" simply had not increased minority group representation in the past and, by itself, was unlikely to do so in the future.

Having thus disposed of the racial issue with surprising alacrity, the court then tackled the related claim that the whole law school admissions policy lacked constitutionally adequate standards to guide the allocation of a scarce resource among many applicants. Counsel for DeFunis had argued with some force that the law school was acting irrationally and arbitrarily in departing from strict numerical ranking of applicants. The court's response here too was unequivocal: Even without any special minority program, the admissions committee need not (indeed should not) have based its selection on purely mathematical rankings. Consideration of nonquantitative factors was appropriate and essential to the admissions process. Moreover, the court rejected "the assumption that a minority applicant is ipso facto 'less qualified' than a nonminority applicant who has a higher predicted first year average." Determination of "qualification" involved more than simply a comparison of paper records. There was no certainty that the potential contribution of a law student or attorney would correlate precisely or even closely with academic performance. The court cautioned: "Law school admissions need not become a game of numbers; the process should remain sensitive and flexible, with room for informed judgment in interpreting mechanical indicators."

There remained for brief disposition the claim that DeFunis should receive preference as a Washington native and taxpayer. Nothing in the constitution or laws of the state compelled the university to give any special breaks to residents as against out-of-staters. The legislature had in fact accorded certain benefits to Washingtonians— for example, by making them eligible for financial aid, and indirectly by charging much higher fees to nonresident students. But there was no authority for giving to resident applicants the very sort of preference that DeFunis claimed was illegal when it came to race or ethnicity.

Three majority justices added a brief concurring opinion on admissions matters. They simply wanted to take the occasion to point out "the desirability of more complete published standards for admission." Publication of such standards, they suggested, "would insure not only the complete fairness of the process, but also the appearance of fairness." This comment may have represented a mild slap on the law school's wrist.

Two justices dissented at length. They reviewed quite critically the process by which the student members of the admissions committee had been chosen—an issue that had been discussed nowhere else and did not seem central to the case. The dissenters fastened upon several comments by admissions committee members which seemed to reveal a taste for applicants with a background of activism and social commitment. Such comments would ordinarily not have come to the court's attention at all. They had, however, been made available in the trial court and remained in the record. James B. Wilson, the Washington Assistant Attorney General who represented the university and tried the case, explained later:

> The confidentiality accorded the admissions files by the law school was of no help in efforts to keep individual files out of evidence. Nor were objections sustained on the basis of irrelevancy on the theory that it would be improper for the court to probe the mental processes used by members of the committee in reaching their conclusions. Thus, the pencilled comments of student members of the committee on several files, including Mr. DeFunis', became a part of the trial record and a basis for the dissenters' claim that the procedure for determining admittees was arbitrary and capricious.

Despite later attempts to set the matter straight, considerable damage had been done by the rather free use of these internal comments to taint the whole admissions process.

The precise status of DeFunis himself was also thrown into limbo by the Washington decision. Technically he could have been dismissed from the law school at once, since the court decree under which he was admitted had now been overturned. But such an action would have made the case moot, and would have prevented the resolution of issues that obviously went well beyond the state of Washington. DeFunis and his lawyer were also anxious to keep the case alive for more immediate and personal reasons. They promptly petitioned Mr. Justice Douglas to issue an order maintaining the status quo while the case was being appealed to the United States Supreme Court. Such an order was issued, and served to keep the case alive. As DeFunis had entered law school under Judge Shorett's order, he now remained in school—almost to the conclusion of the case—under Justice Douglas' stay.

The state supreme court decision provides a good opportunity to appraise the relative positions of the parties. Both DeFunis and the university had gained something, but each had also lost in the process. There were some beneficial side effects of the *case,* if not so much of the *decision.* In late 1973 the University of Washington law faculty adopted a new and detailed set of admissions policies—a model for other law schools to follow. Published policies now spelled out clearly both the rationale for and the appropriate degree of departure from mathematical criteria in judging minority applications. Because of the troublesome "advice" given to DeFunis in the spring of 1970 (to wait a year and then apply again), administrators and faculty became more reluctant to say anything that might falsely raise the hopes of anxious applicants. The degree of accountability of everyone involved in the admissions process was thus enhanced.

Yet the university's victory in the state courts was also a pyrrhic one. We have already noted the damage done by the dissenting judges' disclosure of pencilled comments on confidential admissions files. As a result of the merciless scrutiny to which the admissions process had been subjected, the law school decided in the fall of 1973 to cut back sharply the student role. The lack of input impaired student confidence in the process, and apparently led to charges that women applicants were not being fairly judged. A new suit challenging the admissions process on grounds of sex was threatened for a time but never materialized. Another suit did reach the courts during the year, and produced an order that the University of Washington law faculty must henceforth make public all meetings involving admissions and many other vital matters. (As though to add insult to injury, the court commented that the faculty's consistent past violation of the open meeting law could be excused because it had acted in good faith on the advice of the Attorney General's office!)

The most pervasive and most serious consequence of the *DeFunis* suit is also the hardest to define. There had been various signs of a hardening of the admissions process since the early stages of the case. The new admissions policies, in the Dean's words, required "more strict adherence to rank order of PFYA's except where it is felt that the numbers wouldn't predict accurately." Some flexibility remained, but significantly diminished. The reluctance of faculty and administrators to counsel applicants as freely as they would once have done, the diminution of the student role in admissions decisions, heightened tensions and strained relations within the faculty—all these results provide the clearest evidence of the deeply divisive effect of the *DeFunis* case.

For Marco DeFunis, too, it was a mixed experience. He was still in law school and now within sight of the coveted Juris Doctor degree, even though the state's highest court had rejected his constitutional claims. His status was truly ironic. Far from being the *victim* of preferential minority admissions, he was in fact a major *beneficiary:* Had there been no special minority program, DeFunis would never have been admitted, since there were many more whites above him on the waiting list than the number of places given to preferred minorities. Thus it was only the existence of the preferential program, and the trial court decision striking it down, that put DeFunis in the law school of his choice.

Yet for DeFunis, too, the taste of victory was partly soured. For one thing, the drawn out litigation was expensive. While Diamond and his firm had waived all *professional* fees, they expected DeFunis to bear printing, filing, and other out-of-pocket costs, which had already reached some $10,000. This figure exceeded by far the total cost of attending law school in Oregon or Idaho. Interpersonal relations, too, had been complicated by the notoriety which the lawsuit brought to DeFunis. On several occasions in the law library he encountered a group of black students who pointed him out as the "house bigot" and promptly got up and left. Such experiences quite likely imposed a higher price than DeFunis ever expected he would have to pay for seeking the aid of the courts to get him into law school. About his inner personal feelings, one can only speculate. When asked whether he had regrets or second thoughts about bringing the suit, DeFunis says simply, "That's my secret."

CHAPTER TWO
THE SUPREME COURT DECIDES NOT TO DECIDE

Whichever way the Washington Supreme Court had decided, the case would certainly be taken to the United States Supreme Court. Already the word "DeFunis" had come to symbolize preferential admissions, reverse discrimination, and, in the minds of many, the total mounting conflict between racial minorities and white ethnic groups. "It's been notorious from the beginning," Washington Assistant Attorney General James Wilson later said of the case. Thus it was no surprise when Josef Diamond filed his final appeal with the clerk of the Supreme Court.

There were two obvious possible dispositions. In view of the clear significance of the issues it presented, the Supreme Court might well have agreed to review the case and reach a decision on the merits. While the number of students affected by preferential admissions was not known, most major law schools, and graduate schools in other fields, did consider race or ethnic status in the admissions process. Thus the potential reach of a decision either way was vast, and could affect many millions of dollars of financial aid funds as well as the fates of many thousands of students and the policies of hundreds of colleges and universities.

On the other hand, it seemed more likely that the Court would decline to review the case on its merits. Each year more than six thousand cases reach the highest Court. While many of these are frivolous or repetitive appeals in criminal cases, at least two thousand petitions present serious and substantial questions. The Court can only review and decide merits on about 150 of these cases each term.

Clearly it cannot reverse every judgment of a lower court that looks erroneous. (Many years ago, when the docket was about one-third of its present size, Justice Felix Frankfurter asked a young lawyer from Boston why he had not been to the Court recently. The young man replied, "I've tried, Mr. Justice, but you even refused my petition last month, when I thought I had a very strong case." The Justice recalled the case and agreed: "You were clearly right, of course, and the decision below was wrong, but the case just wasn't important enough.")

Apart from the high numerical odds against review of any particular decision, there were several other constraints in *DeFunis*. This was the first case in its field. Usually the Court waits until the lower courts have worked over the issue for some time, unless (as in the Pentagon papers or the Nixon tapes case) there is a critical need for an early decision. Moreover, the Washington Supreme Court opinion in *DeFunis* was a strong and well-reasoned one; if the Supreme Court were inclined to affirm, there would be little point in taking the case just to reiterate the same points. Finally, two procedural barriers might have reduced the Court's interest in the case: the fact, on one hand, that DeFunis was challenging a preferential program that really had not caused his own rejection (since he was well down on the waiting list); and the prospect that he might graduate before the Court could decide the case, since the Washington court had taken so long to reach its decisions. Thus, on balance, many observers felt the Court probably would not take the case.

What the Court actually did was to adopt neither expected approach but instead to pursue a third and quite improbable course. The justices initially agreed to hear the case, invited briefs, and listened to two hours of oral argument, but then announced late in the spring that DeFunis' imminent graduation made the case technically "moot." Even though something might still happen to prevent the awarding of the Juris Doctor degree, the university had agreed that it would allow DeFunis to finish the semester whichever way the Court decided. Thus, a bare majority (5–4) of the justices concluded there was really nothing left for them to decide. Four members of the

Court dissented vigorously; the liberal bloc of Brennan, Douglas, and Marshall, plus Justice White, felt that the refusal to decide the case did a serious disservice to all who sought guidance in this troubled area of the law. We will review the implications of that dissent a bit later. First we must try to understand how the Court could back away after having decided to resolve the merits of preferential admissions.

Before appraising the decision, it is worth studying the case as an example of a major constitutional test suit. The massive briefs by the two parties served to apprise the Court of virtually all the major constitutional and policy issues. Yet an additional thirty or more briefs were eventually received from more than fifty organizations and groups appearing as amici curiae or friends of the Court. The *DeFunis* case produced strange bedfellows among these friends of the Court. The National Association of Manufacturers and the AFL-CIO filed —perhaps for the first time—on the same side (opposing racial preference). Meanwhile, national Jewish organizations that had stood together through the civil rights cases of the 1950s and 1960s now divided sharply—the American Jewish Congress, the American Jewish Committee, and the Anti-Defamation League of B'nai B'rith supported DeFunis, while the Union of American Hebrew Congregations and the National Council of Jewish Women took the opposing point of view. (The fact that DeFunis was himself Jewish, although widely known by this time, probably played no part in this split. The same division would have occurred regardless of the plaintiff's ethnic status.)

Certain minority student organizations and civil rights groups were predictably on the university's side of the case. Less predictable was the commitment of such major amici curiae as the state of Ohio, the Association of American Law Schools, the Association of American Medical Colleges, a group of sixty law school deans, the United Steel Workers, the American Civil Liberties Union, and Harvard University. (The Harvard brief was particularly impressive. Its principal author was Archibald Cox, who had turned to the legality of preferential admissions very soon after he had been discharged by President Nixon as Special Watergate Prosecutor.)

Yet even on the university's side of the case there was some minor falling out among "friends." Where a number of legal organizations (the American Bar Association, the National Bar Association, the Law School Admission Council, and the Council on Legal Education Opportunity) had collaborated on a single brief in the Washington Supreme Court, each group now felt compelled to file a statement of its own distinctive views. (The refinement of positions was not the only cause of this fragmentation. In the interim, the ABA passed a new rule forbidding co-sponsorship of a brief with anyone else. Undoubtedly, too, some groups that had been willing to share the credit in the lower court felt they must have their own forum when the case reached this highest level.) Whatever the reason, the array of briefs was large and diverse.

Apart from giving vent to the views of an organization, do friends of the Court briefs really serve any useful function? Of course the secrecy by which the Supreme Court works permits little insight into the role of amicus briefs. But there are several notable examples of the impact they may have. In 1939, the Supreme Court had before it a case involving the validity of a federal district court pre-trial discussion order. This was the first such case under the new rules of civil procedure. The recalcitrant party was sentenced to jail, and he promptly appealed. The case went all the way to the Supreme Court before a former Solicitor General of the United States noticed for the first time that the new rules did not include imprisonment as a sanction for noncompliance. He so advised in a letter to the Supreme Court and the case was decided accordingly. This was truly a "friend of the Court" since he was helping the justices rather than supporting either party.

There are other examples of the seeming impact of amici curiae. When the Court held in 1961 that evidence obtained through illegal searches could no longer be admitted in any criminal trial, this was a bombshell. The lower courts and the parties had been concerned only with a substantive issue, the validity of the state obscenity law. One of the amici did, however, suggest that the case would be a good vehicle in which to extend the exclusionary rule to the state courts if the justices were inclined to do so. While the result might well have been the same without this suggestion, the forethought of at least one amicus must have been reassuring to the justices.

Another example of the amicus role comes from the sit-in cases of the early 1960s. For several years, civil rights groups pressed the Court to sustain the rights of demonstrators on the broadest possible grounds. While the Court had decided to reverse the convictions of blacks who had protested segregation at lunch counters and other public places, only Justice Douglas seemed ready to make sweeping pronouncements about demonstrators' rights. What was obviously needed was a narrow basis on which the convictions could be reversed without deciding the ultimate constitutional issue. It was the briefs of the Solicitor General of the United States, amicus curiae, which supplied precisely that narrow ground in 1963 and again in 1964. Perhaps here too the Court could have found such a *ratio decidendi* on its own, but there is no doubt that its work was facilitated by the government's timely and friendly participation.

Against this background, it is puzzling that the United States did *not* file a brief in the *DeFunis* case. Surely there was no lack of awareness in Washington agencies of the pendency of the case or its importance. The Equal Employment Opportunity Commission actually sought at one point to file a brief which would have supported preferential admissions. Solicitor General Robert Bork (who administered the *coup de grâce* to Messrs. Cox and Richardson) wrote to the Clerk of the Supreme Court urging that the brief be disregarded since its filing had not been authorized. The Supreme Court acceded and did reject the brief. Bork himself apparently wished to file a brief on the other side. Meanwhile, the Civil Service Commission was reportedly as anxious to file a brief on one side as the EEOC had been to file on the other; HEW would like to have been able to support the university.

As the cross-pressures mounted, a decision was made in the White House that because the case was simply too hot to handle, the government must remain officially neutral. Solicitor General Bork so advised the Court. The University of Washington, which was under intense scrutiny for its affirmative action program, felt betrayed by the government's silence. "It seems," remarked James Wilson, "that the U. S. Government ought to be on our side."

The briefs afforded an opportunity for parties and others interested in the case to tell the Court virtually everything they wanted to say about the case. But briefs are only the prelude to the crucial oral argument. A case is rarely decided until after the argument, and preliminary impressions of the justices can be profoundly altered by appearance of counsel before the bench. So critical is the argument, in fact, that some justices used to refuse to read the briefs in advance so they could receive them with a completely open mind. Felix Frankfurter was the last justice to follow that practice; today every member of the Court will typically study at least the briefs of the parties (if not all the amici) before the argument. The questioning often follows the briefs rather closely.

The oral argument of the *DeFunis* case was a major event in legal circles. A Harvard undergraduate law class rode an overnight bus to Washington and lined up on the steps of the Supreme Court at 4:30 A.M. to get seats in the courtroom. Many who came later could not see or hear the argument; the corridors as well as the chamber itself were crowded to capacity. After the arguments, lawyers who had supported preferential admission in the case were invited by the dean and minority students at Georgetown Law School to a reception and symposium in the school's faculty lounge. The event clearly had a rather festive air.

Those who did witness the argument firsthand felt it was worth the wait. Washington's Attorney General, Slade Gorton, had taken the case over from Wilson and had mastered a complex record in a remarkably short time. (During the oral argument and on a television debate two weeks later he recalled unfailingly such technical data as the attrition figures for minority and nonminority students in DeFunis' class.) The atmosphere in the courtroom was understandably tense, for the issues were deeply divisive. Mr. Justice Marshall (whose position on the merits could be predicted) at one point posed a question to Diamond. About the same time a question came from the other end of the bench, and Diamond appeared to ignore Marshall. Later the lawyer looked in Marshall's direction again and asked the justice to restate the question. Marshall, seemingly piqued, responded, "You have my permission to forget it." But there were some lighter moments as well. Eventually Chief Justice Burger, reflecting on his own legal career and that of other members of the Court, asked Gorton whether any study had been done "to determine whether grades had a direct correlation with success and effectiveness in the practice of law." Gorton replied that the quantitative measures "predict nothing about the contribution you will make to the bar, the contribution you will make to the law school, how much income you will make in the bar or what kind of legal career you will seek." The answer evoked mild laughter and provided relief.

Questions from the bench seldom reveal the sympathies or leanings of the questioner. Justice Blackmun (who would presumably oppose preferential admissions) asked Diamond whether he would condone a program giving preferential admission to medical school applicants who were committed to practicing in rural areas. Diamond conceded that "at that level I think an affirmative action program is good, valid, and I'm all for it." On the other hand, Justice Douglas (whose earlier views would suggest sympathy for preferential admissions) asked Gorton whether he was urging a policy similar to that of the Indian constitution, which set aside a fixed number of seats for the untouchables. Gorton replied, not altogether responsively, that test scores and grades "are not invariable and totally accurate predictions of success, nor do they solve the problem of ending the effects of racial discrimination."

Although the oral arguments gave no clear indication of any justice's views, there were a few straws in the wind. Anthony Lewis, who had once covered the Supreme Court for the *New York Times,* was most struck by a question from Justice Lewis Powell, a moderate conservative on most issues. Powell asked Diamond whether "formal grades are the only thing that can be considered" in law school admission—whether other matters such as employment records and personal recommendations were proper factors. Diamond responded that numerical predictors were not the sole desiderata. Lewis observed in a column several days after the argument: "The exchange suggests that the Court is not going to clamp any 'iron rule' on university admissions, eliminating discretion to seek varied student bodies. On the other hand, it is probably safe to predict that the Court will not approve a frank quota system—one in which all admissions are based on grades except for a disadvantaged group."

Almost two months to the day later, on April 23, 1974, the unexpected happened: the Supreme Court announced that the case was moot and was therefore being dismissed. The possibility of mootness had earlier occurred to many observers. In fact, about a month before it decided to hear the case, the Supreme Court asked for the views of both parties on this very issue. Diamond and Wilson agreed that the case was not moot. Although DeFunis was still in law school, he remained there under court order—first that of the trial court, later the decree of Mr. Justice Douglas—and his status was thus uncertain. While the university argued that the appeal should be *dismissed,* they did so on the merits and not on ground of mootness. Diamond, meanwhile, had more practical concerns: If the Court dismissed the case before his client's graduation, "the injunction and stay would cease to be effective and there is nothing that would prevent the University from terminating his enrollment." Both parties insisted the case was not moot. Thus when the Court agreed in November to hear the case, it implied a willingness to reach the merits.

The possibility of mootness surfaced once again during the oral argument. DeFunis had by that time begun his final quarter of law school in good standing. In response to questions from the bench, Gorton gave his assurance that DeFunis' status would not be altered even if the Court finally decided against him and Justice Douglas's stay thus expired. It was this pledge on which the majority of the Supreme Court later seized: "In light of DeFunis' recent registration for the last quarter of his final law school year, and the Law School's assurance that his registration is fully effective, the insistent question again arises whether this case is not moot. . . ." After reviewing recent decisions on the subject of mootness, the Court concluded that this case must be dismissed: "Because the petitioner will complete his law school studies at the end of the term for which he has now registered regardless of any decision this Court might reach on the merits of this litigation . . . the Court cannot . . . consider the substantive constitutional issues tendered by the parties."

Four members of the Court—Justices Brennan, Douglas, White, and Marshall—vigorously dissented. They argued that the majority was right on neither technical nor public policy grounds. The dissenters pointed out that DeFunis "might once again have to run the gauntlet of the University's allegedly unlawful admissions policy" —if for any reason he did not graduate during the year but withdrew and later sought to reenroll. Moreover, the university in no way had abandoned or even modified its preferential policy by its ad hoc commitment that DeFunis would be allowed to graduate even if he lost the case. The dissenters argued that the case fell within a long line of decisions holding that "the mere voluntary cessation of allegedly illegal conduct does not moot a case." The minority also invoked a "public interest" exception by which the merits might be reached even if there were a more serious technical hurdle:

> Few constitutional questions in recent history have stirred as much debate, and they will not disappear. They must inevitably return to the federal courts and ultimately to this Court. . . . Because avoidance of repetitious litigation serves the public interest, that inevitably counsels against mootness determinations, as here, not compelled by the record. . . . Although the Court should, of course, avoid unnecessary decisions of constitutional questions, we should not transform principles of avoidance of constitutional decisions into devices for sidestepping resolution of difficult cases.

The doctrine of mootness is rather seldom invoked in major constitutional cases. Perhaps the most relevant precedent comes from a case in the late 1940s challenging the reading of the Bible in New Jersey public schools. A group of parents and taxpayers claimed the Bible reading breached the principle of separation of church and state. When the case was argued in the Supreme Court, the children of the parent-plaintiffs had already graduated from high school. Thus, said the Court, "obviously no decision we could render now would protect any right she may once have had, and this Court does not sit to decide arguments after events have put them to rest." If one of the parties to a case dies before a decision can be rendered, dismissal on ground of mootness will also be appropriate—although occasionally the Court has been persuaded that the need to clear the family name would suffice to keep the matter alive. And in one case, where the death of a convicted narcotics offender was known only after a Supreme Court decision in his favor, the Court kept the opinion on the books. In short, doubts about mootness have often been resolved in favor of adjudication because the public interest in the outcome extends well beyond the immediate parties.

This abhorrence of genuinely moot cases is not, however, simply a reflection of judicial choice. The limitation goes to the heart of the federal adjudicative power. Article III of the Constitution gives federal courts jurisdiction over "cases and controversies." Where a real dispute no longer exists because the parties have settled or one of them has dropped out of the suit, the courts have held that no "case or controversy" survived. It would therefore be an excess of jurisdiction to reach the merits of the case, no matter how important or interesting the judges might think the issue. Moreover, when the Supreme Court lacked the control it now has over its docket, and was effectively required to hear every case brought before it, a strict application of mootness and other jurisdictional limits helped to reduce the burden. Yet it is not always clear when a case has become moot—as several recent cases, including *DeFunis,* make clear. Even though the Court must dismiss a case when it clearly is moot, the determination of mootness does allow considerable latitude.

Only a week before *DeFunis,* the Court decided another mootness claim quite differently. The substantive issue in the case was whether New Jersey could deny welfare benefits to workers who were on strike, as New Jersey law required. The case began in the trial court while the strike was in progress. By the time it reached the court of appeals, the strike had been settled, and the case was dismissed as moot. But the Supreme Court, by a 5–4 vote, disagreed. Mr. Justice

Blackmun, joined by the four *DeFunis* dissenters (Brennan, Douglas, Marshall, and White) held that the suit was still alive; although the particular strike was over and the individual workers' claims had thus lapsed, the issue was still important and might return in the event of a future strike.

It is hard to reconcile this holding with *DeFunis.* In one case, the case remained alive even though the strike had ended; in the other, the case was dead even though the plaintiff had not yet graduated. Surely the *DeFunis* controversy was not technically moot, as if the student plaintiff had actually graduated. Thus it was if anything less moot than the case in which the strike had ended. Even if the case had been technically moot, the "public interest" exception might well have justified retention of the merits in view of the extraordinary time and energy devoted to briefs and arguments, and the need of the academic community for clear guidance.

The history of the *DeFunis* case strengthens the impression that the Court may have been seeking an escape route through mootness. When the parties were asked to brief the mootness issue, the university had made clear that if DeFunis began the final quarter in good standing, he would be allowed to complete the year and get his degree. The only contingency was whether he would register for that quarter. If the real concern were the effect which that registration might have on the status of the case, why not decide at that point whether or not to take the case? It is possible, of course, that old doubts were revived during the oral argument, despite a conviction in November that the case was and would remain alive. Even then, a dismissal order would presumably have been announced the week after the argument. Occasionally the Court does decide to review a case and then discovers during oral argument that it has made a mistake—the record is poor, the legal issues have been misunderstood, or some procedural barrier stands in the way of reaching those issues. When this happens, the dismissal is announced as soon as possible thereafter—typically the first of the next week—so that the parties will know where they stand. If the *DeFunis* case was dismissible on this basis in late April, it was equally dismissible in February.

The only event which would make the case any more clearly moot than it was would be the conferral of the degree at graduation. A court wishing to avoid the merits through mootness might well have held the case through commencement and then dismissed on this basis, since the university ended its year some weeks before the Court rose for the summer. Had the case been handled this way, the resulting dismissal might have seemed dilatory or disingenuous, but at least it would have been technically defensible. The actual disposition had neither the virtue of promptness nor that of precision. There must be a better reason for the Court's choice of so bizarre a route.

Alternative explanations are needed since "mootness" really will not wash. At the start, we must remember that the *DeFunis* decision rested on the narrowest possible margin, a 5–4 vote. The position of one member of the Court—Mr. Justice Blackmun—is especially critical since he voted the other way on the mootness question in the New Jersey strike benefits case. Thus we might examine several factors that could explain the votes of the entire majority, and then consider Justice Blackmun's position separately.

For one thing, the state of the record was rather poor. Although the Washington court assumed that a "compelling interest" underlay the university's preference for minority applicants, there was no solid evidence to support that claim. There had been no testimony, for example, about the cause or the effects of minority underrepresentation in law schools or in the legal profession in Washington or anywhere else. It was precisely because of the poor state of the record that one of the amici curiae—the Harvard Center for Law and Education—warned the Court not to decide the merits in *DeFunis.* The Center's brief urged that the case should be dismissed as "improvidently granted"—a signal that the Court has simply made a mistake in agreeing to hear the case—or as moot. This plea undoubtedly reflected a tactical perception on the part of the Harvard Center, for it would undoubtedly have supported the university on the merits.

Whether any member of the Court was influenced by the condition of the record is problematic. It is true that the lack of testimony on the causes and effects of minority underrepresentation was known much earlier than the third week of April. But that is equally true of the facts which supported the mootness finding. And it is quite possible that the significance of data absent from the record did not become apparent until after the oral argument while the justices were writing (or trying to write) an opinion about the validity of the state interest in using racial preferences.

A second possible reason for avoidance has already been briefly noted. Usually in an area of such sensitivity the Supreme Court prefers to have the lower courts first wrestle with the issues. In the context of so-called de facto school desegregation—suits over the racial composition of public schools in the North and West—the Supreme Court consistently refused to become involved despite a large volume of litigation and even despite direct conflicts among the federal courts of appeals. Earlier, the Court had taken a case involving the constitutionality of state antimiscegenation laws but had then quickly backed away. Seven years later, after much more lower court litigation, the Court did take up the issue again and struck down interracial marriage and cohabitation laws. These precedents do suggest one possible explanation of the avoidance in *DeFunis*. It was with a sense of relief that the *Christian Science Monitor* editorial applauded the dismissal for providing "time and opportunity for further individual and national consideration of problems not easily solved by fiat."

A third explanation may lie in the relationship of *DeFunis* to other pending legal and constitutional disputes. When the Court decided to take the case in the fall, it may have assumed that preferential admission to law school was a distinct and separate constitutional issue. As the briefs came in, it became increasingly clear that a decision in this case would have far-reaching effects upon public employment, public school desegregation, and perhaps other sectors. The city of Seattle filed in support of the university because it feared a decision against preferential admissions would cripple its affirmative action program. The AFL-CIO and the National Association of Manufacturers both filed on the opposite side because they saw in *DeFunis* a chance to attack before the Court the validity of hiring quotas and goals—an issue which the Court had consistently declined to consider when presented directly. As the roster of amicus briefs swelled, therefore, the broad implication of a decision on the merits became increasingly apparent. Since the Court did not wish to rule inadvertently or obliquely on the constitutionality of hiring quotas or special minority training programs, postponement of the narrower issue may have seemed the wiser course.

The briefs may have had another effect on the Court which helps to explain the "mootness." Mr. Dooley, the mythical Irish sage at the turn of the century, once quipped that "th' Supreme Court follows th' eliction returns." Whether the charge is fair or accurate—for example, in connection with the Court-packing plan of 1937 and the supposed "switch in time that saved nine"—it is not impossible that at least one justice weighed factors that were not precisely legal. Few persons could have anticipated the bitterness which the *DeFunis* issue would engender, especially among white ethnic groups. There was the unprecedented division among Jewish organizations which had stood together throughout the civil rights struggle. There was also the sudden emergence of various antiminority organizations—not outlandish Klan chapters but organizations of concerned, middle class Italians, Slavs, Poles, and other Eastern European nationals. A banner headline in the *National Observer* late in the spring—"Scram White Man!" —captured in irony the resentful mood of many groups that felt themselves victims of affirmative action in employment as well as education. This bitterness found its way into the briefs. In his argument on the merits, Diamond used this language:

> The predominance of whites in the University law school may well be explained by a lack of inclination or aptitude on the part of blacks for such studies. . . . By the same logic that impels the preference of less qualified minorities to achieve racial balance in law, it might be argued that special treatment should be given to whites to achieve racial balance in athletics.

Minority groups also showed intensity of feeling around the case. On the other side a leading black columnist ventured that "the fight against affirmative action programs designed to help blacks and other minorities into the American mainstream is being led by Jews. . . . And it may be that attempts at making campuses more representative of the country are seen by Jews as attacks on their special preserve." With the battle lines thus potentially drawn, the Court might have begun to fear that a decision either way on the merits of *DeFunis* could have alarming consequences for intergroup relations. Of course the bitter opposition of southern whites to the school segregation cases never dissuaded the Court from doing what it believed right. But the country was far better prepared for those decisions and the division ran along much more predictable lines.

In addition to these general theories, we need special insight into the thinking of Justice Blackmun, who voted differently on two mootness claims only a week apart. Blackmun was obviously deeply troubled by *DeFunis*. When the oral argument came to an end—an event marked by the illumination of a red bulb on the podium telling the lawyer to rest his case—the justice offered a moving and highly personal comment:

> If the Chief Justice will permit me, with the red light on, let me get away from this racial aspect a little bit. Let's speak of our sister profession of medicine, with which I have a little familiarity in the past. [For years before becoming a federal judge, Blackmun had been general counsel to the Mayo Clinic in Minnesota, and has a strong interest in medical affairs.] There's been a good deal of talk about the need for newly trained physicians to get out into small communities. Suppose [for] the University of Washington Medical School, there were some applicants who said, "I would like to go into the mountains or into the desert . . . and I don't desire to specialize in orthopedics or neurosurgery. I just want to be a general practitioner." And yet his qualifications, his undergraduate work, grade-wise, was less than a number of others who wanted to specialize. Do you think this factor . . . the need for general practitioners . . . would be something that the Admissions Committee of the Medical School could validly take into consideration?

For Justice Blackmun, the case may thus have posed a uniquely acute dilemma. On the one hand, he must have been uneasy about allowing preferential consideration of race in the admissions process. Yet he was clearly concerned about the consequences of overreliance on numerical predictors, and sought a way of validating some forms of preferential admission. Rather than seizing either horn of the dilemma in *DeFunis,* Justice Blackmun may have found avoidance the most attractive option.

One can only speculate how much any of these factors explains the Court's decision to defer consideration of the merits in *DeFunis.* All that is clear is that the stated basis for dismissal—mootness resulting from the imminent end of the final quarter of law school—is remarkably unpersuasive. One has the feeling there must be more to the story than this. Yet no one of the alternative theories suggested here would fully justify the avoidance. Whatever the actual reasons, it may be that mootness was the only stated ground of dismissal that would even command five votes. It will not do to have one justice say he thought the case improvidently granted, and another state that he thinks the record is poor, and still another say that he feels adjudication would be premature until the courts have struggled with the issue. While mootness may not have appealed greatly to any member of the majority, it may have been the only theory on which all could unite.

The dissenting opinion of Justice William O. Douglas was something of a voice in the wilderness. A loner in many respects, Douglas was the only member of the Court to address the merits of preferential admissions. The case created an acute dilemma for him. On the one hand, he believed the equal protection clause of the Fourteenth Amendment precluded explicit racial classifications: "So far as race is concerned, any state-sponsored preference to one race over another . . . is in my view 'invidious' and violative of the Equal Protection Clause." Admissions criteria must, he insisted, be applied in a "racially neutral way." Moreover, "there is no constitutional right for any race to be preferred"; every applicant for admission "had a constitutional right to have his application considered on its individual merits in a racially neutral way."

Yet Justice Douglas was troubled by the social and educational problem which preferential admission policies tried to ameliorate. He recognized that racial minorities were underrepresented in the law schools and in the practicing profession. He also acknowledged that numerical predictors, especially standardized tests, served to exclude disproportionate numbers of minority applicants. Such tests seemed to have a cultural bias disadvantageous to nonwhites. Thus, while insisting that explicit racial preference would be unconstitutional, Justice Douglas also ventured that "a separate classification of these applicants [blacks, chicanos, Indians and Asians] is warranted, lest race be a subtle factor in eliminating minority members because of cultural differences." Against this paradox, Douglas urged a compromise solution to the *DeFunis* suit itself: "The case, in my view, should be remanded for a new trial to consider, inter alia, whether the established LSAT tests should be eliminated so far as racial minorities are concerned."

Meanwhile, resort to various alternatives might in Justice Douglas' view avoid the dilemma created by preferential admissions. In addition to abolishing the LSAT, law schools might develop substitute admission tests that would be culturally fairer and more neutral. Greater reliance might be placed on interviews with individual applicants. Performance in such summer institutes as those sponsored by the Council on Legal Education Opportunity (the principal program for recruitment and financial support of minority students) might also carry considerable weight. A greater promise of legal service "to communities that are not now adequately represented" might also be persuasive. Justice Douglas came closest to validating racial preference when he suggested it would be constitutional for a law school to consider in the admissions decision "an individual's prior achievements in light of the racial discrimination that barred his way. . . ." While granting that such alternatives might be cruder and more cumbersome than the preferential admissions policy, "we have never held administrative convenience to justify racial discrimination."

Unlike Judge Shorett or the judges of the Washington Supreme Court, Justice Douglas found the *DeFunis* case a supremely difficult one. Strong forces pulled in both directions. On the basis of his earlier writings, one would have expected from him an unequivocal statement of support for the university's position. In 1956, for example, he anticipated the constitutional issues that would eventually reach the courts:

> Experience shows that liquor has a devastating effect on the North American Indian and Eskimo. It is, therefore, commonly provided in the United States and Canada that no liquor should be sold to those races. Other regulations based on race may likewise be justified by reason of the special traits of those races. . . . What at first blush may seem to be an invidious discrimination may on analysis be found to have plausible grounds justifying it.

Moreover, in the civil rights cases—those involving school desegregation, sit-ins, and the like—Douglas' voice had been as strong and unequivocal as that of Justice Thurgood Marshall in support of minority group rights.

There is, however, a deeper dimension. If Douglas could *understand* the plight of the rejected minority student, he could actually *feel* the hurt of Marco DeFunis. He, too, had grown up as a poor boy in the state of Washington. He had once considered going to the university, but realized he could not afford it. Instead he attended Whitman College because it offered him a scholarship; even with this aid he had to work full time at various jobs. When it came to law school, he did go east to Columbia, but lacking the money for transportation had to travel ten days on a freight car with a load of sheep to get as far as Chicago. His incredible performance during and after law school, ending with his appointment to the Supreme Court at the age of forty-one, represented a triumph of merit and industry, with no special help from anybody. Douglas has always displayed deep compassion for disadvantaged and oppressed minorities, in other lands as well as in this country. Those feelings were evident at many places in the *DeFunis* opinion. But there was an unaccustomed ambivalence to this opinion, reflecting the pull between equality and meritocracy. In a real sense Marco DeFunis working forty hours a week to put himself through college and graduate school *was* William

O. Douglas, many years earlier, waiting on tables and carrying two other jobs in Walla Walla stores to put himself through college and support his widowed mother.

The press greeted the *DeFunis* judgment with a mixture of relief and frustration. The level of expectation had been so high that a nondecision was clearly anticlimactic. Headlines revealed some of the dismay and anger. "COURT REFUSES TO RULE IN 'REVERSE DISCRIMINATION' CASE"; "DEFUNIS: SOUND AND FURY, NO DECISION"; "THE UNSETTLED DEFUNIS CASE"; "A REMARKABLE NONDECISION ON REVERSE DISCRIMINATION"; "DEFUNIS NON-DECISION." The *New York Times* observed editorially the next morning that "the Supreme Court appears at first glance to have run away from the emotion-laden issue." The *Christian Science Monitor* that afternoon suggested that if the case really were moot, "the court might have reached a similar decision sooner, forestalling the expenditure of time, money and emotion during the period of mounting controversy." Marco DeFunis himself, although now assured of receiving the law degree he had so vigorously pursued, said he felt that "the court should have made a decision one way or the other."

Justice Douglas drew the plaudits of the press, not only because he had spoken to the merits at all, but because what he said struck a responsive chord. "Precedent as well as logic will steer the Supreme Court in this direction," predicted a *Washington Post* editorial, "whenever it comes to grips with the merits of a case involving educational discrimination, reverse or otherwise." The *New York Times* concurred: "It will be infinitely better for the Universities' future independence to seek solutions which are at once nondiscriminatory and humane than to rely on rigid administrative procedures which invite court-ordered management of the academic community." In a *Saturday Review* article several months later, senior education writer Fred Hechinger suggested that the chief value of the Douglas opinion may have been almost inadvertent:

> What Justice Douglas overlooks, perhaps deliberately, is the fact that administrative convenience has historically dominated far

too many, if not most, institutional arrangements in education. The judicial torpedo he fired at that tradition, almost as an aside, may turn out to be his most valuable contribution toward cutting through the knotty controversy of quotas and reverse discrimination.

It is important at this point to understand clearly what the constitutional issue was—the issue on which the Supreme Court declined to pass. The question was not whether preferential admission of minority students was wise or unwise as a matter of educational or public policy. The much narrower question was whether the University of Washington acted unconstitutionally in taking race into account in its admissions process—or perhaps even more specifically, whether taking membership in a racial minority into account deprived members of the majority like Marco DeFunis of any constitutional rights. It is easy to confuse the policy issue and the legal issue as one gets deeper into this complex of argument and counterargument. But it is vital to understand that courts usually have no power to decide policy questions and can adjudicate only the legal issues that are brought to them.

In disposing of *DeFunis,* the Supreme Court expressly invited further litigation. "If the admissions procedures of the law school remain unchanged," said the majority, "there is no reason to suppose that a subsequent suit attacking those procedures will not come with relative speed to this Court, now that the Supreme Court of Washington has spoken." By the start of the fall 1974 term, several new cases had been filed. Other suits filed at or even before *DeFunis* had been held in abeyance and (if not mooted by graduation) could also be revived.

Meanwhile, the courts were not the only locus of debate about preferential admissions. About a month after the *DeFunis* decision came down, a congressional committee was routinely reviewing the refunding of the Council on Legal Education Opportunity. Representative James O'Hara, D.-Mich., suddenly introduced a set of amendments designed to forbid any preferential practices in legal education. Under his proposals funding would be denied to any educational institution having "any criteria for admission which accord any preference or pose any disadvantage on account of race, color, national origin, or sex." No student could be excluded from, or *admitted to,* any funded program on the basis of race.

The measure eventually passed the House without any such restrictive amendments. As the bill reached the floor, however, the accompanying committee report warned that the underlying issues of admissions policy had simply been deferred. It had seemed inappropriate to resolve basic constitutional issues through merely technical amendments. Such legislation might also be unfair to students already enrolled in specially funded programs. But to the minority members of the committee (including O'Hara) refunding of a program for the support of "disadvantaged" students was "clearly discriminatory." As though to bring the matter full circle, the minority added a constitutional caveat that sounded strikingly like Judge Shorett's simplistic "color blind" test:

> In practice, it [the preferential policy] is a quota program that is unconstitutional under the Fourteenth Amendment (as would probably have been made clear had the Supreme Court agreed to hear the *DeFunis* case). Each American deserves equal protection under the law, without regard to race, creed, color or national origin.

To make certain the message would not be lost, O'Hara announced that hearings covering many facets of college admissions would resume in the fall. The distinct possibility thus emerged that Congress might well do what the Supreme Court had declined to do, and might overrule the Washington Supreme Court as effectively as by judicial reversal. The power of Congress to produce such a result is beyond doubt. Few institutions could afford to continue a preferential program if the cost of doing so were to forfeit eligibility for federal subvention. Should government funding be cut off because of race conscious policies or programs, the abstract constitutional issue would *truly* become moot in the minds of most higher education administrators. Thus the ultimate locus of decision in this as in many other matters of educational policy may shift from the Court, which refused to decide when it had the chance, to the Congress, which appears less squeamish.

CHAPTER THREE

PREFERENTIAL ADMISSION AND HIGHER EDUCATION

Shortly after the *DeFunis* case was filed, a law professor at another west coast university was talking with the college-age daughter of a neighbor. He described the problems created by the geometric rise in law school applications, which had just closed out at something over 5500. Since the law school could admit less than 300 students each fall, the selection process demanded the full time of one assistant dean, and preempted many days of commitment for faculty and student members of the admissions committee. Many brilliant and promising students (who would easily have been admitted in the past) were being turned away. More than half the magna cum laude graduates of Harvard College, for example, were being rejected. The average LSAT score for accepted students was well up in the ninetieth percentile. For every student admitted, there were at least ten fully qualified applicants who were turned away.

As the professor described the situation, the neighbor's daughter looked increasingly puzzled. "I don't understand," she said at length. "A good friend of mine, whose grades and test scores aren't that good, was just admitted to your school. He says it isn't that tough to get in." The professor at once asked the name of the fortunate applicant. As he might have guessed had he thought about it, the friend was the grandson of the university's president emeritus, who had built the institution to its present eminence, and to whom even the younger faculty paid homage and reverence. The admissions committee and eventually the whole law faculty had wrestled with this one, since the paper record would have placed the young man about three thousandth out of five thousand. But they eventually decided to admit him anyway, as a gesture of gratitude and admiration for his grandfather's accomplishments. (Needless to say, the professor did not explain all the circumstances, but let the matter pass. Three years later, the grandson earned his law degree in due course—not with great distinction, but with a solid record around the middle of the class.)

The import of this episode is quite clear: Consideration of factors other than paper records and test scores in college admissions is neither recent in origin nor limited to disadvantaged minority students. Admissions officers, at least in selective institutions and programs, have long realized that intelligent and responsible choices among applicants cannot be made solely on the basis of quantitative, impersonal factors. This chapter will first explore the background, nature, and extent of nonracial departures from rank ordering in the admissions process, a necessary prelude to understanding the kind of preference that gave rise to the *DeFunis* case. We will then examine recent trends and current opportunities for minority students in American higher education, with special attention to legal education. (This choice is made both because law is the academic sector involved in *DeFunis* and because the data about legal education are richer than for any other field.) This analysis will then set the stage for a consideration of the legal and constitutional factors impinging upon the admissions process.

The Admissions Process

Only the most naive observer would believe that applicants for admission to college or graduate school are admitted in strict rank order. Except where an open door policy mandates acceptance of every student with a diploma or degree, the process is a highly complex one. Even in relatively routine cases, many factors may play a part. In addition to high school or undergraduate grades and scores on standardized tests (which are nearly universal prerequisites these days) numerous other elements may be and are considered. Among these elements are letters of recommendation from former teachers, counsellors, family friends, clergymen, and others; appraisals by a principal or dean or some other administrator; personal interviews with an admissions officer or an alumnus; the applicant's own statement of aspiration or career goals; and the record of extracurricular achievements, community service, and the like.

Not every factor will be considered in all cases, of course. Easy cases at the top and bottom of the academic performance scale may essentially be resolved on the basis of the mathematical predictors— either because the applicant displays little or no potential of satisfactory academic work or because the promise is so great that any institution would grab him up. (Even here, though, some caution is appropriate. Law schools have found, for example, that the voluntary drop-out rate is strikingly high among those with LSAT scores over 700—the very highest scoring group. Perhaps these students become bored more easily, or are subject to more frequent changes of career choice. No one knows the reason for this curious attrition phenomenon.)

In other instances a *nonacademic* factor may be singled out for special emphasis. Colleges and universities have always made concessions for holders of particular, nonquantifiable skills—the ability to compose a sonata, launch a political organization, or win a debate. The presence of such uniquely talented persons in the student body, it is thought, may bring both distinction and diversity to the institution. Thus the admissions officer may well believe that a high school student body president will, despite a mediocre academic record, become prominent in business or government and thus distinguish himself and his alma mater better than a classmate with higher grades but less charisma or drive. The decision to favor the former applicant over the latter is, unquestionably, a departure from strict numerical ranking and thus a clear form of preferential admission.

When it comes to athletic skills, the willingness to waive academic criteria is often limited only by the rules of the National Collegiate Athletic Association. The preferential admission of persons whose promise lies in kicking or throwing a ball or running on a track or field is so common and well-accepted as not to require mention.

(Carl Rowan remarked wryly after the *DeFunis* decision that critics of racial preference "don't complain about 'reverse discrimination' if it's a 230-pound tight end with a C average who gets in ahead of a bookworm.")

Less widely publicized is special consideration often given to children of alumni or powerful friends of private universities, or legislators and other public officials in the case of state institutions. In these cases, as with the grandson of the president emeritus, the name alone will usually attract the attention of the admissions officer; if it does not, a phone call from a prominent person on the applicant's behalf will serve the same end. One recent study of admissions practices notes that "all colleges give extra consideration to the children of alumni. Some carry it to the extent of automatic admission of alumni children who meet the entrance requirements; others go no further than giving alumni children the benefit of the doubt." Moreover, it is no secret that the child of a faculty member sometimes receives a special break when he or she wishes to study where the parent teaches, since preference in admission (as well as free or reduced tuition) is an effective weapon in the competition for faculty talent. All such preferences are justified by the desire of the institution to retain or attract a resource which is deemed vital to its welfare.

Relaxation or adjustment of admissions criteria has also been thought to be warranted where the applicant is literally handicapped —through blindness, deafness, a serious physical disability, or recent migration to the United States after growing up in a non-English-speaking land. In such cases it seems only fair to weigh high school grades and test scores differently, either by discounting them altogether and applying other measures of potential, or by adding to the raw scores a kind of "handicap" which will offset the effect of the disability.

Then there is the occasional case of the student who simply does not do well on standardized tests but has all the other indicia of ability and promise. John P. Roche, political science professor at Brandeis University and White House "intellectual in residence" during the Johnson administration, has observed:

Over the past quarter of a century I have known perhaps a hundred students who were extremely talented but tested badly; two years ago I had a young man who graduated summa cum laude, did brilliant work in constitutional law, and persistently turned up in the 40th percentile on tests.

Under normal conditions he would not have been admitted to the Zonko Law School, but my faculty colleagues and I mounted a full court press in his behalf. We wrote to the admissions committees of several distinguished law schools, explaining that Mr. X went catatonic when faced by those tests . . . and that we were confident that he would do well in law school. He was admitted to a top school and, last I heard, was well on his way to being editor of the law review.

Every college teacher knows of such cases, and has probably at some time in his career interceded for the student who blocks on standardized tests—even though no cultural deprivation or other obvious extenuation exists.

Preferences based on sex represent a quite different matter—and one that is now in violation of federal law. Many state colleges and even universities that evolved from former teachers' colleges or normal schools sought in the years after World War II to maintain rough parity between male and female students. Because of the dominance of elementary-secondary education as a field of study, and the preponderance of women in that field, artificial control was required to achieve the desired mix. Several of Ohio's former teachers' colleges simply set quotas for women students and rejected all applicants beyond that number. As a result, the paper qualifications of the women would turn out to be substantially higher than for the men in the same class. The California state colleges (now state universities) took a subtler route: The ratio of grades and test scores was adjusted, on the basis of experience, to ensure the desired sex balance. Thus the admissions process appeared to be sex blind, since it lacked any quotas. Although further back in the process and subtler in form, the "preference" for male applicants was no less pernicious in the California system. Indeed, it may have been even more damaging because of the superficial appearance of nondiscrimination and the elusiveness of the bias. Such practices as these are now forbidden by federal law (Title IX of the Higher Education Amendment of 1972), whether they are obvious or subtle. But for decades discrimination against women has been a major factor in college admissions. No women appear ever to have been the beneficiaries of any comparable preference. (In addition, of course, women have been indirectly disadvantaged in higher education by financial aid policies, the inflexibility of course schedules, the absence of part-time study options, and the unavailability of child care facilities.)

Finally, there is the selective role of geography in the admissions process. The residence of an applicant has operated quite differently in public and private institutions. Private colleges and universities have increasingly sought students from remote places to add variety and distinction to their student bodies. In his *DeFunis* brief for Harvard University, Archibald Cox explained:

> The belief that diversity adds an essential ingredient to the educational process has long been a tenet of Harvard College admissions. Ten or twenty years ago . . . diversity meant students from California, New York and Massachusetts; city dwellers and farm boys. . . . A farm boy from Idaho can bring something to Harvard College that a Bostonian cannot offer. . . . At the same time the [Admissions] Committee is aware that if Harvard College is to provide a truly heterogeneous environment that reflects the rich diversity of the United States, it cannot be provided without some attention to numbers. It would not make sense, for example, to have 10 or 20 students out of 1,100 whose homes are west of the Mississippi.

This is not to say, of course, that a private university would admit an applicant solely for the sake of geographical variety; simply, where other factors are roughly equal, the student from afar is likely to be favored over the area resident.

The policies of tax-supported institutions run in almost precisely the opposite direction. A century ago the enrollment of the University of Michigan came two-thirds from out of state. As the educational claims and aspirations of Michiganders increased, the nonresident

percentage declined. In the late 1960s, partly because of student unrest, the legislature decreed that out-of-state enrollments must not
exceed 15%. Since the actual percentage was well above that level at
the time, severe restrictions were imposed. As a result, the academic
records of the few nonresidents admitted were far above those of the
in-staters who benefited from the quota. Meanwhile, other states have
built different kinds of fences around their public colleges and universities. Some states have nonresident tuition levels that are almost
prohibitive, and do not need percentage limits. The University of
California consistently admits no more than about ten percent out-of-
state freshmen, simply because the qualifying grade point levels are
set in such a way as to ensure the admission of only the cream of
nonresidents. Perhaps the crudest of all residential restrictions was
that adopted by Purdue University in 1969. In order to tighten up on
nonresident enrollments, the university took particular aim at the
New York City metropolitan area. It first announced it would accept
only students from that area who were children of Purdue alumni and
were especially well qualified. The following year the rule was
modified, so that New York and New Jersey received a quota match-
ing the ratio of those states' population to the total national population. Whatever may have been the goal of this policy, its effect was
especially harsh on Jewish students, who came disproportionately
from the New York area. The Anti-Defamation League of B'nai
B'rith, concerned about declining Jewish enrollments at major midwestern universities, did an extensive study of nonresident enrollment
limits. The conclusion was that a new, and probably unintended, form
of de facto anti-Semitism had been imposed. Since this study was
completed the year before the *DeFunis* case was filed, the special
concern of ADL in that case may have been an outgrowth of the study
—although, ironically, DeFunis had argued for an *in-state* admission
preference.

The relationship between geography and admissions is thus a
rather complex one. In effect, private colleges and universities often
prefer students from other parts of the country, while most public
institutions are now required to prefer residents of the state through

grade point or tuition differentials or outright quotas. Here as in other areas, the use of preferential admissions policies is well established, widely accepted, and evokes little controversy in or out of higher education. The use of qualitative rather than quantitative indicia is quite clear. The novelty of the new policies of the 1960s, therefore, was not the departure from strict numerical ranking of applicants, but rather the addition of race to other factors on which preference had long been based. As Marco DeFunis' complaint itself illustrates through its discussion of residence, it was not the *concept* of preference that was objectionable but only the particular racial element.

To this point we have talked about "preference" as though there were some clear, simple formula for favoring one applicant over others. Obviously this is not the case. The term "preferential admission" may imply many things, even within a single institution or admissions office. At one extreme, a preference could mean no more than tipping the balance in favor of one group or applicant when all other factors are equal. Some choice must be made when it comes down to the wire, and it is technically correct to label as a "preference" the criterion by which the tie is broken. This is, of course, the very mildest form of preference. At the opposite extreme, there is the fixed quota—the guarantee that a certain number of residents of the state, male students, Catholics, veterans, or children of alumni will be admitted regardless of where they rank or even whether they are qualified.

There is a wide range of options between the tie-breaking factor and the fixed quota. Preference may sometimes be given by adding points to a test score in the manner of a handicap when the raw score would unfairly predict performance. Or a test score may be discounted or disregarded altogether in judging the potential of members of certain groups. Sometimes applicants from one group will be admitted on the basis of some qualification not generally shared—for example, graduate work in a special field, military service, or a particular kind of business experience. An applicant who would otherwise be rejected outright may effectively be preferred through *conditional* admission—that is, by acceptance conditioned upon completion of a preparatory course or program. Finally, the same criteria may be used for all candidates but their relative weighting or ranking varied in such a way as to mitigate the effect on one group of an otherwise detrimental factor. Thus there are many possible forms through which preference may be accorded in the admission process. Any one of these approaches might be considered a form of "preferential admission." We shall not attempt to define the term here with greater precision.

Minority Students in Higher Education

Now that we have surveyed the broad scope of preferential admission practices, we turn to the special arena of current controversy—the role of race in admissions decisions. One cannot discuss racial preferences without some awareness of the forces and conditions that have given rise to such preferences. Thus we need to look back into the history of higher education opportunities for minority students. The search for adequate information is difficult for several reasons, not the least of which is the recency with which any data about minority enrollments were gathered.

"A few years ago," observed the vice president of the Educational Testing Service recently, "we did not have the problem of black students because we did not have the students and did not know enough to worry about not having them. We still do not have the students but we worry about it a great deal." Until the late 1960s minority students matriculated in substantial numbers only at the traditional black colleges (and a few emergent institutions like Federal City College); at the community and junior colleges located in or near the ghetto and the barrio; and at a handful of socially conscious elite private liberal arts colleges like Antioch, Oberlin, and Wesleyan. (Many private colleges, especially in the South, had racially restrictive clauses in their charters or gifts from their principal sponsors that were not broken until the late 1950s or 60s. In addition, state law sometimes banned voluntary efforts to integrate higher education. Berea College in Kentucky was one of the few that actively sought to recruit black students to a predominantly white campus. A Kentucky statute, however, actually made it a crime to educate white and colored students in the same place at the same time. In 1908, the United States Supreme Court upheld that law against Berea's constitutional claims. It was several decades before black and white students could lawfully study together on the same Kentucky campus.)

The gathering of accurate data about minority enrollments has been extremely difficult. Many states only recently passed laws which forbade asking questions about an applicant's race or demanding a photograph—laws designed to help minorities by forbidding subtle discrimination. Thus when the federal government first set out in the fall of 1967 to conduct a national survey of minority enrollment, major reliance had to be placed on crude approximations and "sight surveys." The claimed purpose of this survey was to determine the extent of compliance with Title VI of the 1964 Civil Rights Act, which forbade discrimination in the use of federal funds. A similar study was made by federal officials the following year, and then another two years later. Since that time the government survey has been done biennially, in the fall of even-numbered years. Meanwhile, other sources of minority enrollments have emerged—a study of their own member institutions by the National Association of State Universities and Land Grant Colleges and the Association of American Universities and a national study of all freshmen done annually by the American Council on Education.

The overall results of these studies indicated fairly steady increases in minority enrollments through 1972, although at slowing rates of growth. Unexpectedly, the American Council on Education noted a downturn in the fall of 1973, which continued in 1974–75. Black freshmen made up 8.7% of all entering students in 1972, but dropped to 7.8% in 1973 and fell further to 7.4% the following year. New students from all minority groups (blacks, Spanish-surnamed, American Indian, and Asian) dropped from a high of 14.8% in 1972 to 13.0% of the 1973 freshman class. In an attempt to explain the unexpected downturn, David B. Kent, Jr., the executive director of the National Scholarship Service and Fund for Negro Students, put the blame on the general economic condition of higher education. "Everything is tightening up," he observed, "as the institutions of higher learning are looking at their budgets and trying to survive. There is a feeling in the country that low-income students are getting more than their share at the expense of the middle income students." Not everyone was surprised by the minority enrollment drop, however. As early as the spring of 1973 college admissions and financial aid officers attending a conference at Oberlin College had warned that many institutions were retreating from their earlier commitment to increase nonwhite enrollments. Primary blame was placed on the already worsening financial situation. (This explanation is confirmed by the fact that not only minority students, but all lower income students, lost ground between 1972 and 1973. Freshmen from families with incomes below $6,000 constituted 14.1% of entering students in the fall of 1972, but only 11.1% a year later.)

The feeling of uneasiness has now become, in some quarters, a sense almost of despair. A national conference of persons concerned with minority higher education declared in the fall of 1974 that "the future existence and development of meaningful minority participation in education, especially at the post-secondary level, is now in serious jeopardy and question." (The very makeup of the conference intensified the anxiety of its sponsors. A thousand persons had been expected, but only five hundred actually registered. Leaders of the meeting blamed both the poor turnout and the general situation on a growing apathy: "Blacks are not pushing now as they did in the late 1960's," claimed David Kent, who also lamented the lost commitment of liberal whites who "were once on our side" but whom "you just don't see any more.")

These gross data tell very little about the distribution and educational role of minority students. Broad summaries mask wide variations between types of institutions, levels of enrollment, and localities. Such comprehensive figures on minority enrollments of course include *all* institutions. Between one-third and two-fifths of all black students still attend traditionally black colleges, although the fraction is declining. For this reason, minority enrollments on nonblack campuses are less impressive than the total figure might suggest. Moreover, a small group of institutions bear a disproportionate share of the total load. Universities like Temple, Wayne, or the City College of New York each have five thousand or more black students, with Southern Illinois, Pittsburgh, Chicago Circle, and Cincinnati all above three thousand. While small private colleges like Antioch, Oberlin, Wesleyan, and Swarthmore have made valiant efforts and achieved impressive percentages of black enrollments, they simply cannot contribute anything approaching the numbers of the large urban campuses.

Not only are the minority students disproportionately concentrated in the major urban commuter campuses. They also tend to be better represented at the lower end of the collegiate system than at the upper end. To understand more clearly the distribution of minority enrollments, and to translate enrollment trends into educational opportunities, we must go back some years. Remarkably little is known about minority enrollments before the 1960s. During that decade, black enrollment increased from 5.3% of all students to 6.5%. In those years, however, access of minority students to highly selective institutions apparently diminished as a result of pressure from white students which far exceeded the growth of those campuses. The case of San Francisco State College (now University) is illustrative. In the late 1950s, just before the California Master Plan consigned students in the lower half to junior colleges, black enrollment at San Francisco State was about 12%. By the late 1960s that figure had dropped to 4% as a result of rising admissions standards (as well as the expansion of the nearby City College). One can only speculate, but this trend may have contributed in some way to the intense bitterness of the black student uprising at San Francisco State in 1969 and 1970.

Other public university systems that were once relatively open have experienced similar constriction of opportunity. In fact, truly nonselective policies are found hardly anywhere today. Even the open admissions program of the City University of New York does not guarantee to every freshman a chance to matriculate at a four-year college. Only the state universities of Kansas and Ohio are still legally required to accept any state resident with a high school diploma, but even they have the option of assigning marginal applicants to branch campuses or two-year career programs. Despite the historic faith in the "openness" of our system, the pressures of the 1960s simply forced the admission threshhold up and thus out of reach of many previously admissible students.

The picture that emerges from this deeper analysis is already more complex than the impression created by the raw enrollment surveys. We must carry the inquiry at least one level deeper to get an accurate picture of minority prospects in higher education. Without further qualification, the survey results might generate undue optimism. Particularly for the minority student, it is a long way from matriculation to graduation. Thus it is not surprising to find minority enrollments larger in the lower than in the upper division. The demography of the City University of New York just before the advent of open admissions provides a pertinent illustration. Minority enrollments had risen steadily through the 1960s to an impressive 15% overall at the close of the decade. But the black and Puerto Rican students tended to be concentrated in the two-year units, notably Bronx and New York City Community Colleges. And far more nonwhites than whites were classified as "nonmatriculated," which meant that they probably were not in regular degree programs even at the four-year campuses. Thus the minority shares of full-time enrollments at the four-year campuses were not much higher than those of public universities elsewhere—three percent black and Puerto Rican at Brooklyn and Queens, and a bit above 6% at City College and Hunter. (Baruch, which had a black president and special programs, did post a somewhat higher 14%.) Moreover, current *attrition* rates are substantially higher at the predominantly minority campuses—70% for Hostos, and 60% for New York and Bronx Community Colleges as compared to 30% for Queens and 35% for Brooklyn. (These more recent figures do reflect the actual impact of open admissions, which have increased the number of high-risk students in the community colleges.) The experience to date, sketchy and confusing though it is, seems to confirm the view of John Egerton of the Race Relations Information Center: "A disproportionate number of black students in predominantly white institutions are freshmen, and there is ample reason to suspect that their attrition rate is higher than that of white freshmen." When we develop more effective and reliable ways of measuring attrition and retention, we will be better able to confirm this impression.

The data we have reviewed to this point relate almost entirely to *black* students. We have far less information about other minority groups—Puerto Ricans, Mexican-Americans or chicanos, and American Indians. A few general conclusions are apparent, however. The conditions in the elementary and secondary schools in the barrios (both rural and urban) seem to be worse than those in the black ghettoes; studies of educational prospects for both chicanos and Puerto Ricans, though several years out of date, support this impression. Rates of graduation (and therefore prospects for higher education) are lower in the nonblack groups than for blacks. These groups face serious language barriers to learning in an English-dominated educational system—barriers which blacks encounter to a degree because of differences in dialect or vernacular vocabulary, but at least within a common grammar. Early in 1974 the Supreme Court held that supplemental English-language instruction must be provided for pupils who have grown up speaking another tongue. The lower courts have gone even farther in facilitating opportunities for non-English-speaking children, but the impact of these decisions would not be felt for years even if implementation were immediate.

There is an even greater difference between the higher educational prospects of blacks and other minorities. While several campuses (e.g., East Los Angeles City College, Hostos Community College, New Mexico Highlands University) now have substantial numbers of Spanish-speaking students, no system of chicano or Puerto Rican colleges exists comparable to the network of black colleges in the southern and border states. There is no private support system equivalent to the United Negro College Fund. (For Indians, of course, the situation is quite different. Apart from the initial—and recently rediscovered—commitment of Dartmouth College to educate Indians, there are special institutions of higher learning like Carlisle Indian College. Moreover, the Bureau of Indian Affairs has sponsored educational programs for graduates of reservation schools. But the numbers of Native American students who benefit from such programs has been rather small, and even more remote from the academic mainstream than the students at the rural black colleges.) Thus it is hardly surprising that the higher education experience of other minority groups seems to have been even less encouraging than that of blacks.

Our analysis has focussed mainly on undergraduate enrollments, about which the earliest information was available. We now have fairly accurate data about graduate minority prospects as well. A 1974 survey by the American Council on Education shows that for all fields overall minority enrollment has now reached 7.2%. This figure consists of 4.4% black, 1.1% Spanish-surnamed, .3% American Indian, and 1.4% Asian American. Minority enrollments tend to be largest in institutions that have the largest graduate programs, and those that receive the highest levels of federal government support. There are also significant relationships between fields of study and the various minority groups. Not surprisingly, Asian Americans are best represented in the natural and physical sciences and engineering— about 3% in each area, with negligible representation in the social sciences and humanities. Black and American Indian graduate students appear most heavily in fields like education (7.2%), sociology (5.8%), and the health professions (5.5%). (This study did not include professional enrollments in law and medicine, which have been extensively studied elsewhere.) Blacks constituted only about 1%, however, of those scientific and technical fields in which Asians were best represented. The distribution of Spanish-surnamed graduate students roughly paralleled that for blacks. American Indians showed up in more than token numbers only in the health professions.

It is almost impossible to trace any *trends* in the graduate area. The most comprehensive previous survey showed that in 1969 minority groups made up about 3% of all graduate students, and that perhaps as many as half of these students were in predominantly black institutions. Since neither of the two principal black doctoral institutions was included in the 1974 survey, it is clear that substantial improvement has been made within the last four or five years. But we are measuring only *access* to graduate study, and not actual entry into the learned professions and disciplines. Until we have better information on the number of minority degree holders in these academic fields, we cannot meaningfully assess net progress.

Minority Students in Legal Education

The one field in which we do, in fact, have quite extensive data about minority enrollments is that of law. Legal education provides a particularly appropriate microcosm because of its relevance to the *DeFunis* case and because the demand for admission to law school has risen so dramatically.   -

Concern about minority access to law school goes back to the late 1940s. When a black student sued the University of Texas seeking to gain admission to its all-white law school, the Association of American Law Schools filed a brief broadly condemning racial segregation. The Supreme Court held in the student's favor and ordered the university to admit him. The decision not only initiated changes in southern legal education, but paved the way for the Supreme Court's *Brown* decision striking down all de jure school segregation.

About fifteen years later, the Law School Association revived its concern about minority opportunities. Although there were still no accurate surveys, not more than 1% of the American bar was black, and the representation of other minority groups was infinitesimal. Thus the association created a Special Minority Groups Project in 1965 to study the situation and submit recommendations. The first survey revealed that there were only about 700 black students in all the accredited law schools of the country—a shockingly low 1.3% of law school enrollments. Even that figure was distorted, since more than one-third of this number (267 students) attended the several black law schools. (Euphemistically, these institutions were called "predominantly" black, though white students were nonexistent there. Since that time, a substantial number of whites have enrolled at Howard, which has always been the largest and most prestigious member of this group. The other black schools are Southern University in Baton Rouge, North Carolina Central University in Durham, and Texas Southern University in Houston. At the time of the first survey, Florida A. & M. University also had a law school, which has since been phased out.)

In the mid-60s, therefore, black students formed well below 1% of the enrollments at the accredited, predominantly white law schools. Even at that time, black undergraduate enrollment was over 5%, and blacks made up at least 2% in other graduate and professional schools. Thus legal education was behind most other fields—a fact which particularly embarrassed a profession sworn to enforce and apply the guarantees of equal opportunity. Steps were soon taken to remedy the situation. In the summer of 1965 the Harvard University Law School conducted the first of many summer institutes for pre-senior black students. The Law School Admission Council began to administer its entrance test without charge to students at black colleges—partly to reduce one of the major barriers to law study, and partly to gather data about the fairness of the test for minorities. In 1967, the Field Foundation provided support for special summer institutes at Emory and Denver Universities—the former mainly for southern black students, and the latter primarily for chicano students in the Rocky Mountain area. The number of minority students attracted to law school through these special recruitment, preparation, and financial aids had begun to increase.

Early in 1968 came the creation of a major catalyst, the Council on Legal Education Opportunity. The Council (CLEO for short) was a joint venture of the Association of American Law Schools, the American Bar Association, the National Bar Association, and the Law School Admission Council. (The La Raza National Lawyers Association joined several years later.) Initial funding for summer prelaw institutes and scholarships for minority students was provided by the Legal Services Program of the Office of Economic Opportunity and by the Ford Foundation. Other funds and private groups later contributed to the work of CLEO—the American Bar Endowment, the Rockefeller Foundation, the Field Foundation, and a number of corporations. From the outset the active support of such a venture by the "establishment" of both legal education and law practice was critically important in answering charges from educators, legislators, practitioners, and others who were either skeptical or downright hostile to such an explicitly minority-focussed effort. Frequently during the late 60s and early 70s, presidents of the American Bar Association and the Law School Association would affirm their public support of special recruitment, training, and financial aid for minority students interested in studying and practicing law.

CLEO was by no means the only evidence of commitment to increase minority opportunities for law study. Many foundations continued to give for special scholarships and fellowships long after the Ford grant to CLEO expired. In the spring of 1974, just before the death of the former chief justice, an Earl Warren Legal Training Program was launched for black students wishing to study law in the South, funded by $1.2 million from the Carnegie and Rockefeller Foundations.

Most important of all was the growing commitment of the individual law schools to special minority recruitment and support programs. As of the fall of 1973, nearly forty law schools described special minority student programs in the PreLaw Handbook, and many others reported substantially increased minority enrollments. During the first seven years of CLEO, over fifty law schools had participated in summer institutes across the country and graduates of those institutes had attended more than a hundred law schools. Thus the commitment had become pervasive.

The proof of all such efforts is, of course, in the product. Thus we must review what has happened in law school enrollments during the critical period. Recall that there were 700 black law students enrolled in the fall of 1964, including 267 at the predominantly black schools. By the fall of 1973, that number had increased to 4,817—a figure which was, incidentally, almost 50% larger than the number of black attorneys admitted to practice throughout the United States. Comparable growth has occurred for other minority groups. In the late 60s, there had been but 412 chicano students, 61 Puerto Ricans, 72 American Indians, and 480 Asian Americans. Four years later the chicano figure had tripled to 1,259, while other groups had comparable increases—slightly more than triple for American Indians, somewhat less for Asians. The grand total minority enrollment in accredited law schools, which had been 1,122 in 1968–69, and 2,933 the following year, reached 7,601 by the fall of 1973. (Since all enrollments grew prodigiously in these years, the *percentage* increases are a bit less spectacular. By 1973, blacks composed very close to 5% of all law students in approved institutions, while the total minority share exceeded 7% in that year. Of course the figures included expanding enrollments in the predominantly black schools as well. If black students in those schools are subtracted from the total, black representation in the predominantly white schools falls just below 4%, and all minority enrollment is closer to 6%.)

This dramatic increase in minority enrollments doubtless reflects many factors. The attractions which lured so many students from all ethnic groups into law during this period may have been especially relevant for minority persons—the role of the law in redressing injustice, the opportunity to shape social institutions, the burgeoning of neighborhood legal programs, and the like. In addition, the funds available to minority students wishing to study law increased far faster than general scholarship funds during these years, thus making legal education especially attractive to students who had unusually heavy financial burdens after college. Moreover, law was more aggressive than other professions and moved earlier in recruiting minority applicants, and thus probably lured many prospects away from other graduate areas. Minority attorneys and judges became increasingly visible as role models during this period, and participated actively in CLEO institutes and other recruitment programs. Thus a profession which in the mid-60s had a reputation for being closed or hostile to minority groups was rapidly transformed.

Mere changes in recruitment and financial aid policies alone would not, however, have wrought so dramatic a change in enrollments. Indeed, had no change in admissions *policies* accompanied the other catalysts, the minority share would have increased little. The efforts to attract more minorities came at the very time of the dramatic rise in white-Anglo student interest in law school of which we spoke earlier. Since historically the application of numerical predictors— LSAT scores and undergraduate grades—had kept minority enroll- ments to token levels, the situation would barely have improved dur- ing the law school rush of the late 1960s. Indeed, there was a real danger that the newly attracted minority groups might simply have been squeezed out by the rapidly rising entrance criteria, had special consideration not been given to race and ethnic group membership. In a system that was oblivious to color, minority enrollments (at least at the most prestigious law schools) might actually have declined during these years of the application boom.

One can only guess to what extent special consideration was in fact given to race or ethnic status in law school admissions. While minority enrollments have been surveyed annually since 1967, the basis for admission has seldom been probed. In the fall of 1968, law school admissions officers were asked how many of the minority students they reported had been specially or preferentially admitted —that is, "in the judgment of the Admissions Officer or person com- pleting this questionnaire . . . would probably not have been admitted had they not been members of a minority group." For the then first-year class, about 40% had been admitted at least partly on the basis of race. (Smaller percentages of second-year and third-year minority students were also said to be preferentially admitted, but the total numbers in the upper classes were so small that less significance should attach to the report.)

There is one other rough index of the extent of preference in law school admissions. A survey by the American Bar Association asked how many "disadvantaged" students were admitted to all law schools in the fall of 1970. While not all schools responded, those with the largest minority enrollments did complete the survey. A total of 1,042 disadvantaged students, of whom all but a handful were minorities, were reported in the entering class. (A "disadvantaged" student was one who had been "admitted under a program designed to take into consideration prelegal and LSAT score deficiencies resulting from economic, social or cultural circumstances and backgrounds." These students were compared with their classmates who "gained admittance by virtue of their earned competitive standings.") The *total* enrollment of minority first year students that fall was approximately two thousand—a figure which must be interpolated from the preceding and succeeding years since no general minority survey was taken in 1970. Thus almost exactly half the entering minority students were classified as "disadvantaged"—a term virtually synonymous with "preferentially admitted." Unfortunately we do not have such data for later years, and extrapolation from these two limited samples might be risky.

There are two caveats to this single report about the extent of preferential admissions. First, the questionnaire did not ask the number of students (if any) deemed unqualified but nonetheless admitted, but only the number who would not have been admitted had they been white or Anglo in that year. A student preferentially admitted in 1968 to a major national law school would very likely have been admitted in ordinary course two or three years earlier. It was only the flood of applications, and the precipitous rise in paper records, in other words, that made such a student a "special admit."

Moreover, it is clear that one school's marginal applicant would be a prime prospect at a less prestigious campus. John Egerton had observed that "a risk for Harvard, where the median SAT score is about 1300, would be a prize catch for many an institution which accepts any high school graduate." Not quite the same can be said of legal education, of course, since by the late 1960s there were very few schools willing or able to accept anyone who applied. This comment does, however, suggest a point that some critics have argued: Preferential admission, instead of increasing the total pool of minority students, may simply redistribute that pool by moving minority students a notch or two above where they would be in a color blind system. Undoubtedly some such redistribution has resulted. But the total number of minority persons in the system has unmistakably increased as a result, and the most promising minority students have had a far wider range of opportunities than before. It is also impossible to tell how many people may have been encouraged to apply for law school because special minority opportunities were widely publicized.

As preferential admission became increasingly common throughout American higher education, excesses and abuses were inevitable. In several notable instances, the careful assessment of preferential needs and entitlement gave way to crude and simplistic quotas. (The distinction between a goal and a quota can be simply stated and will be discussed again in Chapter 7. For now it is sufficient to say that a goal simply declares an objective, which will be met only if a sufficient number of qualified persons apply, while a quota specifies the number to be admitted from a given group regardless of the pool of qualified applicants.) A widely publicized case of abuse was the announcement by an administrative assistant at the Center for Human Relations of the University of Massachusetts (Amherst) School of Education that "our quota for non-minority students has been filled" but that "applications from minority persons are still being processed." The Anti-Defamation League protested this policy to the Boston Regional Office of HEW, and the university wisely agreed to reprocess some three hundred rejected applications under a proper nonquota standard. There are a few other examples of excessive reliance upon racial or ethnic factors in the admission process. But they are remarkably few, considering the intense pressures to which that process has been subjected during a turbulent period in higher education. The fact is that most policies cited as "quotas" are not rigid numerical formulas but more flexible goals for the improvement of minority opportunities. The wonder is not that there have been some abuses, but that there have been so few.

Increases in minority enrollment are not, however, the ultimate objective. No matter how impressive the growth in the numbers of minority students, what really counts is the number of minority graduates and professionals. We know relatively little about the performance in law school and on the bar examination of such students. We do now have the results of one study, done by Professor George N. Stevens under the auspices of the Association of American Law Schools Bar Examination Study Project. The study concentrated on the law school and bar examination experience of the 1,042 "disadvantaged" students admitted in the fall of 1970. The performance of this group was followed carefully through the three years of law school and on through the bar examination.

Superficially the results were not very encouraging. Of the 1,042 "disadvantaged" students who entered law school in the fall of 1970, 408 graduated on schedule in the spring or summer of 1973. An additional 178 were still in law school in good standing and expected to graduate—either enrolled in four-year programs, having taken a year out and returned, or having stretched the regular three-year curriculum. A total of 154 minority students were dismissed for academic reasons at some time during the three years—a rate higher than that for white-Anglo students, but undoubtedly lower than would have been predicted for the minority students on the basis of strictly numerical criteria. An additional 167 students simply disappeared from view; their status is unknown, and some of them may already have graduated while others would do so a year or two later. Finally, about one hundred of these students withdrew voluntarily during the three years.

The study followed the 408 graduates through the bar examination in the summer and fall of 1973. Here the data became sketchier because the law schools did not keep files in the same detail for graduates as for students currently enrolled. The records of the disadvantaged students were compared with those of their regular minority classmates. The results of this comparison is in one sense encouraging; 56% of the regular blacks passed, but only 46% of the disadvantaged blacks; for chicanos, the success rate of the disadvantaged students was about half that of the regular students; but among the American Indians, disadvantaged graduates actually fared better (80%) than the regular minority graduates (50%). A partial explanation for these confusing data is the relatively small size of the sample for all minority groups other than blacks. Moreover, it is always hard to compare composite bar examination results because success rates for all groups vary so much from state to state and year to year. Finally, it is much too early to judge from these returns how many members of the disadvantaged minority group entering in the fall of 1970 will eventually become members of the bar. It will take similar surveillance for another several years before anything like a final accounting can be rendered.

Legal education does, then, provide a useful microcosm of recent experience with minority admissions and enrollments. We know a good deal more about what has happened in this field than we do in most others—partly because the number of institutions is somewhat smaller, and partly because better data have been kept on minority enrollments since the mid-1960s. Against this background, it is now time to explore some of the legal problems and issues that may be raised by consideration of race in the admissions process.

CHAPTER FOUR

THE CONSTITUTION AND RACIAL PREFERENCE

When Judge Shorett found the *DeFunis* case on his docket, he went to the law books in search of precedent. He quickly discovered there was no Supreme Court decision in point. The absence of constitutional guidance was surprising, for the issue had been much discussed in the press and in law journals. As early as ten years before, there had been much debate over the legality of "benign quotas" in housing projects, but no court decisions. Thus the *DeFunis* case was what lawyers call a case of "first impression." The decision that Judge Shorett would soon render would have to create, rather than follow, legal precedent.

The slate was not completely blank, however. The relevant provision of the United States Constitution was that section of the Fourteenth Amendment which guarantees to all persons "the equal protection of the laws." This clause was adopted in 1868, with obvious primary concern for the rights of the recently freed former slaves. (The Fourteenth Amendment was closely tied to the Thirteenth, which essentially wrote the Emancipation Proclamation into the Constitution.) Through a curious twist of fate, the first major test of the equal protection clause involved not freedmen in the South but Chinese laundry owners in San Francisco. While these people were not citizens, the Supreme Court held that they could not be discriminated against on racial or national lines in the granting or denial of licenses to operate laundries. (The equal protection clause speaks not of "citizens" as do other constitutional guarantees, but of "persons" and thus extends to aliens as well.)

71

Over the years the equal protection clause was invoked to strike down various forms of racial discrimination—mostly against blacks, but more recently against other ethnic groups as well. Although the primary focus has always been on race, the Fourteenth Amendment has also afforded protection to the victims of many other forms of governmental discrimination. Where a law operates harshly against the poor, as in the case of the poll taxes that once existed in many states, the Supreme Court has held such classifications to be a denial of equal protection. The courts have also enjoined discrimination against lawfully resident aliens—in access to public employment, welfare benefits, and education. Recent cases have established the principle that illegitimate children may not be discriminated against, solely because of the accident of birth out of wedlock, in regard to inheritance, social security, and other benefits. Equality has also been extended to the right to vote; the Supreme Court held in 1964 that citizens of heavily populated areas were entitled to equal representation in Congress and state legislatures. These cases and many others over the years make clear the broad reach of the equal protection clause. Although clearly intended by its framers to protect the rights of newly freed blacks, the Courts have found in this clause a flexible weapon against various types of discrimination. Aliens, poor people, city dwellers, illegitimates, and others have been the beneficiaries of the post–Civil War concern for the former slaves.

In all these areas, however, the issue is discrimination *against* a particular group rather than in *favor* of anyone. There is simply no Supreme Court decision in the one hundred year history of the equal protection clause that deals with preferential treatment or so-called reverse discrimination. Legal commentators have cast about for dicta and even vague references that might shed some light on this issue in the absence of any clear precedent. Much has been made, for example, of the views of the first Mr. Justice Harlan, who observed in 1896 that "our constitution is color-blind, and neither knows nor tolerates classes among citizens." He added that "in respect of civil rights, common to all citizens, the constitution of the United States does not . . . permit any public authority to know the race of those entitled to be protected in the enjoyment of such right."

More than a half century later, in reversing the conviction of a black person by an all-white jury, the Court said that "the defendant is entitled to be tried by a jury in which there has been neither inclusion nor exclusion on the basis of race." But it would be unwise to attribute to the "inclusion" reference any judicial foresight on the racial preference issue. For one thing, the particular case dealt only with systematic *exclusion* of blacks from voter lists or jury rosters. In fact, sixteen years later a lower court took a quite different view of a case in which blacks had been deliberately *added* to the jury rolls to avoid racial imbalance. Moreover, it would be unwise to claim much significance for so casual a reference to "inclusion" in a single Supreme Court decision. Although the question of racial balance on juries came before the Court many times in the ensuing years, the "inclusion or exclusion" phrase never reappeared.

Such was the state of the law when Judge Shorett turned to the law reports for guidance in deciding *DeFunis*. For him the case most closely in point was the Supreme Court's 1954 decision declaring that public school segregation violated the equal protection clause. That case, Shorett believed, "decided that public education must be equally available to all regardless of race. After that decision the Fourteenth Amendment could no longer be stretched to accommodate the needs of any race." While the *Brown* case did concern the relationship between race and public education, that was about the extent of its applicability to *DeFunis*. The focus of *Brown* was a state policy directed *against* Negroes—in fact, barring them solely on grounds of race from a substantial part of the public school system. Like most of the other equal protection precedents, *Brown* involved racial exclusion, not inclusion. Indeed, it could be argued that *Brown* supported, rather than forbade, policies designed to integrate public education. (The Court had spoken in *Brown* of the isolation of the black child in a segregated school system; a major goal of preferential admissions policies was to overcome the past effects of such isolation and to prevent further racial isolation at the graduate level.) Thus the *Brown* decision failed to provide the guidance Judge Shorett sought. As the Washington Supreme Court later recognized, the constitutionality of racial preferences was one of first impression. In this chapter we seek to unravel some of the pertinent strands of constitutional law.

Equal protection issues have been approached under three quite different constitutional tests. One test is termed the "per se" standard, which holds that any use of race by government is invalid, regardless of the purpose or effect. Under this test, preferential classification would be as objectionable as racial discrimination. At the opposite extreme, there is the standard that has been used for classifications in the business and economic area—any distinction is valid so long as the government can show some rational basis for it, and so long as it is not wholly arbitrary and irrational. Under this test, almost any racial classification that did not harm minorities would probably pass muster. Then there is a third possibility, which would permit some but not all racial distinctions: in order to be constitutionally valid, a racial classification must be supported by a very strong or "compelling" governmental interest, which cannot be served without using race. The Washington Supreme Court decided upon the third test, but without really considering and rejecting the other two. What we shall do in this chapter is to explore all three standards in an effort to understand why the Washington court reached the conclusion it did reach in *DeFunis*.

The Per Se Test: All Racial Classifications Are Invalid

A literal reading of Justice Harlan's "the constitution is color blind" would mean that a governmental agency could never use race per se to differentiate among persons for any purpose. That view has at least some superficial appeal, since the Fourteenth Amendment sought to establish racial equality and to eliminate distinctions based on race. Yet the Supreme Court has repeatedly resisted invitations to espouse that view. Even when striking down racial classifications that were plainly harmful to minorities, the Court has consciously avoided such a rigid test.

The clearest indication of this reluctance has come in the cases dealing with racial intermarriage and cohabitation laws. Such laws once existed in virtually all southern states. Despite a number of earlier forays, they did not reach the Supreme Court until the 1960s. Although the penalties applied equally to the white and nonwhite partners to the interracial marriage or affair, the Court held such laws to be violative of the equal protection clause. More important than the result was the ruling constitutional standard. Throughout the opinion Chief Justice Warren spoke of "the very heavy burden of justification which the Fourteenth Amendment has traditionally required of state statutes drawn according to race." Such classifications, said the Chief Justice, "if they are ever to be upheld, must be shown to be necessary to the accomplishment of some permissible state objective, independent of the racial discrimination which it was the objective of the Fourteenth Amendment to eliminate." In an earlier case involving a similar issue, the Court had observed that such racial classifications are "constitutionally suspect" and "in most circumstances irrelevant to any constitutionally acceptable purpose."

Yet the Court stopped short of holding racial distinctions per se invalid, even though miscegenation laws (a) were directed against racial minorities, and (b) imposed criminal penalties for their violation. It would have been so easy and so natural to adopt a per se test that the Court must have had some very good reason for not doing so.

Around the same time another case gave added evidence of that circumspection. A federal district judge in Virginia had reviewed a number of state laws classifying people according to race. Most of these provisions had been held unconstitutional. But in one area— notations of race on divorce decrees—the judge sustained the use of race as an aid to the maintenance of vital statistics. When the complex decision was appealed to the Supreme Court the entire package was affirmed without opinion. One should be cautious about giving much significance to such actions; in the course of each year the Court affirms several dozen such lower federal court decrees without argument or opinion. Such judgments are, however, entitled to greater weight than the routine denials of discretionary review about which we spoke earlier; a memorandum affirmance is nonetheless an approval on the merits and may be cited as such. Moreover, the one portion of the lower court decision upholding one use of race was much less important than those sections striking down other Virginia racial classifications. The particular use of race—in the recording of divorce decrees—was so innocuous, so neutral, that it should not receive much attention. Yet the conscious approval by the Court of *any* racial classification has some meaning.

Perhaps the Supreme Court left open the validity of racial distinctions only to cover neutral practices like notations on divorce decrees. This inference would be plausible but for two factors. Although the miscegenation cases came after the divorce records case, no mention of the latter was made in the former. Moreover, the divorce records case is hardly strong enough by itself to create or define support of a major exception to the Court's general abhorrence of racial distinctions. It is improbable that a hole large enough for a trailer truck has been kept open to allow passage of a small wagon.

Support for a broader view of this exception comes from other quarters. In the past several years the validity of considering race has been recognized both in public education and employment. Here we find the courts increasingly willing to accept racial classifications to the extent necessary to promote equality or erase past racial injustice.

In the school segregation area, the courts have come a long way from the *Brown* decision. The pace of desegregation has been slow despite the command of the Supreme Court; there has been much more "deliberation" than "speed" in meeting *Brown*'s mandate of "all deliberate speed." The Supreme Court has been increasingly impatient in striking down remedies that did not promise substantial relief of segregated conditions. In 1971, the Court approved broad remedies decreed by the district court in Charlotte, North Carolina. These remedies required classification of students on the basis of race as a prerequisite to their reassignment in ways that would relieve racial imbalances. The Court approved such race conscious approaches, noting: "Just as the use of race must be considered in determining whether a constitutional violation has occurred, so also race must be considered in formulating a remedy."

Even before the Supreme Court had spoken this way, a number of lower federal and state courts had upheld race-based remedies. State laws in Massachusetts, Illinois, California, and New Jersey, for example, required affirmative steps to relieve and prevent several racial imbalances in the schools, and the state courts of all four states sustained the implicit but essential use of race in the assignment of pupils. Lower federal courts also allowed or even mandated race conscious remedies in public school systems. A signal example was the decision of the federal court of appeals sustaining a Newark, New Jersey, plan to promote minority administrators. Since the plan implied a departure from the regular eligibility list derived from test scores and experience, some white candidates who had been bypassed brought suit challenging the program's constitutionality. The federal courts upheld the plan despite the preferential use of race: "State action based partly on considerations of color, when color is not used per se, and in furtherance of a proper governmental objective, is not necessarily a violation of the Fourteenth Amendment."

Such judgments were not confined to school segregation. Consideration of race in awarding of radio and television licenses, planning for urban redevelopment, choosing jury panels, and other areas of government action has been upheld by the courts. Perhaps the clearest statement of the rationale comes from a federal court of appeals decision involving a racially conscious relocation plan for the central area of Norwalk, Connecticut:

> What we have said may require classification by race. That is something which the Constitution usually forbids, not because it is inevitably an impermissible classification, but because it is one which usually, to our national shame, has been drawn for the purpose of maintaining racial inequality. Where it is drawn for the purpose of achieving equality it will be allowed, and to the extent it is necessary to avoid unequal treatment by race, it will be required.

The context in which racial classification has played the most decisive role is that of public employment. Many lawsuits have recently been brought to challenge public employment practices that disadvantage racial minority groups. In most cities the percentages of blacks and Spanish-surnamed persons in the police and fire departments fall far below the general population figures. Such an imbalance results not from any conscious or explicit refusal to hire minorities, but rather from the use of civil service examinations, height and weight limits, and other entrance criteria that appear fair and neutral but in fact operate to the detriment of minority groups. In these cases the courts first review the criteria to determine whether they keep out minority applicants. If they do operate in that fashion, the agency must prove that they are "job-related"—that is, test abilities or qualifications necessary or relevant to the performance of the task for which a selection is being made. If the criteria are not job-related, they may not be used. Most such cases have gone against the government, for failure to show, for example, why a fireman must have an extensive knowledge of current events, or that a policeman need be well versed in American literature. In order to overcome the past effects of using such discriminatory employment criteria, the agency must sometimes hire a prescribed number of minority applicants or candidates—one out of every two, or three, or four persons employed. Such varied municipal agencies as the Boston, Philadelphia, and Erie police departments, the Minneapolis, San Francisco, and Bridgeport fire departments, and the Alabama and Mississippi highway patrols, among many others, have been ordered to practice "quota hiring" to alleviate persistent racial imbalance.

One of the most sweeping of these decisions recently sustained a Massachusetts regulation requiring private contractors who did business with the state to increase minority employment. Any contractor who refused to comply would lose all public contracts. A group of contractors brought suit in the federal court to challenge the constitutionality of such a requirement. The courts upheld the law even though it required racial preference. The opinion of the court of appeals explained the results:

> It is by now well understood . . . that our society cannot be
> completely color blind in the short term if we are to have a color
> blind society in the long term. After centuries of viewing through
> colored lenses, eyes do not quickly adjust when the lenses are

removed. Discrimination has a way of perpetuating itself, albeit unintentionally, because the resulting inequalities make new opportunities less accessible. Preferential treatment is one partial prescription to remedy our society's most intransigent and deeply rooted inequalities.

Given such decisions in the public employment area, it would be anomalous to proscribe use of race in college admissions. Indeed, the school and employment cases go somewhat substantially further than preferential admissions in two major respects. On the one hand, most of the employment and some school cases *require* use of race rather than simply permitting it. Moreover, the employment cases involve strict quotas based only on race; a preferential admission policy involves simply consideration of race, along with many other factors, to achieve a general goal. Thus it would appear that other types of decisions have gone well beyond the commitment to race challenged in the *DeFunis* case.

The analogy between employment or school desegregation and graduate admissions may, however, be imperfect. Some of the organizations supporting DeFunis as amici curiae argued that the quota hiring and school cases were distinguishable—in part because they used race only for the purpose of overcoming past discrimination, and in part because such race conscious remedies did not hurt the majority. Both distinctions deserve careful consideration.

The first argument—that the quota hiring and school segregation cases use race only to overcome past overt discrimination—seems tenuous. Surely there is such a background in the case of the Alabama Highway Patrol or the Mississippi State Police. But the situation in the Boston Police Department or the Minneapolis Fire Department is quite another matter. Racial imbalance in the civil service of northern and western cities is caused not by formal segregation but by the use of superficially neutral tests on which minority persons score less well, or by height and weight limits which keep out most chicanos, Puerto Ricans, and Asians, or simply from inadequate recruitment efforts. Thus the situation is in fact much closer to the situation in which preferential admissions policies are used.

Moreover, to the extent that race conscious remedies do assume a background of overt discrimination, the analogy is closer than may at first appear. Colleges and universities in the North and West do not deny admission to minorities. But in many southern states, dual higher education systems for blacks and whites have existed for decades and are just now coming under attack by the federal government—long after the major efforts to desegregate elementary and secondary schools. The range of programs, courses, and degrees available at the undersupported black colleges in those states falls far short of parity. Thus to the extent that a history of racial discrimination is necessary to sustain the use of racial preference, such a history can in fact be found in many parts of American higher education.

Suppose, however, that this distinction was accepted. Consider the bizarre results that would follow if race could be used for ameliorative purposes only where there had been a history of discrimination. The University of Texas at Austin, where racially exclusionary policies were once held unconstitutional, could admit preferentially, while the newer campuses at Dallas, El Paso, and San Antonio could not, even though the minority populations of those communities are in fact larger than in Austin. Much the same situation would occur in Missouri: The Flagship campus of the state university system at rural Columbia would be allowed to consider race in its admission policies because the Supreme Court once struck down its discriminatory practices. The newer urban campuses in Saint Louis and Kansas City, however, could take no account of race since they had never formally barred black applicants. In the Georgia system, the University at Athens could admit preferentially because there has been a history of racial exclusion; the new urban center in Atlanta, whose creation postdates official discrimination, could never adopt such a policy. Demographic conditions, common to all the public institutions in a single state, would thus become constitutionally irrelevant. So perverse a result could surely not have been intended by the courts.

The second distinction suggested between the employment and school cases and the issue of higher education admissions seems equally unpersuasive. Its premise is that racial hiring quotas and school bussing decrees are valid because they do not hurt the majority, while preferential admissions harm the majority to help the minority. This suggestion simply does not accord with reality. If anything, the distinction may argue the other way. The white parents who have brought suits to stop school bussing—not to mention those who have taken to the streets in Flint, Boston, and other communities—would be puzzled by the suggestion the minority is being helped without hurting the majority. White workers passed over by preferred minorities—like the San Francisco and Newark school administrators, the Suffolk County police candidates, and many others—would also find perverse the proposition that minorities are being helped without jeopardizing majority interests. The fact is that any race conscious remedy which aids minorities may in some way disadvantage others. The amicus curiae brief for the AFL-CIO in the *DeFunis* case saw clearly the connection between preferential admissions and quota hiring. The real reason for the national union's filing in support of DeFunis was to attack quota hiring, especially in the building trades. The AFL-CIO brief reviewed the recent cases upholding government plans to force private contractors to adopt minority hiring programs. Where other amici (e.g., the Anti-Defamation League) tried to distinguish the cases, the AFL-CIO insisted upon their assimilation. The brief spoke of "the harm to the majority [worker] who is . . . unemployed" as a result of "minority preference" and rejected the balm of one federal court that an affirmative action plan would not "eliminate job opportunities for White tradesmen. . . ."

In fact, the rejected law school applicant may be better off than the bussed white child or the displaced white worker. Take the very case of Marco DeFunis as an example. Though rejected by the University of Washington, he was accepted by four other law schools, including one or two that were academically comparable. His preference to remain in Seattle, for financial reasons, was after all much more a personal than an educational one. Had he been willing to work full time for a year, presumably he could have gone to Oregon and his wife could have found work as a dental technician in Eugene. A white family's option to leave the city and move to a suburb in order to avoid bussing is surely no less costly or painful. The white construction worker who is passed over by a preferential hiring program may be even less mobile, though presumably his number will come up on a future job. Preferential admission cannot, therefore, be distinguished from school desegregation and quota hiring as a more "benign" form of racial classification.

We have now wandered somewhat from the original issue—whether the equal protection clause requires a holding that all use of race is per se unconstitutional. The foregoing discussion should suggest several reasons for rejecting the per se test: First, because the Supreme Court has carefully and consistently avoided such a rigid rule, even where racial classifications harmed minority interests; and second, because the lower courts have extensively allowed and even required the use of race in areas (notably school desegregation and public employment) which turn out to be comparable to preferential admission. Thus unless the Court were ready to reverse field on school desegregation and to overrule all the quota hiring cases, the per se test should be rejected.

A Rational Basis Test: Use of Race Is Valid if Any Rational Basis Exists for the Classification

At the opposite extreme, it has been argued that courts should be rather lenient with classifications which help minority groups. In most cases involving distinctions between citizens or groups, the Supreme Court has required proof of no more than a "rational basis" —that is, some plausible governmental interest, and minimal rationality or logic behind the classification. New York City once passed a law permitting trucks to carry on their sides advertising for the owner, but not for anyone else. The Railway Express Company objected, since most advertising on their trucks was for other companies (e.g., "I'd Walk a Mile for a Camel" at the time of the case). The United States Supreme Court rejected the claim, finding that New York must have had *some* rational basis for drawing this strange distinction—perhaps a belief that owner-advertisements were less distracting to other drivers than advertisements for other businesses. In most contexts, the courts have upheld classifications upon proof of a rational basis or minimal governmental interest. More recently, for example, the Supreme Court has upheld "flat grants" in welfare programs, which treat large families less well than smaller families, and state school financing systems based on the property tax, which differentiate sharply between rich and poor communities in a single state. Even though important human interests were affected in both cases—welfare levels in one, and the quality of public education in the other—the court held that a "rational basis" was enough.

The Supreme Court has imposed a harsher standard only in certain specifically defined situations—where the classification affected the right to vote, the right to travel from state to state, or the exercise of some other "fundamental" human interest. The Court has also taken a stricter view of classifications that are "invidious"; chief among these are racial classifications which harm or disadvantage minority groups. But where neither a fundamental interest is impaired, nor the basis or effect of the classification is invidious, the courts have been quite lenient. Thus there is at least a superficially plausible argument that racial classifications designed to help rather than to harm minorities should be upheld if any rational basis can be found. Such classifications have been called "benign" to distinguish them from discriminatory classifications.

Under such a test, any policy designed to aid minorities would be valid if any rational basis for it could be shown. Separate grading systems, racially restricted financial aid programs, segregated dormitories, special courses and the like would be permitted under this test (regardless of their effects on others or the availability of alternatives); at least as substantial a basis could be found for any such distinctions as for the New York City ordinance on truck advertising, the welfare maximum grant limit, or the property-tax based school financing system. So long as the purpose or effect was to help minorities, and so long as some rational or plausible basis existed, that would be the end of the inquiry.

Shortly before *DeFunis,* the Supreme Court decided one case that suggests the rational basis test may be appropriate to racial classifications. The case involved a federal statute which requires the Bureau of Indian Affairs to give preference to Indians in filling certain jobs. This law was challenged both on equal protection grounds and under the 1964 Civil Rights Act. The Court disposed of the constitutional claim on the ground that the Indian preference was "reasonably and directly related to a legitimate, nonracially based goal"—a standard that sounds very much like "rational basis." But there are several difficulties with using this case as a precedent to show the constitutionality of preferential admission. For one, the Court said that the preference was not "racial" but rather applied to Indians on the basis of tribal membership and because of the special status of those tribes under federal law. Moreover, the Court traced evidence of the congressional concern for Indians back to the adoption of the Fourteenth Amendment. If the Court now held that such evidence justified a looser standard of constitutional review, a difference would be drawn between the two groups for whom Congress did provide special protection—Indians and blacks—and the newer minority groups (Spanish-surnamed, Filipino, Asian) for whom no such concern exists. Yet the need for special consideration may actually be greater in the case of these newer minority groups, for whom language as well as cultural barriers exist. Thus the Indian preference decision does not give constitutional support to the use of a "rational basis" test.

There are other reasons why a racial classification, however benign, should not be allowed without a test stricter than a "rational basis." Racial distinctions are perhaps the most dangerous and volatile of all distinctions among citizens. Racial classifications are inherently divisive. They tend to evoke the latent and overt prejudices of people on both sides of a line that all know exists but which gains added importance from governmental recognition or sanction. Moreover, racial distinctions are indelible and are clearly beyond an individual's control, even when government does not draw added attention to them. To recognize a class based on ethnic group membership is to reinforce barriers that should be minimized wherever possible if we are to enhance equality in our inescapably pluralistic society.

Further, the power to classify on the basis of race is always dangerous, no matter how carefully it may be exercised. Courts should avoid any standard of review which allows racial distinctions to become too easily embedded in the law. Today's majority may become tomorrow's minority, and the group that claims protection today could turn out to be tomorrow's oppressor. Finally, the legislature that enacts laws based on racial distinctions may appear to many citizens to have departed significantly from the neutrality which government must maintain.

There is a further and more practical reason why benign racial classifications should not be lightly judged. Clearly *some* racial distinctions—those that disadvantage or harm minorities—must be strictly scrutinized. If the difference between benign and nonbenign classifications is to have constitutional significance, then we must be able to distinguish very clearly between the two. Yet the courts have warned repeatedly against resting constitutional distinctions on legislative motive or intent—partly because legislative history does not always yield satisfactory evidence, and partly because motive or intent varies widely among the members of a lawmaking body. The Supreme Court observed over a decade ago: "Judicial inquiries into Congressional motives are at best a hazardous matter, and when that inquiry seeks to go behind objective manifestations, it becomes a dubious affair indeed." Thus, as much for practical as theoretical reasons, any constitutional test that depends on divining legislative motive should be rejected.

It should be clear that the "rational basis" test opens the door much too wide in the racial area. If the only issue were whether the classification helped minorities, then "reverse discrimination" could run rampant. Segregation could conceivably be reimposed in the name of ending the effects of segregation. The effects upon nonminority groups would be irrelevant. The availability of alternatives that avoided such consequences would also be immaterial. Clearly, then, something more than a "rational basis" seems to be required.

The Compelling State Interest Test

There is a third standard, between the other two, which would permit some but not all uses of race. In the *DeFunis* case, the Washington Supreme Court simply announced that "the burden is on the law school to show that its consideration of race is necessary to the accomplishment of a compelling state interest." The origin of this standard is far from clear, and the Washington opinion cited no relevant authority. Many years ago the United States Supreme Court used a similar test in upholding the Japanese relocation orders, which were harmful to minority groups on an explicitly racial basis. In the miscegenation cases, where the Court struck down the racial classification, a similar standard appears: A racial classification must be proved "necessary to the accomplishment of some permissible state objective, independent of the racial discrimination which it was the object of the Fourteenth Amendment to eliminate." Most recently, the Supreme Court has allowed the use of race in fashioning remedies for school desegregation, but has announced no constitutional standard.

The Supreme Court's occasional statements about the strength of relevant governmental interests have not been particularly helpful. In cases that involve restrictions on freedom of speech or the press, the Court has insisted upon "a substantial regulatory interest" or "an appreciable public interest"—though in these cases the particular constraint has always been held unconstitutional. A bit closer to the mark are recent cases holding that classifications which burden "fundamental rights" of individuals must show unusually strong justification. Several years ago, for example, the Court held that residence restrictions or "waiting periods" imposed on new applicants for welfare who came from other states were unconstitutional because they deterred the right of free interstate travel. The majority declared that "any classification which serves to penalize any exercise of the [right to move freely between states] unless shown to promote a *compelling* governmental interest, is unconstitutional." The Court analyzed several interests advanced by the states—preventing fraud, getting needy people into the work force, stabilizing the welfare rolls, among others —but found none of these "compelling." In later years the Court applied the same analysis to strike down state residence requirements on registration of voters and on access to free medical care.

In fact, the Court has never upheld a classification which had to meet the "compelling interest" test. Thus it is hard to know what sort of governmental claim would pass muster. There is but one oblique hint in recent law. After striking down a Connecticut law which prevented students from other states from ever qualifying as "residents" for state college tuition purposes, the Court suggested that ordinary tuition differentials—under which students may be reclassified after a year or so—were valid. Indeed, the Court had earlier affirmed without opinion two lower court decisions so holding. In the Connecticut case, the Court summarized the interests which underlay those holdings: "We fully recognize that a State has a legitimate interest in protecting and preserving the quality of its own colleges and universities and the right of its own bona fide residents to attend such institutions on a preferential tuition basis." The value of this comment for our current discussion is, of course, rather limited. The case in which it appears actually *struck down* the classification, and did so on grounds of due process rather than equal protection. There is some uncertainty whether the "compelling interest" test applies at all here since the Court held that education is not a "fundamental right." Yet this brief clue gives about as much insight as we have into what interests the Court deems "compelling."

Before we accept this standard of review we must account for Justice Douglas' curious comment in his *DeFunis* dissent:

> The argument is that a "compelling" state interest can easily justify the racial discrimination that is practiced here. To many, "compelling" would give members of one race even more than pro rata representation. . . .
>   If discrimination based on race is constitutionally permissible when those who hold the reins can come up with "compelling" reasons to justify it, then constitutional guarantees acquire an accordionlike quality. . . . So far as race is concerned, any state-sponsored preference of one race over another in that competition is in my view "invidious" and violative of the Equal Protection Clause.

A literal reading of this statement would leave no option but the per se test which we rejected at the start—a test which Justice Douglas himself has carefully avoided in earlier cases. Moreover, the compelling interest test had provided a useful tool for deciding the cases involving the right to travel and to vote—where the protection of human rights and liberties has proved anything but "accordionlike." Nor would a per se test comport with Justice Douglas's own earlier writings—for example, his suggestion in 1956 that "regulations based on race may . . . be justified by reason of the special traits of [particular] races." Finally, the very opinion containing this statement strongly implied the validity of racial distinctions—for example, "a separate classification of [minority] applicants . . . lest race be a subtle force in eliminating minority members because of cultural differences." Thus it seems unlikely that Justice Douglas really meant to read the compelling interest test out of the equal protection clause. He was understandably troubled about the subjectivity inherent in any test which would sanction any use of race. Yet of all the justices he would be almost the last to insist that government could never display special concern for the needs of a disadvantaged or deprived group. The contradictory character of the *DeFunis* dissent simply deprives us of the reconciliation which will presumably appear in later decisions.

Whatever language one uses, something like the "compelling interest" test offers the only acceptable middle ground between the rational basis and the per se tests. Yet the courts have given little guidance in the dimensions or application of the "compelling interest" formulation. From analogous situations we can infer the elements which constitute such a test, and which will presumably be spelled out when the courts devote more time and thought to the constitutional context than they have done to date. Four factors seem essential—not because any court has so specified, but because the compelling interest test would be meaningless without them.

First, the classification must be compatible with the objectives of the Fourteenth Amendment. Any classification that is subject to strict scrutiny by the Court—that is, any classification that uses a suspect factor like race or geography or that affects a fundamental right—must serve or promote the aims of the equal protection clause. Most of the race classifications reviewed by the court have failed even to meet this first criterion. Laws forbidding racial cohabitation or intermarriage, for example, may indeed serve a plausible governmental interest, but they do so by penalizing persons who live or marry across racial lines. It is this kind of discrimination which the equal protection clause sought to eliminate. Thus there is a clear conflict between such classifications and the objectives of the Fourteenth Amendment. A court need go no further where such dissonance is manifest. The only exception to this precept is the thirty-year-old Japanese relocation cases, which may best be explained as a wartime aberration. (At least two members of the Court who were involved in that episode in different ways—Justices Black and Clark —later wrote them off on this basis.)

Second, the state interest must be substantial if not absolutely central to the governmental process. In the welfare residency cases, for example, the Court rejected both administrative convenience and welfare cost reduction as interests falling far short of "compelling" even though they might suffice to meet a lesser test. On the other hand, in the Connecticut tuition case the Court apparently found compelling the desire of a state to limit access of nonresidents to their state universities. That interest was not simply economic or administrative, but had vital educational dimensions as well. Yet the quest for criteria of substantiality is largely speculative. Since the Japanese relocation cases—where the interest was seen as the protection of a nation at war from enemy espionage—there is no holding precisely on the point. The Washington Supreme Court in *DeFunis* not only failed to state any test of substantiality; the fact is that the court did not even spell out in much detail the governmental goals it found "compelling." Thus we are still pretty much on our own in this area.

Third, there must be a rational relationship between the classification and the governmental interest or interests. Indeed, the Supreme Court said in the miscegenation cases that the classification must be "necessary" to implement the interest. In the welfare residence cases, the fatal flaw was not so much the basis of the classification or the insubstantiality of the asserted interests, but the weakness of the connection between the two. The defendant states had argued that waiting periods for newcomers promoted accurate welfare planning. The Court replied that since no such waiting period was imposed on long-term residents of the state who were newly in need of welfare, the restriction did not rationally serve the alleged objective. Nor was there any logical connection between the waiting period and the need to verify information about applicants.

On the "linkage" or "nexus" issue, we do have a little law in the racial area. In the interracial cohabitation cases the Court recognized that states had a valid interest in deterring promiscuity and premarital intercourse. But the use of race for this purpose—presuming that interracial couples posed a greater threat than monoracial couples—was not rational in terms of the stated and valid objective. By contrast, the Court has underscored in the school desegregation cases the close nexus between race and effective remedies: "Just as the race of students must be considered in determining whether a constitutional violation has occurred, so also race must be considered in formulating a remedy."

Fourth, the governmental interest must be incapable of being adequately served through nonracial means. No cases involving racial classifications actually impose such an obligation, to be sure. Elsewhere, the Supreme Court has said not only that a suspect classification must be "necessary" to a valid governmental end, but that less onerous means (if available) must be employed. In the voting residence case in 1973, the Supreme Court declared that "if there are other, reasonable ways to achieve those goals with a lesser burden on constitutionally protected activity, a state may not choose the way of greatest interference." Similarly, the welfare residence cases indicated that the challenged classification could not be used where "less drastic means are available, and are employed [elsewhere] to minimize the hazard."

Obviously the validation of racial preferences will be more difficult if this fourth element of the test must be met. Yet there seems no doubt about the appropriateness of imposing such a burden. As we indicated earlier, all racial classifications are inherently dangerous and should be sanctioned only for as long and to the extent they are absolutely essential. Whatever the courts might say, one cannot over-look the highly charged political context in which this debate has unfolded. If the pursuit of less suspect classifications were not required by the courts, legislators and political figures would insist upon them in any case. Mr. Justice Douglas has already stated his view that nonracial alternatives are constitutionally relevant even if they are less effective than racial preferences. Thus it would be pointless for a court or a commentator to adopt the compelling interest test without this fourth tenet.

With a constitutional standard before us, we proceed in the next three chapters to apply that standard to the problem of preferential admission in higher education. Chapter 5 will summarize the case in favor of preferential admissions and show that the state does have a compelling interest; Chapter 6 will consider the nonracial alternatives and show that they do not suffice; and Chapter 7 will review and appraise the arguments against preferential admissions.

CHAPTER FIVE

THE CASE FOR
PREFERENTIAL ADMISSIONS

In the fall of 1968 a black law student at UCLA was recalling his own educational background to a faculty group. He had grown up in Watts, attended entirely black schools and lived most of his life in the ghetto. Of his high school class of several hundred, only three graduates went on to college. At that time there were no nearby junior or community colleges and higher education was simply out of the question for most people in that part of Los Angeles. Of the three who had gone to college, all graduated with high distinction. One was now a fourth-year medical student at USC, the speaker was in his final year of law school, and the third was about to receive his Ph.D. in political science, also at UCLA. This remarkable account tells several things about the higher education of minority students in the period before preferential admission policies were adopted. First, the barriers (both educational and financial) to matriculation were so high that very few students from the ghetto or barrio even began college; most of the small minority population on white-Anglo campuses came from middle class backgrounds. Second, those who did make it into college from severely disadvantaged backgrounds were extremely good risks and were likely not only to survive but to distinguish themselves. (In the late 1960s, a survey of attrition rates at the medical school of a midwestern state university showed that the drop-out rate for white-Anglo students was almost ten times that of minority students; the number in the latter group was pitifully small, but those who managed to get that far stuck it out.) The third lesson that emerges from the UCLA student's experience brings us to the central focus of preferential admissions: without some selective consideration of the special backgrounds, needs, and potential of disadvantaged minority students, no substantial increase in their numbers is likely to occur. The essence of the case in favor of preferential admission is that little would have happened without such policies. But the matter is obviously much more complex than that, and deserves a chapter of its own.

The Effects of Minority Underrepresentation

We discussed earlier in some detail the historic exclusion of minorities from higher education and particularly from graduate and professional programs. This condition by itself would not be a cause of national concern if it did not have harmful collateral effects. Education is, after all, not an end in itself. Indeed, we learned from the recent student protests that many young people have attended college who should have done something else. A national television documentary (entitled "Higher Education—Who Needs It?") raised the most basic doubts about the value of the general baccalaureate degree. Many of the new jobs anticipated within the next decade will demand technical skills rather than liberal education. Thus it is fair to question whether mere underrepresentation of minorities in higher education is a critical problem.

While the United States is far short of having universal higher education (matriculation seems to have peaked at about 50% of high school graduates) both the college experience and the baccalaureate degree remain vital for many reasons. Christopher Jencks and David Riesman, wise commentators on American higher education, have observed that "the bulk of the American intelligentsia now depends upon universities for a livelihood and virtually every would-be member of the upper middle class thinks he needs some university's imprimatur, at least in the form of a B.A. and preferably in the form of a graduate degree or professional degree as well." What is true for the majority is especially true for the minority. Much as with immigrant groups earlier in the twentieth century, upward mobility almost demands higher education, whatever may be the intrinsic merit of a liberal arts degree.

Even if a college degree were simply window dressing, the collateral effects of restricted minority access would be disturbing. Persons with college degrees do enjoy earning capacity far above non-degree holders; the ratio which obtains in this regard for the population as a whole also exists in the minority community, although the income figures are lower. Access to graduate and professional schools (and of course to the professions they serve) are effectively limited to college graduates. As we have seen earlier, the percentage of minority students in the graduate schools is lower than the corresponding undergraduate percentage. The number of minority persons holding graduate and professional degrees is not only lower than the proportion for the entire population; graduate-undergraduate ratios are substantially lower *within* the minority sector of the academic community, a fact which reduces the prospects for increases in minority group teachers and professional practitioners. Indeed, it seems that even an arithmetic expansion of minority participation in the learned professions would require an almost geometric increase in the number of minority undergraduates.

The nature of the underrepresentation and its effects can best be understood by taking the legal profession as a microcosm. Today there is roughly one white attorney for every 630 persons, but only one black attorney for every 6,000 black citizens. Despite the vigorous recruitment efforts and the substantially increased number of minority students, not more than 2% of the American bar is black. Minority representation in the legal "establishment" is even less substantial. A 1973 survey of the seventeen largest law firms in Chicago reveals that of 1,364 attorneys, there are but one black partner, thirteen black associates, and eight Spanish-surnamed persons (of whom seven are in a single firm with a substantial Latin-American clientele.) These results are especially depressing because of the large and increasingly well educated black population in Chicago, and the very special efforts (and monetary contributions) of the Chicago bar to support minority legal education.

The situation in particular regions is even more extreme than the national averages suggest. Several years ago there were only seventeen black lawyers in Mississippi to serve a black population of nearly a million. Today there are forty-nine black attorneys admitted to practice in the state—an improvement, but still a ratio of 1:16,000 compared to 1:450 for white lawyers to white Mississippians. In Georgia, the situation is superficially somewhat better than in Mississippi. But since about one-third of the black attorneys in Georgia work for the federal, state, or local governments, the number actually available for private clients is smaller than the total lawyer population would indicate.

Moving to the opposite corner of the country, the situation in the state of Washington is illustrative. One of the groups supporting DeFunis argued there was no need for preferential admission because the percentage of black students in the law school (2.2%) at the time the program was adopted matched the racial makeup of the state. The relevant comparison, of course, should be to the minority representation in the bar, which presents a quite different picture. According to 1970 census figures, there is one white lawyer for every 720 white Washingtonians; one black lawyer for every 4,195 blacks, one Indian attorney for each 6,677 Indians, and at most one Mexican-American lawyer for every 35,000 chicanos.

As the Washington state data suggest, other minority groups are even less well represented than blacks. Take the case of the Spanish-speaking population in California, the state's largest minority group. The ratio of lawyers to clients for California as a whole is 1:530. In the Mexican-American community, however, there is but one attorney for every 9,482 persons. Across the country, a similar situation exists for the Puerto Rican population of New Jersey; the state appears to have only three Spanish-speaking lawyers for a population of some 300,000.

Figures for the medical profession show a similar, if slightly less acute, underrepresentation. At last count there was one white physician for every 750 persons in the general population, but only one black doctor for every 3,500 black citizens. There appear to be only 250 Mexican-American and 56 American Indian physicians in the entire United States. Thus the extent of the underrepresentation in the professions seems beyond dispute.

The cold statistics do not, however, tell the whole story. Much more significant in terms of governmental interest are the social, psychological, and economic effects of underrepresentation. The correlation between income and education seems obvious. The significance of this factor has been heightened by recent economic trends. During the 1960s the gap between incomes for blacks and whites narrowed, and at one point the black median was 61% of the white median. During the 70s the gap has begun to widen again, moving back by 1973 to the ratio of 1966. Meanwhile, the Spanish-speaking community has fared no better. Recent Census Bureau data show that Spanish-speaking groups have been losing ground in purchasing power vis-à-vis the general population, and that educational attainment for this group is even lower than for blacks. (Of Mexican-Americans, 27.8% have finished high school, a figure slightly better than the 26% of Puerto Ricans.) The pressures of inflation which have pressed all groups have hit the minority community particularly savagely. Savings are lower there and unemployment (even in good times) is higher. Thus the consequences of lower levels of educational attainment and opportunity are felt with particular force by minority groups.

Socioeconomic status is by no means the only collateral value. Professional status is a vitally important factor in shaping minority group self-respect and capacity for effective civic participation and self-government. There have, to be sure, been dramatic strides in black political involvement and participation. By 1974 there were just short of three thousand black elected office holders in the country. But this figure is still less than one percent of all elected officials in the country. It is only in the federal and state civil service that blacks begin to be represented meaningfully, though even there at typically lower salaries and classifications. Obviously not all elected officials are lawyers, and a law degree is no prerequisite to political success. But lawyers are disproportionately represented at all levels of public life, and exert legislative power even beyond their numbers. Thus in the most direct sense the underrepresentation of minorities in the professions impairs the capacity for civic involvement and self-government.

Minority professionals and educators also serve a vital function as role models for younger members of the community. Success and achievement suggest to minority youths that there are ways of "making it" within the system that do not require resort to self-help or more drastic means. Such sanguine prospects might profoundly reduce the high school attrition of minority students, despite the segregation and overcrowding which will probably persist in the inner city schools for some time. The promise of success through higher education may also have a salutary effect on crime and violence in the minority community, where the principal victims of lawlessness are the members of those communities themselves. Conversely, there is little question that the closing off of opportunities will breed frustration, resentment, and anger at the predominantly white-Anglo society. Columbia University political scientist Charles V. Hamilton has shown that a major cause of urban violence is the exclusion of minority groups from the decision-making process. "People do not," he observed, "blow up or burn down what they feel they are a legitimate part of."

Let us take a closer look at the effects of minority underrepresentation in the legal profession. Clearly the bar as presently structured does not fully meet the needs of the poor and especially of the minority poor. "Legal services are still the preserve of middle and upper incomes," notes Virginia law professor Ernest Gellhorn, one of the earliest proponents of increased opportunity for minorities in law. "Government sponsored and voluntary legal services programs, while expanding, do not fill the need. They are not available in all parts of the country, are limited by an inability-to-pay test, and do not provide representation in all types of cases." Superficially it might appear that this need could be met simply by expanding the number of white-Anglo lawyers with a commitment to serve the poor. That is, however, only partially accurate.

While many white lawyers do admirably serve the minority community, there are certain things they cannot do as well as a person who comes from that community. Supreme Court Justice William J. Brennan once observed that black lawyers "most clearly understand the problems and difficulties found by members of the Negro community." The director of the southern regional office of the American Civil Liberties Union believes that many racially oppressive practices would have gone unchallenged but for the presence of native southern black lawyers; even highly competent and committed white attorneys "would not have understood or would not have raised the racial issues."

What is true of the black community is even more true in the Spanish-speaking community. New Mexico Governor Roberto Mondragon has written eloquently of that special need from his own chicano background:

> When these people are forced to resort to Anglo law and counsel, the language and cultural differences result in the most difficult communication imaginable. In cases where the Spanish-speaking American resorts to Anglo counsel, the Spanish-speaking, because of his suspicion of the Anglo value-oriented legal system, will relay only that information which he feels is relevant to his case and withhold all other information which may indeed be vital. Despite any good faith representation by the Anglo attorney, lack of information will in many cases result in the loss of the suit. This in turn escalates and deepens the fear of the Spanish-speaking American in the legal process. . . .
>
> To carry the situation one step further, the prevailing feeling in the barrio and the pueblos is that the courts are insensitive to their social and cultural values. To them the legal system is used to perpetuate injustices rather than to protect their legal rights. This feeling is reinforced by many very unfavorable contacts that these people have with the courts and law enforcement agencies.
>
> The legal profession itself has closed the door to the Spanish-speaking and Native American. In many cases the legal rights of these people go unprotected because attorneys are unwilling to represent them either because their cases are so controversial or because they are unable to pay the high cost of legal assistance. Furthermore, until recently, the legal profession has for the most part been indifferent in protecting the civil rights of these people.

If there remains any doubt about the importance of getting more minority students into college, there should be little doubt about the need to get more of them out and into those professions where they can play a unique role. In short, there does seem to be a substantial governmental interest in increasing the number of minority students and graduates because of the intrinsic value of having more and better educated members of the minority community. This is the first and undoubtedly the most obvious interest underlying preferential admission policies in higher education. It is not, however, the only argument a college or university might advance for giving special consideration to minority group members. We now turn to several other possible governmental interests.

The Effects of Traditional Entrance Criteria

The causes of minority underrepresentation are more complex than the consequences. There has been extensive debate about the fairness of standardized tests such as the Law School Admission Test. The Educational Testing Service and its various branches have conducted considerable research on this subject. What emerges from these studies is a set of beguilingly simple propositions that set the stage for this discussion: First, that the use of standardized tests (and grades) has served to exclude disproportionate numbers of minority applicants who have lower than average scores and grades. Second, however, standardized tests do not underpredict the performance of minority students, and may in fact slightly *overpredict* the performance of minority persons. Third, such tests appear valid and reasonable criteria for selecting among nonminority applicants; while they do not correlate perfectly with later performance, their record is sufficiently good to warrant their retention for most groups. Obviously the juxtaposition of these three propositions creates a paradox for the admissions officer who wants to be both fair and rational in selecting among applicants.

The issue before us is not whether admissions should be based *solely* on grades and test scores. No responsible institution, no matter how large the applicant group, would invoke exclusively quantitative measures in this sensitive area. While mathematical factors may operate at the high and low ends of the scale, hard choices in the middle range must be resolved with the help of other factors. The question here is whether a college or university may validly take race or ethnic status into account in deciding what weight to give the grades and test scores—or possibly to adjust the resulting performance predictor on the basis of race. The real issue is therefore much narrower than the question many people associate with *DeFunis*—whether the numerical rank ordering can be varied or departed from at all. As we saw in Chapter 3, all sorts of exceptions and variations have long been recognized for reasons that have nothing to do with race. The issue now before us is only whether race can be added to the list.

If we agree that standardized tests (a) exclude disproportionate numbers of minority students but (b) neither have inherently biased content nor are unfair as predictors, how do we resolve the paradox? It is relevant first to note that the organizations which devise and administer the tests and report the results have not only cautioned against excessive reliance on test scores but have suggested that race or ethnic status might properly be weighed along with numerical indicia. The Law School Admission Council filed a most significant brief in the *DeFunis* case, supporting the University of Washington's preferential policies. The brief reviewed the growing concern of the Council over the underrepresentation of minority students, despite its confidence in the accuracy and fairness of the LSAT for the general run of students. Particularly in a time of rising applications for professional study, the Council recognized the need to temper the admissions decision with nonquantitative factors. With particular reference to the use of standardized test scores the brief urged:

> The handicaps visited on members of minority groups bear directly on the appraisal of their pre-law educational attainments. . . . A proven capacity to catch up in learning, and the distance between where he started and where he now stands, may be more important to prediction than a comparison of his present level of attainment with that of others who had no headwind to overcome. Standardized testing is not so familiar in segregated or vocational schools, where college preparation is not emphasized, and the verbal abilities measured by such tests—and by the law school examinations—are seldom developed in such an environment.

The LSAC also argued that "predictions based on test scores and college grades must be ameliorated for minority backgrounds which restrict opportunities to acquire or to demonstrate academic abilities."

It would be ironic if a court were to insist that a law school give greater weight to test scores than the organization reporting those scores believed was warranted. In addition, much experience with preferential programs confirms that many applicants who would have been excluded by rigid adherence to numerical ranking are in fact well qualified and will succeed if given the chance. (In the very class of which Marco DeFunis was a member at the University of Washington, for example, the attrition rate for minority students—all of whom were preferentially admitted—was virtually identical to the attrition of nonminority students, most of whom were admitted on the basis of more traditional criteria.) Thus the denial of infallibility to the tests accords not only with the convictions of admissions officers, but with recent practical educational experience as well.

It is important to note that we are dealing here with two quite distinct theories that may lead to the same conclusion. The view of the testing experts is that race should be taken into account in an "ameliorative" way even though the tests are fair to, or even slightly favorable to, minority groups. The other theory, reflected in Mr. Justice Douglas' *DeFunis* opinion, is that such tests should be disregarded for minorities (or even for all applicants) because they are culture-bound, biased, or whatever. Douglas's sweeping view on this issue is revealing:

> Insofar as LSAT tests reflect the dimensions and orientation of the
> Organization Man they do a disservice to minorities. . . . My
> reaction is that the presence of an LSAT test is sufficient warrant
> for a school to put racial minorities in a separate class in order
> better to probe their capacities and potentials.

Neither theory really explains the paradox—that standardized tests exclude disproportionate numbers of minority applicants and thus should be weighted differently even though their content may not be racially biased and even though they may predict academic performance about as well for minority and majority students. Several factors offer hope for reconciliation. First, a negative correlation between test scores and law school or college performance would be surprising in view of their symbiotic development and validation. Professors David Kirp and Mark Yudoff have recently written:

> That standardized test scores and higher education performance are highly correlated is unsurprising, for the tests are meant to mirror institutional requirements. They stress the very linguistic and logical skills the university prizes.

A negative correlation would be most puzzling in view of the homogeneity of the factors being compared—traditional admission standards and traditional grading policies and curricula. Both curricula and grading standards have been designed to deal with a predominantly white-Anglo, middle class student population whom the traditional admission tests have brought to American campuses. As the students change, the curricula will presumably change in some degree, and the correlation of performance with admissions standards should also change. Where curricula and evaluation procedures have been redesigned to reflect the special needs and interests of minority students, rather different correlations seem probable—i.e., standardized test scores might be found to be underpredictive for minority applicants.

Second, most of the validation studies involve freshmen or first-year grades rather than total performance. Adjustment to the strange and sometimes hostile environment of a white campus takes longer for the minority than the majority student. The freshman year is undoubtedly traumatic for many students, but is especially so for students from the ghetto or barrio. Correlations which stop with freshman year grades may thus in fact be biased in a rather subtle but damaging way.

Third, the populations being compared in most validation studies are simply not comparable. When one contrasts the performance of all minority students in a class with that of all other students, the pairing is superficially sound. In fact, however, a much higher percentage of the minority students come from inadequate elementary and secondary schools; many more are poor and must work at outside jobs; a far higher proportion will either have heavy and time-consuming family responsibilities or will lack the reinforcement and support that white families typically derive from stable home environments. Thus a fairer comparison would be between minority students and similarly disadvantaged white students, of whom there are in fact far too few on most campuses. The critical issue would be how well the test-performance correlation for poor black students from, say, Cleveland's East Side compares with the same data for children of poor Czech steelworkers from the West Side—not whether blacks do better or worse than Shaker Heights graduates with the same predicted first year averages. Until we have comparisons of truly comparable samples, the issue must remain conjectural.

Finally, the validation studies have dealt almost entirely with blacks, who are after all English-speaking minority students. Even if heavily verbal standardized tests are completely fair for these students, their application to students who grew up speaking Spanish or an Indian tribal tongue may be quite different. In recognition of that difference, several courts have held that Spanish-speaking children may not be classified as "educationally mentally retarded" on the basis of English language tests, because of the linguistic bias. (San Francisco school officials acknowledged several years ago that when a group of chicano children who had been so classified were retested in Spanish, 45% of them proved to be of average or above average intelligence.)

Special consideration of the test scores of minority applicants would be warranted, however, only if there are reasons—unrelated to ability or college potential—why all or most minority students tend to score lower. In the case of students from non-English-speaking backgrounds (chicanos, Indians, and some Asians), the explanation seems obvious. The tests are in English, and rely rather heavily on facility in our native tongue. In the case of black students, the explanation is more elusive. There are variations in vernacular language, to be sure, and cultural differences between black and white community life are significant. But black children surely have an advantage in this regard over their Spanish-speaking counterparts, and the pervasive effect of television has also blurred the differences. In the case of blacks there is a different factor: The deplorable condition of the urban ghetto public schools, which within the last decade have become increasingly racially isolated despite formal attempts at desegregation. These schools are often overcrowded, housed in old and run-down plants, with equipment, programs, and extracurricular activities of a quality far below those of the middle class and suburban schools. The rates of retention and graduation even from these schools are often much lower than for the general school population. But even graduation rates tell only part of the story. It is well known that high school counsellors and advisers tend to channel minority youth into technical and vocational tracks that may render them ineligible for college. (In New York City, about one-quarter of the students graduating from eight high schools in the most depressed areas of the city received "academic" or college preparatory diplomas in 1957. A decade later the percentage of academic diplomas in the same schools had fallen to thirteen.)

Experience in taking standardized tests (and the likelihood of success on them) varies inversely with such conditions endemic to the ghetto or barrio school. Students in noncollege bound classes obviously will not practice on college board exams. At a higher level, postsecondary students in technical and vocational programs will have far less experience in writing essay examinations than their contemporaries in liberal arts and sciences programs. Since the general condition of minority education militates against the experience that helps middle class white-Anglo students perform well on such tests, a different weighting of the scores seems entirely appropriate.

This last point suggests that the use of standardized tests which exclude disproportionate numbers of minority applicants may even be constitutionally vulnerable. Many recent decisions have invalidated the use of such tests in employment, where minority groups have been underrepresented in the workforce. The Supreme Court several years ago held that when such a condition exists, "if an employment practice which operates to exclude Negroes cannot be shown to be related to job performance, the practice is prohibited." At least one lower court has extended this theory to school testing. In that case, in which the use of tests was attacked because a disproportionate number of minority students ended up in the educationally mentally retarded track, the court required the school authorities to demonstrate the educational relevance of the tests, which they were unable to do. The failure of such justification rendered the continued use of such tests unconstitutional in this context.

The case that is most nearly in point leans the other way, however. San Francisco has one highly selective, city-wide college preparatory school, Lowell High School. Admission to Lowell from other schools is based on grades in four college preparatory subjects. The proportion of minority students entering Lowell is considerably lower than minority enrollment throughout the district. A group of parents brought suit to challenge this procedure, claiming that the Lowell admission (or transfer) policy denied them equal protection. The federal court of appeals in the summer of 1974 rejected the claim and upheld the use of grades despite the tendency to exclude larger numbers of minorities. The court found it conclusive that "conditioning admission to Lowell upon the level of past academic achievement substantially furthers the district's purpose of operating an academic high school." Moreover, the students excluded from Lowell were not denied a quality, or even college preparatory education, elsewhere in the San Francisco system. (The effect of the policy was in fact mitigated by a preferential minority transfer policy adopted about the time the suit was brought. While this program played no part in the holding, the court may have been influenced by the voluntary steps already taken to diversify the Lowell student body.)

Despite the paucity of pertinent court cases, an argument can be made for the unconstitutionality of entrance criteria which disproportionately exclude minority applicants. The parallel issue in employment has countless times been resolved against the maintenance of racially or ethnically detrimental criteria that are not clearly job-related. Perhaps it would be easier to prove the "education-relatedness" of grade point averages and standardized tests in college admissions, as the Lowell case suggests. It is one thing to require a college degree of one who seeks to become a lawyer or a physician; it is another to require a candidate for a police or fire department job to be versed in Shakespeare and Mozart. In any case, the time is not far off when courts will call upon colleges and universities to justify in educational terms any entrance standards which disfavor minority groups.

To summarize this discussion of the effect and validity of standardized tests: Even if traditional entrance and admissions criteria are not *discriminatory* (that is, biased in content), there is little question they are *exclusionary* to minority groups. This fact alone suggests that colleges and universities have a valid interest in weighting test scores differently for members of these excluded groups, even without finding the tests themselves invalid. Substantial numbers of minority students will not be enrolled at predominantly white campuses unless one (or more) of the following changes occurs: (1) the quality of secondary education for minority students improves dramatically; (2) financial and social barriers that now impede advancement of minority students are dramatically reduced; (3) alternative tests and predictive measures are developed that do not disproportionately exclude minority applicants; or (4) the use of traditional admissions criteria is adjusted to overcome the effects of their uniform application. Of these possibilities, the fourth appears the only one immediately attainable. Thus there appears to be a strong state interest in doing precisely what the Law School Admission Council and other groups suggest—taking race or ethnic status into account in the use of test scores and grades.

Compensation for the Effects of Past Discrimination and Segregation

A third and quite distinct governmental interest in preferential admission policies derives from educational history. There is little question that past racial segregation partially explains the present minority underrepresentation. Higher education in many states has been until quite recently organized along explicitly racial lines. In fact, "dual" higher education systems in the southern and several border states remained segregated far longer than the elementary and secondary systems. Racially divided public college systems are not unique to the South. In addition to states like Missouri, West Virginia, and Kentucky, publicly supported black colleges persist in such states as Pennsylvania (Cheyney and Lincoln) and Ohio (Central State). While many blacks have pursued higher education only because these colleges existed, the range of offerings, quality of faculties and facilities, and extracurricular opportunities typically do not match those of the major white institutions. The potential effect of total desegregation upon these colleges and their students is problematic; some black students would undoubtedly benefit from dismantling of these dual systems, while others would be effectively denied even the quality of higher education now available to them through the black colleges.

Quite apart from the perpetuation of segregated public systems, blacks have until recently been denied graduate and professional opportunities that exist only in predominantly white institutions. It was only twenty-five years ago that the United States Supreme Court struck down racial segregation in legal education, requiring the University of Texas at Austin to admit its first black student. James Meredith's battle with the University of Mississippi Law School—then completely white—goes back only a little over a decade. Well into the 1960s some private university law schools still excluded blacks, and at least two institutions had to go to court to nullify racial restrictions in their charters or endowments. Thus if higher education now wishes to remedy the lingering effects of a condition for which it was at least partly responsible, that goal would appear to constitute a valid and substantial state interest.

Even if the academic community had been blameless for the racial imbalances which exist, consideration of race in the admissions process would seem a permissible remedy. As we suggested earlier, it would be anomalous if universities that had once discriminated on grounds of race could now use race preferentially, while newer institutions in the same state could not do so. So long as it is the same evil or condition to which the admissions policy is addressed, the corrective should be equally available. "Just as the race of students must be considered in determining whether a constitutional violation has occurred," the Supreme Court has said, "so also race must be considered in formulating a remedy."

Regardless of past wrongs, a college or university might well regard race conscious admissions as a key element in an affirmative action plan. Institutions which receive federal funds (as almost all colleges and universities do) face a serious dilemma under current federal guidelines. On the one hand they must take positive steps to identify, evaluate, and recruit more women and minorities at all levels; on the other hand they may not "discriminate" in doing so. Federal officials have already taken several academic institutions to task for announcing or using too explicit a racial preference in hiring or admission. The case of the University of Washington poignantly illustrates the dilemma: At the very time the university was fighting Marco DeFunis in the courts to continue to be able to consider race in admissions, federal officials were pressing in hard on the other side and threatening to cut off funds to the university unless it formulated a bolder affirmative action plan for minority recruitment and advancement. For a court to preclude any consideration of race or ethnic status at the admissions level would virtually cripple many affirmative action programs. Surely the right hand cannot so stay the left.

Representation of the Larger Society: The University as Microcosm

There is a fourth interest underlying preferential admissions which relates only indirectly to the needs of minority students. A major function of higher education must be to prepare students for responsible and meaningful citizenship in the larger society. In certain respects, of course, the campus is appropriately cloistered and insulated from practical and political demands. Academic freedom must, for example, be protected in ways that are neither necessary nor appropriate in other kinds of institutions. But when it comes to the makeup of the student body, there is neither need nor justification for failure to reflect the general condition of society. If education is to be more than simply book learning and sterile research, groups present in the total community must also be present in the academic community. Thus a college or university may seek more minority students as much to provide a more realistic learning and extracurricular environment for its white-Anglo students, as to improve opportunities for minorities.

This goal of diversity and representation has been recognized by the United States Supreme Court as a valid governmental interest at the elementary and secondary level. In holding that race could constitutionally be considered in the framing of remedies for past segregation, the Court has said:

> School authorities . . . might well conclude . . . that in order to prepare students to live in a pluralistic society each school should have a prescribed ratio of Negro to White students reflecting the proportion for the district as a whole. To do this as an educational policy is within the broad discretionary powers of school authorities.

The same reasoning has also been applied at the graduate and professional level. A quarter century ago, the Supreme Court held that the University of Texas could not constitutionally exclude black students from its law school. While this decision preceded *Brown* v. *Board of Education* by four years, and paid lip service to the waning "separate but equal" philosophy, the Court did indicate the positive value of integration:

> Few students and no one who has practiced law would choose to study in an academic vacuum, removed from the interplay of ideas and exchange of views with which the law is concerned. . . . With such a substantial segment of society excluded . . . we cannot conclude that the education offered . . . is substantially equal.

While the Court's immediate concern was the effect of isolation on the excluded black, precisely the same argument could be made for the white students on a campus that was demographically unrepresentative of the larger society. In its *DeFunis* brief, the Association of American Law Schools amplified the argument along these lines:

> The quality of legal education parallels student understanding of the ways in which law relates to society. Student perception of legal situations is conditioned by the prior experience, training, background, culture, race and sex of the student body members. A White student from a "good" undergraduate school, amply funded by a well-to-do family, views law and society differently from the way a Black student would with a similar, or different background. . . . Diversity in the law school student body achieves another important interest for state law schools. Law schools serve as the source of training of a bar which must satisfy the legal needs of a heterogenous society.

There are other institutional interests that reinforce the case for preferential consideration of minority applicants. When a selective institution decides to admit a qualified chicano or black or American Indian student instead of a superficially better qualified white-Anglo, the person thus displaced was not expected to excel. Had the class been a bit smaller, or had the number of returning veterans been slightly larger, or had more first choice admittees decided to accept, etc., the rejected applicant would not have got in anyway. The minority student admitted in his place may well have a lower predicted first year average, and may actually do less good academic work. But if the preferred minority student does graduate, the chances are somewhat greater that he will distinguish both himself and his alma mater in later life. Moreover, the prospects for attending graduate school now appear higher (as a result of preferential policies, admittedly) for the minority student who survives than for the white applicant who is supposed to get by with a gentleman's C and does only that. Thus the preference for the minority student may be justified in institutional as well as individual terms.

Minority students may also supply a catalyst for beneficial change. One of the most frequent demands from minority students has been for special ethnic studies program. Black or Afro-American programs and departments are now widespread. Puerto Rican or

Borricua studies and chicano programs are less common but flourish in the relevant regions. There has been much debate about the quality of these programs and their value for *minority* students. Their greatest ultimate impact, however, may be on the majority students who are enrolling in such courses in increasing numbers. Even those who question the worth of ethnic programs generally accept Kenneth B. Clark's view that "it is whites who need a program of black studies most of all." Without the minority students, it is doubtful that pressure for such programs would ever have existed at all.

There is also a substantial interest in the production and recruitment of minority faculty—an interest which is now heavily undergirded by federal affirmative action requirements. There can be no major expansion of the black and Spanish-speaking professoriate until graduate schools turn out many more minority scholars and teachers. Given the competition from other professions, a geometric expansion of minority graduate enrollments may be required to increase minority faculty even arithmetically—at least without decimating the black college staffs. There is a related if subtler factor: The black or chicano Ph.D. has a broad range of options these days and faces a difficult career choice. Other institutional variables being at all constant, he will probably seek evidence of commitment to equality of educational opportunity and will be most likely to find that commitment in a vigorous minority recruitment program.

Finally, the effectiveness of a minority student program may depend in part upon its scope. In the 1960s, a number of smaller institutions—especially those in rural areas like Cornell and Wisconsin at Oshkosh—had disastrous experiences with black student protests. In most cases the student dissatisfaction could be traced simply to isolation and fear. A tiny band of black students in a rural northern community is not likely to feel very comfortable. When issues arose —like the burning of a cross in front of the black women's dormitory at Cornell in 1969—already tense feelings could surface and violence ensue. The program will succeed only when there is a large enough group of minority students—a "critical mass" as some have called it —to provide a community and a source of strength and confidence for the members of the group. James McPherson, a black graduate of the Harvard Law School and a distinguished poet and teacher of creative writing, has observed that the anxiety of black students at predominantly white institutions "can be reduced only when there are enough blacks on white campuses to establish an interdependent, self-sufficient black community."

These latter interests relate mainly to the college or university and to its majority student population. There seems no reason why, from a constitutional point of view, the desire to make the campus a more representative and realistic environment may not stand equal to the goals of overcoming past discrimination or increasing minority participation in the mainstream of American life. In fact these interests are quite closely and logically related; the future of opportunities for minorities depends in large part upon the sensitivity and the values of whites who will continue to make up the majority of our society for the foreseeable future. Thus in some respects the desire to improve the educational experience for the present generation of white-Anglo students may really be the most substantial interest of all.

CHAPTER SIX

NONRACIAL ALTERNATIVES

No court has yet held that nonracial alternatives must be considered and rejected before a racial preference can be used. But the compelling interest test seems to impose such a burden upon proponents of preferential policies. In other contexts where suspect criteria are used or fundamental rights are affected, the availability of less restrictive or intrusive means must be considered. And whatever the courts may require, the *politics* of admissions argue strongly for inclusion of this additional test. If the governmental interests we have just reviewed could be substantially achieved without classifying people on the basis of race, wisdom if not law would counsel using such alternatives. Thus we must explore several possible options.

"Nondiscrimination" as an Alternative

Some have suggested that we need only abolish racial restrictions and formal ethnic barriers to bring about substantial increases in minority enrollments. The short answer to this suggestion is that "nondiscrimination" has been tried and found wanting. At most colleges and universities in the North and West, where racial exclusion has never been practiced, enrollments have remained at token levels until admissions officers became color conscious. The few institutions that have had more than token minority enrollments are either public campuses in urban centers where minority populations are high, or open enrollment junior and community colleges near minority communities, or a few elite liberal arts colleges which have vigorously recruited minority students for decades. Elsewhere "benign neglect" has been the rule, and pitifully low minority enrollments have been the result.

If nondiscrimination by itself would not suffice, the possibility of strengthening *recruitment* policies without redirecting *admission* standards remains to be considered. The amicus curiae brief of Harvard University in the *DeFunis* case suggested an answer, at least at the law school level:

> [Opponents of preferential admission] offer no convincing evidence that by more vigorous recruitment the numbers of minority law students and minority lawyers can be increased substantially within a reasonable time. The low numbers of the past and even the present are themselves deterrents to seeking higher education and a professional career.

This conclusion requires a caveat. It is true that the number of minority students (at least in law) admitted through the regular process has also increased dramatically in recent years. Recall the American Bar Association study of the class entering in 1970. Of the total of about 1,400 black students who entered law school that year, roughly half were preferentially admitted. Thus the total number of students admitted without consideration of race may have been as high as 700. This figure marked a substantial increase from the roughly 300 first-year black students in the 1965 AALS survey. Thus one could argue that even without preferential admission the number of minority students would have increased significantly during this period.

There are several answers. First, the total first-year class increased about 50% between 1965 and 1970; thus if the black enrollment had not increased at least that fast, minorities would actually have lost ground. Second, figures for the entire group of law schools are obviously misleading. A high proportion of the regularly admitted minority students are probably enrolled at the less selective schools, while the preferentially admitted students figure more prominently in the national and regional law schools. Without preferential admissions, the representation of minorities in the latter group of schools would almost certainly have declined in the late 1960s. (The University of Washington provides a case in point. In 1967–68, before preferential admissions, the law school student body was 2.2% black. In the class of 1974, however, there would have been no minority students at all if consideration had not been given to race; the one black who was regularly admitted did not accept and went elsewhere. At a national law school like Washington, some preference thus proved necessary just to maintain the meager minority population of the mid-60s.)

There is a third answer, which cannot be documented but seems persuasive. While some of the regularly admitted minority students might have applied anyway, many probably chose law because they knew that law schools were receptive to such applications and would give them special consideration. The confidence and optimism generated by publicity about special programs, and the experience of other students from the same community, must have had a strong influence on graduate and career choices of minority undergraduates. Moreover, part of the attraction of law has been the availability of special financial aids through the Council on Legal Education Opportunity and other programs. If race conscious *admission* policies were impermissible, presumably special *scholarships* would also be out, and a major incentive for the regularly admissible minority students would disappear. Thus while "nondiscrimination" has a more than superficial appeal, deeper analysis suggests that simply removing racial restrictions would not meet the need. As California state superintendent of education, Wilson Riles, put it some years ago, "Desegregation does not ensure integration."

Abolition of Tests

If the removal of one kind of barrier would not suffice, then what about removing the other barrier that has impeded minority access to higher education? This approach too has some surface appeal. Justice Douglas, for example, thought the *DeFunis* case should be remanded to "consider *inter alia,* whether the established LSAT tests should be eliminated so far as racial minorities were concerned." In an analogous context, the courts have decreed that employers must discard tests which disproportionately exclude minorities and are not proved to be job-related. Thus a possible and clearly nonracial alternative would be simply to abandon all standardized tests and rely on other indicia of potential.

This approach would have the virtue of simplicity, but little else. Given the vast number of applications received by major graduate and professional schools—often five thousand or more for one or two hundred first-year slots—the task of sifting and sorting without the aid of quantitative guides would become unmanageable. Some form of random choice among all who met minimal criteria would be almost inevitable. Moreover, the standardized tests do seem to predict quite well for majority students, and show a high correlation between test scores and actual performance. Indeed, they *predict* reasonably well for minority students too. Thus the remedy is not to abandon tests for all purposes because they have one undesirable effect. Rather the approach should be to try to improve the utility of the tests in judging all students.

Anyone who thinks seriously about abolishing standardized tests should consider the alternatives as well as the consequences. The most likely substitute for tests and grades would be letters of recommendation, personal interviews, endorsements from alumni, etc.—all highly subjective criteria in which racial or ethnic bias is more likely to operate. At least standardized tests and grades have the virtue of objectivity; while they may operate to keep out many minorities, they are not capable of the bias which has often infected more personalized selection systems. Thus the elimination of tests could open the way to use of subjective measures even more harmful to minorities than passive "nondiscrimination" has been.

The remedy is not to throw the tests out but to temper their application while trying to improve them. Much research has been and is being conducted by testing experts to devise alternative tests that are freer of possible cultural bias than some present instruments. While the Educational Testing Service and its component units (like the Law School Admission Council) maintain that present tests are not discriminatory against minorities, they also acknowledge the possibility of improvement. That is why the LSAC has for some years had a special committee working on better adaptation of the admission test to minority applicants. Meanwhile, there are some encouraging signs elsewhere. In New York City, for example, a federal court several years ago invalidated a civil service examination for school principals on the ground that it disproportionately excluded minority groups from administrative positions. While new tests were being developed, principals were evaluated by an on-the-job procedure. This new approach relied upon monitoring and interviewing by university-based panels familiar with the schools and their needs. The first results were most encouraging: by the summer of 1974, rates of success for minority and majority candidates were almost exactly equal. About 94% of the black principals, 97% of the Puerto Ricans, and 93.4% of the whites qualified for permanent appointments under the new procedure.

In time the development of alternative entrance criteria may make race unnecessary and irrelevant in admissions decisions. But surely we have not yet reached that point. Meanwhile, to abandon tests and other predictors which work well for the great majority of applicants would be unwise and counterproductive.

Open Admissions

One racially neutral admissions policy that offers some hope of increasing minority participation is the "open door" policy most closely identified with the City University of New York. Since open admissions was adopted in 1970, there is no question that minority enrollments at all the City University campuses have increased, and quite dramatically in some cases. The retention rates for these students have also been impressive; after the first two years of the program, 70% of the students who entered with the first open admission class were still registered. A year later, 60% of the open admissions students who began at four-year colleges were still enrolled, and 41.5% of those who began at a two-year college had transferred to a senior campus. On the other hand, of those students admitted to the senior colleges in 1970 with grades that would not have got them in prior to open admission, only 10% actually graduated four years later.

Then too, the tangible and intangible costs of supplementing the inadequate secondary education of many of the open admission students have been substantial. Some critics have charged that the commitment of resources to these programs has hurt the more traditional programs and has lowered the levels of undergraduate performance. It is, however, much too early to make any firm judgments about open admissions. We do not even have official detailed data on the first class to go through the program, and it will be some years before we have enough experience to evaluate fairly this new approach to selection of students.

While open admissions has undeniably enhanced minority prospects in New York, it does not offer a viable alternative to preferential policies. The most critical areas of minority underrepresentation are those highly selective graduate and professional programs (like law and medicine) where open admission would obviously be impossible. The University of Washington cannot admit 1,600 law students, as it would be required to do under an open admission policy. While a slight increase in class size may be possible, law schools clearly cannot keep pace with the steady rise in student demand. Nor should they do so in good conscience, because society's need for lawyers is not likely to expand nearly as fast as student interest in becoming a lawyer. Medical schools have even less flexibility, however rapidly the demand for physicians may be growing as a result of Medicare and other new health care programs. Limitations on laboratory space and clinical facilities make expansion of medical education a slow and costly process. Thus in these fields, and in others where career opportunities, faculty time, or study space sharply limit enrollments, open admission obviously affords no solution. Yet it is in precisely those fields—and precisely because of the high selectivity of those schools —that the problem of minority underrepresentation is most acute.

Open admissions would improve minority prospects only in a metropolitan area, like New York City, where minority populations are highly concentrated and have easy access to two-year or four-year campuses. In less densely settled regions, open admissions would benefit only those who can take advantage of higher education under current conditions. The state universities of Kansas and Ohio do have open admissions, perhaps alone among major public educational systems. Yet the ratio of minority students to minority population in those states is little if any higher than in neighboring states where the universities are no longer open to all high school graduates. Even in New York City, the major beneficiaries of open admissions have not been racial or ethnic minorities but Italians, Jews, and other white groups who are better able to seize the opportunity than the blacks and Puerto Ricans. Columbia University sociologist Amital Etzioni, on the basis of an early study, observed that "for every one Black or Puerto Rican who entered the City University [under] open admission, there were two . . . whites who entered the system who would not otherwise have been in it." This is not to say that open admission would not bring more minority students into undergraduate programs in the urban areas than come in under current entrance standards. But this is a crude solution at best, and one that is wholly unsuited to the sectors of most critical need.

Expansion of Junior Colleges

There is little doubt that continued growth of junior and community colleges would increase the share of minority students. Several studies have shown that rates of college attendance for people in lower socioeconomic groups vary in direct proportion to the proximity of a college campus. In California, with its extensive junior and community college system, close to 80% of all high school graduates go on to some sort of college. Ohio, which is demographically and economically comparable to California but lacks the two-year college network, has a college attendance rate barely half as large. Studies of metropolitan areas like Dallas confirm that proximity of a college campus, within easy commuting distance, particularly attracts disadvantaged and minority students. (The density of population and the strategic location of the units is, incidentally, one reason why open admission has worked as well as it has in New York City.)

Yet even an infinite expansion of two-year college systems would not provide a viable alternative to preferential admissions. At best, a junior college can only prepare a student for transfer to a four-year institution, which alone can confer the essential baccalaureate degree. At worst, increasing the numbers of minority students on two-year campuses, especially where technical-vocational programs predominate, will only extend educational "tracking" from the high school into the postsecondary level. (Indeed, it may be more difficult for students who start out in a two-year college to complete the baccalaureate program than for those who matriculate at a senior campus. Limited experience in New York confirms this hypothesis. Open admission students with high school averages under 70 were *more* likely to remain in college if they began at a four-year college than if they entered a community college. There may be extenuating factors, of course, including the very small number of such students in the baccalaureate colleges, and the availability of better remedial instruction. But the higher attrition rates for comparable students starting out at the community colleges are worrisome.)

Clearly there should be more junior and community colleges—not only to bring higher education closer to the minority community, but for the benefit of all groups. And transfer options need to be considerably expanded, through closer collaboration between two-year and four-year campuses, better counselling reaching back into the high schools, clearer guidance on transfer requirements, courses, etc. Like open admissions, the two-year colleges help to get more minority students *into* the system. But they do not offer a viable alternative to preferential admission. No matter how many community colleges existed in Seattle, the University of Washington would still have faced the dilemma that eventually led to the *DeFunis* case.

Black Colleges

Historically the predominantly black colleges have borne a major share of higher education of minorities. Even today, it is estimated that 75% of all black Ph.D.s, 85% of black physicians, 75% of black officers in the armed forces, and 80% of all black judges received their degrees from black colleges or graduate schools. Clearly it would be disastrous if the traditionally black colleges ceased to exist. More recently, opportunities have been enhanced by a newer kind of predominantly black institution—Federal City College in Washington, Malcolm X and Olive-Harvey Colleges in Chicago, Manhattan and Bronx Community Colleges in New York, and Laney, Compton, and Merritt Junior Colleges in California. Such institutions play a critical role in minority group education. Since some of them do offer graduate and professional degrees, they offer a superficially more plausible alternative to preferential admissions than others we have considered.

There are two obvious weaknesses in this suggested solution. While there are many predominantly *black* colleges, there are (except in Puerto Rico) no comparable institutions for Spanish-speaking groups. Recently the Latin enrollments have become substantial at places like East Los Angeles City College, New Mexico Highlands, and Hostos Community College in New York. But there is no Spanish equivalent of Howard, Morehouse, or Fisk. (The situation for American Indians, as we have noted earlier, is different. The Bureau of Indian Affairs does support some special institutions, and others have been privately endowed for this purpose. They are, however, remote from the academic mainstream.) Thus reliance on minority-group institutions would effectively benefit one group but not others in which comparable educational needs exist.

An even more basic argument against reliance on the black colleges would be the complete disregard of such a solution for the value of integration in higher education. The goal of preferential admission, as we noted in Chapter 5, is only in part to get more minorities through college and graduate school. Many institutions have recruited blacks, chicanos, and Puerto Ricans as much in the interests of the majority student population as for the minorities. Indeed, recent federal pressures are rapidly bringing about the integration of state-supported black colleges, which have remained segregated long after integration took effect at lower levels.

Minority students themselves have shown a declining preference for black campuses as new opportunities in formerly closed white institutions have become available to them. North Carolina provides an illustrative microcosm. Since 1970, freshman enrollment at North Carolina Central University, the state's comprehensive black institution, has barely held its own. Meanwhile, black freshmen at the University of North Carolina jumped from 637 in 1971 to 975 two years later. While many black students continue to prefer a black college or even a graduate school, many others will opt for an integrated environment when given a choice.

Finally, these are bad times for the black colleges. Several years ago it was predicted that as many as 50 of the 128 black institutions might have to close simply for lack of funds and students, despite the valiant efforts of the United Negro College Fund and other groups. Subsequent experience has not confirmed so dire a prediction. But it is true that federal funds, so vital to growth and strength in higher education, are distributed on a basis that tends to make the rich richer and the poor poorer. Howard, Fisk, Hampton, Tuskegee, and the Atlanta University complex have all fared well in recent years, but other black institutions have had only the crumbs from the federal and foundation tables. Meanwhile the accelerated quest for black scholars has started a kind of "brain drain" at just the time these institutions are trying to strengthen their own faculties. While some black professors are intensely loyal to their alma maters, black colleges can seldom compete in terms of salaries, libraries, teaching loads, and laboratories with the major universities that now seek minority talent.

Black colleges clearly serve an important function in our educational system and should be maintained. They are a source of pride and hope for many black people. Indeed, there would be intense resistance to the total integration of higher education—as Ohio officials rapidly discovered after a tornado levelled Central State University and the possibility of a merger with a white university was proposed. But black colleges are not even remotely relevant to the goals of preferential admission at predominantly white campuses. Quite apart from the numerical inadequacy of black institutions to the size of the task, the positive value of integration would be disserved by such a solution.

Improving Elementary and Secondary Education

Some critics of preferential admission insist that the solution lies in better precollege education for minority students. There is no question that many such students enter college with seriously deficient backgrounds, and thus require considerable supplemental instruction in reading, mathematics, and other basic skills. Such deficiencies also help to explain the poor performance of many minority students on standardized tests. Everyone agrees that all efforts should be made to improve the condition of ghetto and barrio schools and the instruction provided by them. When (if ever) elementary and secondary education becomes equal for all groups, the need for racial or ethnic preference may well vanish at the college and graduate level.

The only drawback to this solution is one of time. At the rate at which progress is being made toward this goal today, it will take at least a generation and probably more before anything like equality will occur. Indeed in some respects, the very conditions that create the problem are getting worse rather than better. In some large cities, the number of minority children attending schools with high minority enrollments tends to increase. (Of the 537 elementary schools in Chicago, 259 now have black enrollments of more than 90%. Another 104 schools are over 90% white. Between 1972 and 1974, the number of totally black elementary schools increased from 128 to 144. Not only is the figure alarming by itself, but it is the more puzzling in light of (a) an Illinois law which requires efforts to achieve racial balance, and which was upheld by the state supreme court; and (b) increasing federal government pressure on northern and western school districts to integrate the schools.) Insofar as segregated education tends to be poor quality education—and there is a high correlation—progress will take some time. Meanwhile, the Supreme Court's decision in the Detroit case (which prevents a federal judge from ordering desegregation throughout a metropolitan area unless there has been some complicity between the city and its suburbs) will probably slow still further the pace of desegregation in the North and West.

There is no question about the desirability of improving elementary and secondary education for minority children. This is a goal to which colleges and universities can make at least a modest contribution. Meanwhile, the critical problems with which the University of Washington and other institutions have been concerned show no early prospect of being alleviated at lower levels in the educational system.

Preference for "Disadvantaged" Students

A widely proposed solution to the dilemma of the *DeFunis* case is to substitute a general concept of "disadvantaged" for race as the criterion of preference. Such an approach would certainly avoid many of the sensitive feelings and concerns aroused by explicit reliance on race. It would also circumvent the constitutional problem; as Harvard law professor Paul Freund has written, preference would seem valid if extended to "the most disadvantaged segment of the community, whether economically, educationally or politically." Undoubtedly a preference for "disadvantaged" applicants would in fact heavily benefit minorities, since they fall disproportionately into that category.

Such an alternative would, however, face serious practical problems. It would have to be based on some readily identifiable standard like family income; to determine a complex profile of "disadvantage" for each of several thousand applicants to law school or medical school would be an impossible task. To use an economic standard would, however, fall wide of the mark in terms of real needs. Such a classification would, as lawyers say, be both overinclusive and underinclusive. It would include many persons who are simply poor but do not need any special consideration in the admissions process—students who have received a good education, come from a stable family environment, have never been the victims of discrimination—who simply need financial aid but require no other dispensation.

There is an even more basic flaw in the "disadvantage" approach. While it is true that all socioeconomically deprived groups are probably underrepresented in higher education, the critical shortages are those of racial and ethnic minorities. There is no point in adopting a recruitment or admission policy aimed at one group when the primary target is another group, albeit contained

within the larger group. If colleges and universities also seek to attract more poor whites—a commendable goal but distinct from
the goal with which we are concerned—the means of doing so
may be quite different. Rather than modifying admissions policies,
increases in financial aid or remission of tuition are probably more
appropriate. While a general preference for "disadvantaged" students might incidentally help to expand opportunity for minorities,
it would constitute a very crude and imprecise remedy for a specifically defined problem.

In order to avoid both the constitutional and political problems
evoked by a racial classification, it is also possible that special consideration could be given to some applicants on the basis of equivalent
factors. Justice Douglas suggested, for example, that success at special
prelaw summer institutes might be a substitute for racial preference.
A commitment to serve the minority community upon entry into the
profession might also be considered. Or, Justice Douglas ventured, a
law school might consider "an individual's prior achievements in light
of the racial discrimination that barred his way, as a factor in attempting to assess his true potential for a successful legal career." Such
proposals appear to avoid only the form but not the substance of racial
preference. The summer institutes to which Douglas referred are
designed almost exclusively for minority groups; hence a law school
which admitted on the basis of institute performance would be taking
account of race, de facto if not de jure. Much the same can be said
of Douglas's other suggested alternatives: each one in fact recognizes
race through the back door in order to avoid doing so by the front
door. Such avoidance seems disingenuous and is not likely to be
persuasive with critics of admission policies who look to results rather
than to terminology.

There is limited judicial support for the "de facto preference"
approach. Several years ago a federal court of appeals upheld the
lending practices of the Small Business Administration against a
challenge by a rejected white applicant. Although the law permitted
loans to be made to all "socially and economically disadvantaged
persons" the agency treated that language as a euphemism for racial

preference. In the region where the lawsuit arose, 98% of the loans had in fact been made to minority persons. Yet the court sustained the program, without looking at the results, or reaching the racial preference issue, because the statutory language appeared neutral. Another case avoided the *DeFunis* issue on equally tenuous grounds. The participants in a federally funded "Inner City Library Service Institute" turned out to be almost totally black and Spanish-speaking, and the composition of the program was challenged on that basis. The court upheld the selection criteria for the institute since "any segregation which may have occurred resulted solely because of the content of the course dictated by the needs of experimental programs."

Instead of hiding behind language like "disadvantaged" and "inner city," an explicit racial classification would certainly be more candid, wherever the focus of the program is in fact racial or ethnic. Nothing is gained by using neutral language to define benefits for which in fact only minorities can qualify. In fact, such circumlocution may mislead nonminority persons into believing the program includes them when it does not. Conversely, some minority group members might not apply because they did not realize the program was meant for them. When a particular opportunity is genuinely intended for all disadvantaged or socioeconomically deprived groups, such language should be used. But a benefit designed for racial and ethnic minority groups should not take refuge behind euphemisms in order to forestall political criticism or another lawsuit.

One caveat is in order: This discussion is not meant to suggest that expansion of higher education opportunities should be *limited* to racial minorities, or even that other groups should not receive some preference in admission. The proper scope and extent of preference will be considered in Chapter 8. The point here is only that the special and critical needs of minority groups cannot be met through general and broadly focussed preferential policies. The case for expanding collegiate opportunities for poor whites is a very persuasive one. But it is a different case, and the methods of meeting it are also different.

Racial Preference on an Individual Rather Than a Group Basis

As a final alternative, some critics have suggested that the goal of preferential admissions might be achieved by selective review of individual cases rather than by making an entire racial or ethnic group eligible for a preference. There is serious doubt, though, whether this proposal is really an alternative at all. Since it would presuppose consideration of race or ethnic status in the case of some applicants, neither constitutional nor political concerns about broader preferences would really be avoided. More important, this approach differs little from the procedure now followed by responsible institutions with preferential programs. Except where a quota exists, minority applications are screened individually, and admissions decisions are finally made on a number of criteria. Many minority applicants are eventually rejected, including some who might rank higher on paper than those accepted.

When used properly, a racial preference guarantees nothing; it simply serves to alert the admissions officer or committee to certain applicants because they belong to a particular class or group. It is the beginning, rather than the end, of the admission process. Such a preference simply suggests that minority students offer greater promise or potential than their raw paper records would indicate. That inference may be appropriate in some cases, but may in other cases turn out on further study to be unwarranted. Thus the preference merely invites more careful attention to applications that would otherwise be passed over on numerical criteria.

There is also something circular about the suggestion that only certain individual minority students should receive preference. The volume of applications for the professional schools is so large that individual minority applicants will never surface unless some special consideration is given to all members of the group on the basis of racial or ethnic status. Only in this way can those particular applicants with special individual merit be identified. Otherwise it would be impossible to spot potentially eligible applicants whose files did not happen to surface for some nonracial reason—special financial need, outstanding letter of recommendation, personal contact with a member of the admissions committee, etc. Thus if any minority applicants are to be eligible for special consideration on racial grounds, all members of the eligible groups must be individually reviewed. That is essentially what is done now under responsible special admissions programs. Thus the suggestion for individual rather than group preference really implies no change from the status quo.

Finally, there are reasons, suggested in the preceding section, why every minority applicant deserves some special consideration. Racial discrimination has been general and not selective. The potential contribution of minority students to predominantly white campuses is a group rather than an individual attribute. There is a need for diversity among minority students, and not simply between the minority and majority populations. The capacity of a minority professional to serve the community of which he is a part inheres in all members of the group, though undoubtedly in varying degrees. Though not all minority applicants are equally good candidates for admission, all are equally entitled to special consideration at the threshhold.

We have now reviewed a number of possible alternatives to preferential admissions. Many of these proposals are sound and should be favored for other reasons, but fail to meet the needs or goals for which preferential policies were designed. If it is necessary to show that nonracial alternatives will not suffice to help minority group members, this discussion should demonstrate precisely that.

CHAPTER SEVEN

THE CASE AGAINST PREFERENTIAL ADMISSIONS

Opposition to preferential treatment of racial minorities is nothing new in this country. In 1764 a group of disgruntled frontier settlers in western Pennsylvania sent a "remonstrance" to the provincial governor and legislature. The essence of their concern was alleged neglect of their interests by the ruling group in Philadelphia. They were particularly annoyed that white survivors of the bitter Pontiac's Rebellion had been less well treated by the colonial government than the Indians who had plundered and massacred. While the survivors languished, "upwards of an hundred and twenty of these Savages . . . have procured themselves to be taken under the protection of the Government, with a view to elude the fury of the brave relatives of the murdered, and are now maintained at the public expense." Such protests have been relatively infrequent throughout American history —but only because there have been so few instances of preferential treatment. It is hardly surprising that the recent consideration of race as a factor in college admissions has evoked a widespread concern among nonminority groups. The focus of this chapter is on those concerns, their rationale, and their manifestations. Clearly the question of preferential admission has two sides.

The Impact of Racial Preference on Society, Law, and Government

The most persuasive argument against the preferential treatment of minorities may well be the most obvious: any consideration of race, whether to help or to harm minority groups, officially sanctions a distinction we have been trying for decades to minimize. When the first Justice Harlan said in 1896 that he believed the Constitution was color blind, he meant exactly that; the equal protection clause, he went on, "does not permit any public authority to know the race of those entitled to be protected in the enjoyment of [civil] rights." Our most enlightened states only rather recently passed laws forbidding employers and colleges to ask about the race of an applicant, or even to require photographs which might subtly facilitate discrimination. There is an irony in now being told that such efforts to obliterate racial distinctions in the interest of equality must be reversed if equality is to be enhanced.

There are basic philosophical concerns about allowing government to draw or even recognize racial distinctions. Racial classifications are inherently divisive; they tend to evoke the latent and not-so-latent prejudices and hostilities of people on both sides of a line that all know exists but which acquires added importance from governmental recognition. Racial distinctions are immutable and indelible even when government does not draw attention to them. To define a class based on ethnic-group membership reinforces barriers that cannot be crossed, and adds governmental sanction to differences among people for which they are in no way responsible and over which they have no control. (In this respect, distinctions based on race, like sex differences and legitimacy of birth, are more dangerous than classifications based on wealth or geography, although the courts have reviewed the latter as well as the former with very strict scrutiny.)

The power to classify on the basis of race, no matter how "benign" the goal, is always dangerous. Today's minority may become tomorrow's majority, and the tables can easily be turned. It was this risk that Justice Douglas had in mind when he cautioned in *DeFunis* that "constitutional guarantees acquire an accordionlike quality" if classification based explicitly on race is allowed even to serve a compelling interest. Groups that have in the past been victims of racial or ethnic quotas—Jewish groups, as a notable example—are understandably troubled about the principle accepted by any racial preference. Granting that there are vast differences between the Warsaw ghetto and the ghetto of Detroit or Chicago, there are also disturbing similarities.

Most basically, the use of race to allocate benefits or burdens may jeopardize our governmental process. As Stanford law professor John Kaplan has said, "Any legal classification by race weakens the government as an educative force." The legislature that enacts law based on racial distinctions—whichever way they cut—appears to many citizens to have departed significantly from principles of both equality and neutrality. Much as Watergate has undermined public confidence in the *integrity* of government, so racial preference may undermine an equally necessary confidence in the *fairness* of government in dealing with its citizens.

Closely related to these concerns is another fear about racial preference—that it rejects or abandons the historic American commitment to merit and ability in selecting students. In a recent pamphlet on this subject, the Anti-Defamation League of B'nai-B'rith opposes preferential policies (as it did in *DeFunis*) because of an apparent conflict with the merit principle:

> Society has yet to devise a better measure of excellence than performance, or better predictors of excellent performance than qualifications it perceives in those who themselves have performed excellently. When it takes such qualifications and applies them uniformly and without discrimination to candidates for admission and employment, it performs a service to all; when it does not, sooner or later a disservice will have been perpetrated upon all.

In a like vein, philosopher Sidney Hook (a staunch opponent of racial preference) asks rhetorically: "Why not drop all color, sex and religious bars in honest quest for the best-qualified for any post—no matter what the distribution turns out to be?" There is even a touch of meritocracy in Justice Douglas's dissent—"Whatever his race, [the applicant] had a constitutional right to have his application considered on its individual merits in a racially neutral way."

The discussion of "merit" and "qualification" sometimes assumes these terms are virtually synonymous with numerical ranking.

As we observed in Chapter 3, the admissions process has never consisted simply of taking people in rank order on the basis of quantitative achievement. Any responsible definition of "merit" in higher
education has always included nonquantitative and speculative factors. The current consideration of race simply adds a new dimension
to the nonnumerical prognosis. Yet to the critics of preferential admission a policy like that of the University of Washington goes further
in this respect. Colleges and universities have been reaching deeper to
get minority students than has been the practice in the past—save
possibly in the uncontrolled quest for athletic talent prior to NCAA
restrictions. The concern is not so much that "merit" or "qualification" has now been defined in nonquantitative terms, for that has
always been the case. What Sidney Hook, the Anti-Defamation
League, and many others are worried about today is how far afield the
search for minority talent has carried the concepts of "merit" and
"qualification."

A closely related fear is that preference soon leads to quotas,
which are abhorrent to responsible educators. Despite the insistence
that preferential programs seek to achieve "goals" and not "quotas,"
many critics find that distinction specious. They point to several
examples of what are unmistakably quotas, such as the University of
Massachusetts program we discussed earlier. They recount incidents
like the struggle at the University of California (Berkeley) Law School
in 1972: the black students insisted that their "share" of the entering
class be determined on the basis of national demography; the chicanos
insisted on a figure based on California statistics; and the Asian students demanded proportions based on the immediate San Francisco
Bay Area population. Had all three demands been met, half the
entering class would have consisted of minorities, regardless of the
number of qualified applicants from any of the three groups. (The
faculty did not accept these demands, but worked out somewhat more
modest and realistic minority admission goals.) Critics also point to
the decision of the University of Michigan in 1970 to accept demands
from the Black Action Movement to bring undergraduate black enrollment to 10% in several years—suggesting that this policy repre-

sented a quota rather than a goal. There are certainly enough "horror stories" to feed and reinforce the fears of those who do not understand (or do not *want* to understand) the difference between goals and quotas. For groups that have had relatively recent and deeply distasteful experience with ethnic quotas—not only Jews in higher education, but Irish in Boston employment, Asians in West Coast landholding, etc.—the assimilation of goal and quota, and the resulting opposition to any use of race, are understandable.

The distinction between goal and quota can be defined more easily than it can be applied. In essence, a quota sets both a ceiling and a floor, while a goal sets neither. If there are not enough qualified applicants to meet a quota, then some who are not qualified will be admitted. If there are more qualified candidates than the quota allows, as was the case with Jewish applicants to selective universities for decades, then some who are qualified will be rejected for the most arbitrary and irrational of reasons. If needs and conditions change, the quota is unlikely to be altered, since it was initially developed for reasons unrelated to human supply or demand.

A goal is altogether different. Both its rationale and its content should reflect human circumstances. The purpose of a goal is to include, and not (as with most quotas) to exclude. If the number of qualified persons falls short of the goal, it will not be filled. If in the future the qualified pool rises above the goal, then it can be exceeded with impunity. No public official has tried harder to explain the difference between goals and quotas than J. Stanley Pottinger, Assistant Attorney General in charge of the federal Civil Rights Division. In his view the key distinction is "flexibility." Speaking about employment rather than admissions, he has recently remarked of the distinction: "A goal also serves as an objective to be reached, but unlike quotas, a goal should not become carved in stone. Changing circumstances beyond the employer's control, or estimations which prove through experience to have been unrealistic when made, can impair an employer's ability to meet a goal regardless of his good faith efforts to do so."

Even if preferential policies do not necessarily generate quotas, they do require that people be identified and classified by race. The mere process of indicating one's race is abhorrent to some people, both majority and minority members. Some applicants and employees have simply refused to fill out racial identification questionnaires at all, while others have marked them incorrectly, checking "American Indian" as a gesture of defiance. Such surveys are opposed partly because they seek information that some consider within the realm of personal privacy, and partly because the potential uses of such data are objectionable to those who oppose racial classifications of any sort. Legal intervention has in some cases stayed the operation of such surveys or made them optional. Notable in this regard was the ruling of the California Attorney General that the San Francisco School District could not require its employees to provide racial or ethnic identification under oath, with the additional stipulation that "in all cases where race / ethnicity is a factor in matters related to me . . . the entry made here will be used and shall not be changed." Private groups like the Anti-Defamation League have interceded to require government agencies or institutions to abolish racial and ethnic surveys or at least make them voluntary.

A parallel concern has been the very process of racial classification. If benefits are to be allocated on the basis of membership in a minority group, then lines must be drawn somewhere. Persons who call themselves "black" may range in skin color from very dark to very light, and may show considerable difference in other relevant physical characteristics. Even less clearly defined is the category "Spanish-speaking" or "Spanish surnamed"; admission preference is not extended to persons (like Marco DeFunis himself) who have Latin surnames, nor to Iberian immigrants, nor typically to persons who came from middle or upper middle class Cuban backgrounds. Eligibility of "American Indians" or "Native Americans" is more easily determined by reference to the tribal rolls or the records of the Bureau of Indian Affairs; but here too arbitrary and sometimes unsatisfactory distinctions must sometimes be drawn simply to resolve close cases. Whatever the preferred minority group, there may be some difficulty deciding just who fits into that group, and there may not be complete consensus about the resulting classification. (Vestiges of discriminatory classification persist from the nineteenth century. Louisiana still has a law, for example, which forbids defining any person with less than 1/32 "Negro blood" as "colored", "Black", or "Negro." This law was recently sustained by the Louisiana Supreme Court despite claims that its very existence discriminated against blacks.)

Finally in terms of the impact on government and society, preferential admission policies may be bitterly divisive. The division they can create between minority and majority is obvious. Subtler but perhaps even more dangerous are divisions *within* the majority and minority communities. Blacks are by no means of one mind on the wisdom of preferential policies, for reasons we shall explore later in this chapter. Among white organizations, deep divisions were reflected in the *DeFunis* briefs. Organized labor, for example, was sharply split. The national AFL-CIO—making a rather strange bedfellow for the National Association of Manufacturers—filed a strong brief opposing racial preference in admissions. Yet the United Auto Workers, United Mine Workers, United Farm Workers, and the American Federation of State, County, and Municipal Employees all filed on the other side, joining in the master brief of the Children's Defense Fund.

The division within the American Jewish community has been the most intense and troubling. While a number of Jewish organizations filed briefs supporting DeFunis, two groups (the National Council of Jewish Women and the Union of American Hebrew Congregations) filed on the other side. This split among Jewish groups would not be so alarming were it not a unique effect of the *DeFunis* case; throughout the whole civil rights struggle, these groups stood together in the courts and elsewhere for the protection and advancement of minority rights. No segment of white American society has been so clearly committed to equality. The decision to file briefs in support of white interests against policies which benefit blacks was reached reluctantly but with full conviction in the wisdom of doing so.

Clearly, however, the Jewish community has not been monolithic on this issue. Former Justice Arthur Goldberg is among those

Jewish leaders who disagree with the Anti-Defamation League position; "It is tragic," he has said with regret, "that the two most persecuted minorities should fall apart on this issue." Even more vocal has been John M. Lavine, a vice chairman of the Upper Midwest regional Anti-Defamation League and a member of the Wisconsin Board of Regents. Shortly after the *DeFunis* decision, he wrote:

> As Jews we should be the first to realize that we must do
> everything short of quotas to remediate the discriminations of the
> past. Surely, we should know that as long as our black, red, yellow
> and female neighbors can be kept out of America's mainstream, we
> are only a step away from losing our place. If we don't remediate
> these discriminations, we also will lose our country's purpose and,
> at the same time, our commitment to that purpose is then hollow.

The Effect of Preferential Admissions on Nonminority Groups

One explanation for this opposition is a natural fear that if minorities are preferred, and their numbers increased, other groups must be "unpreferred" to their detriment. It has been widely supposed that the opposition from much of the Jewish community reflects such self-interest. The fact is that Jews are today overrepresented in higher education and some of the professions. While nationally about 40% of high school age youth go to college, 80% of Jewish young people do so. Predictably, Jewish enrollment overall is about twice what strict proportionality would ensure, and in the most highly selective professional programs the percentages are even higher. Thus the Anti-Defamation League asks pointedly: "What happens when Jews . . . are restricted to 3 percent of the available openings?"

Yet the explanation for Jewish concern and opposition must lie deeper than mere self-interest. The fact that Marco DeFunis is Jewish may explain the initial interest that Jewish groups took in the case, but it does not fully explain the position they took once they came in. The very combination of ability, commitment, and energy that have brought the Jewish community into the American academic mainstream despite decades of subtle and overt discrimination, suggest that they are not likely to be harmed by special consideration for newer and less established minorities. Even if Jewish applicants were uniformly distributed throughout the entire pool, the effect of admitting more minority students would impair only slightly the prospects for an individual nonminority applicant. But Jewish candidates for selective academic programs are not just average, as their representation in these programs (without any kind of preference or favoritism) clearly proves. Thus it seems unlikely that any diminution of Jewish opportunities can be traced to preferential policies. While no studies yet validate this hypothesis, it seems only logical that those groups already well established—Jews in law and the social sciences, Asians in certain sciences and engineering, etc.—could not be displaced at the top by broadening the base at the bottom.

Yet *someone* must be displaced, if more minorities are admitted to a class of relatively fixed size. The groups most likely to suffer are in fact those most like the minorities in socioeconomic and educational background—the poor Irish and Italians in Boston and New York, Slavic groups in the Great Lakes cities, Appalachian whites in the border states, and rural white-Anglos in the Southeast and Southwest. Just as these groups have been the major beneficiaries of open admissions in New York City—because they most closely resemble the minorities for whom open admission was originally designed—so they are most directly in competition with minorities in the most selective graduate and professional programs. It is for these white groups just beginning to enter the mainstream of American opportunity and achievement that special minority programs may pose the gravest threat.

A related attitude appears in the comment made in 1970 by Representative Roman Pucinski, D.-Ill., during hearings on HR 513 before the Ad Hoc Hearings Task Force on Poverty of the House Committee on Education and Labor: "Many who are now in the forefront of leading the rioting and the unrest in our universities are the very people that have been admitted into these universities at lower standards"—an obvious reference to the Black Action Movement at the University of Michigan in 1970.

Against this background it was not surprising to see on DeFunis' side of the Supreme Court fight such groups as the Joint Civic Committee of Italian Americans, UNICO National (another Italian group), and a Chicago organization of 300 Polish-American lawyers known as the Advocate Society. About two months after the Supreme Court decision, the *New York Times* carried a story entitled "ITALIAN AMERICANS HERE UNITE TO FIGHT 'REVERSE' RACIAL BIAS." The story recounted the emergence and growing militancy of several new Italian ethnic groups formed to protect the interests of persons of Italian ancestry. The Columbia Coalition was instrumental in filing suit in behalf of a young Italian-American woman who was dismissed by the New York State Department of Labor, apparently the victim of an intensified affirmative action program. Other similar cases have been projected. Financial support for the group's activities comes from such notables as Phil Rizzuto, Joe Garagiola, Bernard Castro (of the convertible couch fame), and former New York Secretary of State John Lomenzo. The Executive Director of the Coalition has been working closely with the regional office of the Anti-Defamation League—a link forged by the shared concern of both groups about the implications of affirmative action for their membership.

There is now very specific evidence of the collaboration of these white ethnic groups. In January 1975 two suits were filed challenging the admissions process used by the City College of New York in starting its new biomedical program. One suit was brought on behalf of Italian-American students by the Coalition; the other was an Anti-Defamation League suit filed on behalf of two Jewish students who, like the Italian plaintiffs, had been excluded from the highly coveted undergraduate program. Both suits claimed that the admissions process had been racially tainted, since minority applicants were given special consideration. Like DeFunis, these plaintiffs argued that they would have been admitted to the program in the absence of minority preference. These suits not only sought to compel the admission of the plaintiffs and other students in a similar position. They also asked money damages ($10,000 in one case, and $25,000 in the other) for each applicant who had been excluded from the biomedical program because of any racial or ethnic preference for minorities.

While the concern of the newer white ethnic groups is altogether understandable, it may be exaggerated, at least in regard to college admissions. Surely the charge that whites are rejected on racial grounds is unfounded. (DeFunis, through his counsel, repeatedly argued that he had been *"excluded from* the University of Washington Law School by reason of his race. . . ."* Some of the amici curiae on his side of the case used similar language.) White-Anglo applicants are not excluded on racial grounds from any program like the one involved in the *DeFunis* case itself. Nor are minority applicants *included* solely for racial reasons. It is true that a rejected white-Anglo applicant who is close to the line might have been admitted if there were no minority program. Yet the marginal white-Anglo might also have been rejected if nonnumerical admission factors were weighted differently, if the number of returning veterans was slightly larger, if the quality of the general applicant pool was a bit better, if the rate of acceptance on the first round were higher, or if the size of the class had been set slightly lower for any of myriad reasons. A minority preference is simply one factor among many affecting the probability of admission for any given applicant. The closer that applicant is to what turns out to be the final line, the greater the impact of any such factor. But any notion that such a marginal applicant is finally "excluded by reason of his race" is naive in terms both of causation and of the admissions process.

Moreover, the effects of rejection in such a case must be carefully assessed. Marco DeFunis, denied admission to the University of Washington, could have gone to several other accredited law schools, including the University of Oregon. Even in the highly selective fields, the system is sufficiently flexible that a student who barely missed getting into one law school or medical school will find a place somewhere else. If no alternatives do exist, then it is not preferential admission but the person's own qualifications and potential that foreclose access. It is also well to remember that a student who is "displaced" is not expected to be at the top of the class; the location on the list which makes an applicant vulnerable to a preferential program is based on a careful prediction of first year performance. Such an applicant is therefore "marginal"; whether in or out. Displacement takes place at the bottom, and not at the top of the class.

There is, however, a quite different collateral effect of preferential admission that may hurt majority students. Most minority students come to college or graduate school with special financial needs. If they are to succeed, they must typically receive support at a level far above that required by middle class white students. Some outside funds do exist to defray these costs. Increasingly the major foundations (especially Ford and Danforth) have provided special scholarships and fellowships for minority students. But much of the cost, both of direct aid and of supplemental education, must be borne by the institution itself. Given static or even shrinking financial aid budgets, the money must come from somewhere else. The competition for minority students is such that any school which wishes to attract them in substantial numbers must be prepared to make a major commitment of special resources, and thus provide less generously for the needs of other students. At private institutions and those publicly supported colleges that receive lump-sum budgets, the diversion of resources may come at the cost of improved instruction, better facilities, higher faculty salaries, and other expenditures that would benefit the entire university community. The only answer to this very substantial concern is the high priority which the institution as a whole presumably places upon attracting and keeping more minority students if it is willing to make the commitment in the first place. Surely government should bear a greater share of the special costs of minority group education, but it is unlikely that institutions will soon be relieved of making the hard choices that result from such a commitment.

The Effect Upon Minority Groups and Their Members

It has also been argued that preferential admissions may harm the very groups it is intended to help. Those minority applicants who would be admitted without special consideration, it is said, will be stigmatized when it is known that a preferential program exists.

Thomas Sowell, a black economics professor at UCLA, has expressed this concern as follows:

> What all the arguments and campaign for quotas are really saying, loud and clear, is that Black people just don't have it, and that they will have to be given something in order to have something. . . . Those Black people who are already competent, and who could be instrumental in producing more competence among this rising generation, will be completely undermined, as Black becomes synonymous—in the minds of Black and White alike—with incompetence and Black achievement becomes synonymous with charity or payoffs.

In a similar vein, James McPherson, the black lawyer, poet, and literary critic, once wrote that he and other blacks at Harvard Law School felt that "perhaps we were not authentic law students" and that white classmates "knew that we were not, and like certain members of the faculty, had developed paternalistic attitudes toward us."

While these concerns are genuine, there appear to be several answers. Most basically, much of the initial pressure and continuing support for preferential programs has come from minority students and professionals, including many who would not need any preferences for themselves but do not feel stigmatized because such a program is available for others. It is also true that no minority person is forced to participate in such a program; as the Harvard amicus curiae brief pointed out: "All the law school does is to open an educational opportunity to the minority student which would otherwise be closed; the choice is the student's." Finally, the experience to date does not confirm or validate the early fears. Degrees from the University of Michigan are no less sought or prized because the 10% black goal was set and has been largely attained. In fact, the commitment to preference seems to correlate closely with the prestige and distinction of an institution. It is significant that Harvard and MIT supported the University of Washington in the Supreme Court, as did the deans of the most eminent national law schools.

There is a quite different sense in which preferential admissions might jeopardize minority students. Those students who really need, and would not be admitted without, special consideration may be thrown in over their heads. There were alarming failure rates during the early years of preferential admission in some law and medical schools. The danger is one that drew the concern of John P. Roche, Brandeis political scientist and White House intellectual in residence during the Johnson administration:

> Once the decision was made that Negro or "culturally underprivileged" youngsters would be admitted to first-class colleges without the usual prerequisites, the escalation began. . . . Nobody has actually worried about the anguish of the poor Negro kids who have been dumped into a competitive situation, have been thrown with inadequate preparation into water well beyond their capacity to swim.

Roche's statement was made in 1970. Since that time much attention has been given to more careful selection among minority applicants —made possible in part through expansion of the minority pool; to special supplemental prematriculation programs like summer institutes designed to bridge the skills gap; to more effective counselling both before and during the academic experience (relying largely on older minority students, who are the most effective "teachers"); and to continuing supplemental and developmental instruction in needed skills and fields. Attrition rates have declined dramatically, as the survival of the minority students in DeFunis' own class at the University of Washington suggests. The failure rate for preferentially admitted minority students is still probably higher than for the class as a whole, but far lower than would be predicted on the basis of numerical indicia.

It has also been feared that the special needs of disadvantaged students might lead to a lowering of academic requirements, or even adoption of a dual grading system. Dr. Kenneth Clark, the black psychologist and New York Regent, warned several years ago that "for Blacks to be held to lower standards, different standards or, in some cases, no standards is a most contemptible form of racism." Yet it does not appear that academic standards have in fact been diluted to accommodate preferentially admitted minority students. The Newman Commission, the major federal task force on higher education, whose chairman is now President of the University of Rhode Island, reported: "Different criteria have clearly been used for admission of some minority students, but there is little or no evidence of any change in degree standards." The American Bar Association survey of the comparative progress of "disadvantaged" and "regular" minority law students asked a number of questions about the treatment of students who entered the second year on probation. One question inquired whether all students took the same exams and were graded according to the same standards. All 73 schools reported that the exams were the same for all students; only two schools noted any difference of any kind in the grading standards in favor of minority students. Thus the promising survival rate of the preferentially admitted students seems to reflect the supplemental education programs offered by most of the schools.

If minority students do enter highly selective institutions or programs with inadequate preparation, some special attention is appropriate. The consequences of a high initial failure rate are predictable, not only by shattering the confidence of the students thus disqualified, but also in deterring other students from seeking opportunity through the same route. If grading standards and degree requirements are not to be diluted, then the only remaining option is to design and offer special supplemental programs for minority and/or disadvantaged students. There is now a substantial literature about special and compensatory programs, suggesting a number of approaches that do help dramatically in improving the minority survival rate. Yet there are also risks. The knowledge that one is a "special student" or survives only because of special help can be quite damaging to self-esteem as well as to relations with peers. The creation of special programs for minority students may also jeopardize the very goal of integration by perpetuating the "tracking" system of the elementary and secondary schools. Special care must be taken to avoid too great a gulf between the special programs and the mainstream of the campus.

For the minority student on the integrated campus, there may be additional problems. Financial needs may increase during the college or graduate years, and the anticipated employment may either be unavailable or may conflict with the need to devote more time to academic work in order to survive. Meanwhile, the promises that drew minority students into college or graduate school may prove increasingly elusive. The examinations that one must pass to enter the various professions, even after earning the requisite degree, pose additional and sometimes more formidable hurdles. For minority law graduates, the bar examinations in many states have been a cause of grief, as we noted earlier in reviewing the results of the special ABA survey. Efforts are being made to improve the fairness of bar examinations and their grading, but substantial hurdles do remain. The fact that graduation may not assure entry into the profession should not, however, deter admission of minority students into professional schools—any more than the Harvard Law School should twenty years ago have refused admission to a brilliant applicant because (as an avowed Communist) he was unlikely to be admitted to the bar. If it is true that minority graduates cannot become practicing lawyers without passing the bar, it is equally true that they cannot pass the bar without a good legal education. It is the responsibility of the professional schools to improve opportunities for minorities both by opening educational prospects and by enhancing likelihood of actually entering the profession. Surely discriminatory bar examinations, or poor minority performance on other kinds of licensing tests, should not excuse exclusionary admission policies.

Finally, preferential admission may be unfair to the minority student by placing him in a socially difficult position on the predominantly white-Anglo campus. Early experience in bringing small numbers of urban blacks to isolated rural campuses like Oshkosh, Urbana, and Ithaca were disastrous. A small band of minority students felt alone and isolated in such surroundings, and reacted to what they saw as a hostile and threatening environment. Since the late 1960s, students of all sorts are at least much quieter. Whether they feel better about their surroundings is another matter. Many more institutions today have achieved the "critical mass" of minority students that is necessary to create a community and not just a symbolic group.

Minority students understandably take a less sanguine view of their social role—like the black Yale student who asked the dean for a black roommate because "We're tired of being textbooks for Whites", or the junior at Wesleyan who said he didn't "give a damn for educating white boys about what it's like to be black." Administrators seldom appreciate the time that minority students may devote to just being black, or chicano, or Puerto Rican, or American Indian on a campus where he may still be something of a rarity. To expect the minority student to integrate the institution, and sensitize the whites to intercultural relations, as well as completing the regular requirements for a degree and working a part-time job, may unreasonably burden many who have been preferentially admitted.

Such problems as these do not really argue against preferential admissions as such. They do indicate areas of caution, and the need for supplemental educational programs and opportunities without which admission alone would be a hollow promise. This discussion should prove—in case there was any doubt on that score—that education of preferentially admitted students is likely to be expensive in both tangible and intangible terms. This is hardly surprising; the very factors of discrimination and educational disadvantage that call for special consideration in the admissions process create additional obligations once these students have been admitted. To accept the obligation at one level but not at the other would be irresponsible.

CHAPTER EIGHT

BEYOND *DE FUNIS:* THE POLICY IMPLICATIONS OF PREFERENTIAL ADMISSIONS

In the year that followed, the Supreme Court's expected flood of *DeFunis*-type litigation simply had not materialized. In one suit brought by a thirty-four year old applicant to the Medical School of the University of California at Davis, the judge reached the same conclusion as the *DeFunis* trial judge on the merits of preferential admission, but resolved the issue differently.

The applicant in this case had sued on precisely the same grounds as DeFunis, claiming that he would have been admitted had the school not preferred a group of minority applicants with lower test scores and grades. The Superior Court held in his favor on the abstract constitutional issue—agreeing with Judge Shorett—but declined to order the plaintiff's admission because he was too far down on the waiting list. The judge accepted testimony by the admissions officer of the medical school that the plaintiff would not have been admitted even if there were no minority program. (This is what lawyers call a "standing" issue. A person who is not directly affected by a policy or practice—or who would not be helped by its elimination —may not be a proper plaintiff in a court case.) The court also felt that "the admission of students to the Medical School is so peculiarly a discretionary function of the school that . . . it should not be interfered with by a Court, absent a showing of fraud, unfairness, bad faith or capriciousness, none of which has been shown."

The only other suit to attract any attention was brought by one

Doris Guerriero Stewart against New York University, after she had been denied admission to the university's law school. This case has several interesting features, and provides a useful entree to the issues of our final chapter.

Ms. Stewart (suing on her own behalf and for other persons similarly situated as a "class") had three basic claims in her complaint against NYU: First, she argued for essentially the same reasons as had Marco DeFunis that the law school's publicized minority preference program was unconstitutional. Second, however, she claimed that if the program should be sustained she was entitled to a preference as a woman, since women had suffered "cultural, educational and social deprivation, based on societal, cultural, institutionalized and stereo-typed sexual roles. . . ." Finally, should the preferential policy be upheld by the court, Ms. Stewart insisted that she was entitled to share in its benefits because she came from an economically, socially, and culturally deprived background and thus had suffered similar deprivation. (Although the facts of her previous life and career were not developed in the complaint, she apparently had put herself through college and graduate school with employment and fellow-ships, while earning impressive grades and receiving strong recom-mendations. Her LSAT score, however, was not high, and without some sort of special consideration she would not have been admitted.)

The *Stewart* case provides a natural point of departure to pursue several practical problems and issues we have deferred in our discus-sion of educational policy and constitutional law. These questions are really five in number: *(a)* Who may or should be preferred under such a policy? *(b)* In what form should the preference be extended? *(c)* How much of a preference is appropriate? *(d)* How long should preferential policies last? and *(e)* What are the practical responsibili-ties of a college or university that adopts preferential policies?

One introductory comment is in order before we turn to the specific questions. In Chapter 5 we assumed that a group was "under-represented" in higher education or in a profession if its share of that particular sector was less than its share of the total national popula-tion. That conclusion is almost tautologically correct. But it does contain two assumptions which we must now consider: First, that in the absence of artificial or "structural" limitations, representation would be roughly equal to population proportionality; and second, that a lack of proportionality which results from *artificial* barriers or impediments to the access of minority groups is undesirable, if not unconstitutional.

These assumptions require some clarification of the concept of structural or artificial limitations. In broad outline, we refer here to restrictions and inequalities that result not from differential capacities or desires, but are from external and therefore artificial constraints. If, for example, a particular group is underrepresented in a given area either because it does not *wish* equal access to that sector or lacks the competence to attain equal access, that is one thing; if, however, the absence of equal representation is neither the result of voluntary choice nor of lack of ability, then the limitations are artificial or structural. Not all such limitations are the result of governmental policies. Much of the discrimination and segregation which has denied equality to minorities is the result of private action—housing discrimination, employment barriers, and other socioeconomic impediments. While such nongovernmental restrictions are typically beyond the reach of the constitution—since they involve private rather than "state" action—they have increasingly been brought within the reach of laws which forbid discrimination in housing, employment, public accommodations, and a broad range of activities. Today, in fact, few forms of private discrimination remain beyond the reach of government and law. Someday, therefore, all the structural barriers that currently restrict access will presumably have been removed.

Even if all artificial barriers to access were removed and their effects obliterated, we do not know whether college attendance rates for all groups would be roughly equal. There may be differences both of motivation and of competence. We do know, for example, that Jewish students show relatively little interest in such fields as agriculture and forestry even though no artificial barriers limit their access to those fields. Asian students seem to prefer the science and engineering fields and are underrepresented in the social sciences and humanities, probably through choice rather than by necessity. (The latter generalization must be qualified, in the case of Asian students from culturally limited or deprived backgrounds, for whom preferential admission in law, medicine, and other fields has been found warranted.) Even if all artificial barriers were removed, blacks, chicanos, Indians and other racial minorities would probably choose different graduate and professional fields at differing rates, just as do majority groups today. Thus perfect proportionality of representation would probably never occur, even in a world of completely free choice. The goal of higher education, in seeking to break down the artificial and structural barriers, should be to maximize such choice rather than to ensure that choice is exercised in any particular pattern.

Rejection of strict proportionality of matriculation rates to population does not, however, mean proportionality has no utility at all as a rough goal for admissions policies. We can hardly expect precision in the statement of objectives while actual minority representation in most selective programs still falls so far short of proportionality. There will be time enough to consider fine shadings if and when proportionality comes within view. Until that time, opponents of proportionality have at least an obligation to suggest a better alternative goal. Proportionality also has the virtue of objectivity, and keeps the process of goal determination from being politicized, as it would be if objective criteria were not used. Reliance on proportionality as a guide also avoids the virtually impossible task of determining the extent to which representation has in fact been distorted by structural disabilities. Thus both practical and theoretical considerations point toward proportionality as an appropriate working goal.

Who May / Should Be Preferred?

There are two quite distinct questions under this heading. The question of what applicants *should* be preferred is somewhat narrower than the question of what applicants *may* (legally or constitutionally) be preferred. As a practical matter, it is unlikely that every applicant who could be given preference will in fact be admitted. Limitations of space and financial aid and consideration for the normal admissions process make this unlikely. Thus the University of Washington Law School did not in fact admit every minority applicant; even some qualified black and chicano candidates were rejected simply because the school could not accommodate them all. This pattern will exist almost everywhere a preferential program is in force, except where either space or resources are unlimited. The question who *should* be preferred is a practical one that must reflect institutional needs, conditions, resources, and the like. We must simply set that question aside and move to the more general, and for us much more important, issue of who *may* be preferred.

The question of who may be preferred takes us back once again to the compelling interest test. It would be nearly impossible for a public college or university to show a compelling interest in giving preference to members of every identifiable racial or ethnic minority. Jews in many fields, and Asians in others, have already achieved eminence without any special consideration. Clearly today they need no special help in seeking or realizing higher educational opportunities. Discrimination against such groups undeniably still exists in other sectors, and should remain a concern of government. Although full equality of citizenship has not yet been achieved, equal access to higher education and to the professions does seem to exist, and that is the critical fact for present purposes.

For what groups, then, might a preference reflect a compelling interest? Clearly the strongest case can be made for preferring or giving special consideration to those groups that are not only under-represented in higher education but also disproportionately *(a)* are victims of overt racial or ethnic discrimination; *(b)* are socioeconomically disadvantaged; *(c)* are excluded by standardized tests and other entrance criteria; and *(d)* are graduates of crowded, run down, and poorly staffed public schools where intense segregation persists. Most blacks, Mexican-Americans, Puerto Ricans and American Indians meet these criteria. Some Asians and members of other racial or ethnic minorities meet these tests. Those groups clearly present the most compelling case for special consideration.

Once a group has been identified for a general preference, the next question is whether all members of that group should receive the preference. A specific and difficult problem is raised by members of the group who certainly need no financial help and may have had better preparatory education, e.g., the children of successful business and professional people. Superficially, it would appear that preference for such persons would be unnecessary, if not undesirable. But there are some subtler factors arguing the other way. For one, *all* minority group members have suffered discrimination—perhaps even to a greater degree in the case of the wealthy person who is more likely to have moved in integrated society. Professor Graham Hughes of New York University has put it well: "In the short run at least the mere fact of a person's being Black in the United States is sufficient reason for providing compensatory techniques even though that person may in some ways appear fortunate enough in his personal background." What is true for blacks is true for other minorities as well, though perhaps to a lesser degree for those whose skins are lighter and who speak with no accent.

Moreover, from the institutional vantage point, there may be even greater benefit in attracting middle class minority students. Because of their family circumstances, they will not need financial aid, as will the ghetto or barrio student. The prognosis for their academic survival is probably greater even if they are specially admitted. Middle class minority students will probably assimilate more easily, and may be more acceptable to white-Anglo students who are put off by street language and ghetto lifestyle. While the number of rich blacks and other minorities coming in through any special admissions program will always be small, the argument for including them in that program seems compelling.

Two important groups remain to be considered because they are both underrepresented and the victims of structural barriers to equality. The first of these is women, both minority and majority. While the number of women enrolled in college and receiving baccalaureate degrees throughout the United States approaches proportionality, that is not true for the graduate and professional schools and the careers for which those schools train people. The number of women in law and medicine, for example, remains shockingly low, even though enrollments have shot up in the last several years. It is also true that until recently women were actually barred from some selective professional schools—Harvard Law School admitted its first woman in 1948, for example—and many others faced overt discrimination in the awarding of fellowships, in the use of facilities, and in other regards. (Subtler forms of discrimination have also been widespread in the graduate and professional areas. Denial of opportunities for part-time study, discrimination in placement and career development programs, lack of childcare facilities, etc., have certainly served to reduce opportunities for women in many professional fields.) Finally, there has been a tendency on the part of the white male establishment to take the aspirations of women even less seriously than those of minority group men, and thus to respond less meaningfully to the fact of underrepresentation.

The question, however, is whether these conditions require or justify a preference for women in *admissions*. All evidence suggests that equalization of opportunity, at least for nonminority women, will come about simply through removal of the structural barriers, through equal allocation of scholarships and fellowships, and through positive steps in areas such as part-time study and child care programs. Indeed, a completely sex blind admissions policy would probably produce a larger than proportional number of women in the entering class, since women perform better on many standardized tests and earn slightly better high school and college grades. Finally, women have not sought preference in the admissions process; leaders like Bernice Sandler of the Association of American Colleges insist that equality of opportunity can and should be achieved without such special consideration. At least it would seem proper to remove all the structural barriers first—as the new federal Title IX requires—and then wait to see if equality of choice does not result. Any decision now to give preference to nonminority women would appear premature.

The other group that must be considered—socioeconomically disadvantaged white-Anglo groups—pose a much more difficult issue.

The Southern and Eastern European national groups and the Appalachian whites are both underrepresented in higher education and are victims of environmental and educational disabilities similar in kind if not in intensity to those experienced by racial minorities. Moreover, such people have felt neglected and abandoned by recent efforts to improve opportunity for blacks, Puerto Ricans, and chicanos; in some areas these groups compete with the racial minorities and thus feel they have been further "disadvantaged" by the preference shown for their competitors. We have already reviewed some of the evidence of this feeling—the formation of militant Italian-American organizations to fight "reverse discrimination"; the filing of amicus curiae briefs in *DeFunis* on behalf of Italian and Polish organizations; the critical comments of Representative Roman Pucinski about preferentially admitted minority students, etc. Politically, if for no other reason, these concerns must be taken into account by any college or university that fashions a preferential program. Even beyond politics, the morality and philosophy of higher education demand some attention to the educational plight of these groups.

Obviously the supporting data for these groups are much harder to collect. We have no surveys of enrollments, degrees, and professional participation for Italian, Polish, Czech, or Hungarian Americans. While some crude data could be compiled on the basis of surnames, even that would be impossible for Appalachian whites, whose surnames are indistinguishably Anglo-Saxon. (The only way of identifying Appalachian students in urban high schools and colleges is by tracing parental and grandparental zip codes and counties since certain regions in Kentucky and West Virginia have sent large numbers of migrants to the cities. But this process is both a difficult and a crude measure of a target population.) Even so, the difficulty of gathering information should not preclude the formulation of appropriate remedial measures. The central question is whether such measures are justified.

In an area where white ethnic or Appalachian groups comprise a substantial share of the population, but are underrepresented in the colleges and universities, some special consideration of those groups in the admissions process would seem clearly warranted. To be sure, there are obvious differences between these groups and the racial minorities—in terms of overtness of discrimination, quality of education, family environment, socioeconomic status, etc.—which would justify a college's decision to exclude some or all of these groups in a preferential program. It would be equally defensible from a constitutional point of view to *include* disadvantaged white ethnic groups in the preferred population. And where the underrepresentation in college of these groups is acute—as it is for the Slavic groups in Buffalo, Cleveland, and Detroit, for example—it would be politically and educationally desirable even if not legally mandatory to design a preferential program to take account of factors other than race. If the purpose of preferential admission is to make higher education more broadly available to groups that have been excluded in the past for reasons unrelated to their merit or aspirations, then some degree of preference is certainly appropriate here also.

By What Means Should a Preference Be Extended?

A college or university that wishes to increase its share of minority students through preferential admission might set rough guidelines in one or more of at least three general forms. First, the guidelines might be set as a total or comprehensive minority share, with no breakdown of components. Second, they could be set as a specific group commitment for each of the principal minority groups —an undertaking to seek a black percentage of roughly X, a chicano share of roughly Y, an Indian share of roughly Z, and so on for other disadvantaged and underrepresented groups. The guidelines might also be expressed as a commitment to a single group, with a residual or incidental commitment to other groups. (If Dartmouth, given its special history, decides to devote all its special resources to recruitment and support of Native Americans, that would seem a reasonable decision. The black and Spanish-speaking population of New Hampshire, and all of New England, for that matter, are small; Dartmouth could quite reasonably leave the balance of the task to other institutions.)

The form in which preferential policies will be implemented depends in larger part on institutional needs and practices. As we suggested earlier, preference in admission can mean a multitude of things—ranging all the way from a factor that tips the balance when other elements are equal, to a fixed quota that excludes all other factors. In between these two extremes lie many more moderate forms of preference—different weighting of various admission criteria in minority cases; adding or deleting a particular criterion; setting aside all minority applications for more careful review or for review by a separate group; adding a "handicap" to test scores or grades in minority cases; admission of minority students on the basis of some alternative or supplemental experience such as a summer institute; or conditional acceptance of minority candidates on the basis of expected performance in a special program. All of these admissions devices, and others as well, may be used to implement a decision to prefer a particular applicant group. Clearly there is no one exclusive admissions policy or format.

How Much of a Preference?

Even if proportionality is accepted as the rough short-term guide for preferential admission, *how much* of a preference to extend requires further discussion. A most important factor is the relevant population base. Although a coherent national strategy on the problem of unequal access to higher education would be ideal, it is not likely to occur in the foreseeable future. National population shares are unlikely to provide entirely satisfactory guidance since no institution of higher learning has a truly national student body. What is needed is a more selective approach consistent with institutional setting, constituency, mission, and priorities.

The goal which a college or university sets for minority enrollments should reflect a variety of factors. Among those factors would undoubtedly be the minority population in the area from which the institution draws its students—the metropolitan area in the case of a community college, the state or multistate region in the case of a public university, and possibly the entire nation in the case of a private university or selective liberal arts college. Also pertinent would be the range of institutional resources available for financial aid and special developmental education programs. Proximity to a large city would also enter the picture, since minority populations are increasingly urban and are more likely to attend college in large numbers closer to home. The history, tradition, and mission of the college or university might also affect its enrollment goals; a northern liberal arts college with a long history of concern for minorities will simply be better able to attract minority students than a recently desegregated southern school. Attitudes of the faculty and the nonminority students should also play some role in setting enrollment goals and targets. In addition to these rather obvious elements, many others might be suggested. The point is that there can be no single, simple determinant of an institution's commitment in this area. Each college or university must work out a distinctive approach of its own.

Once an institution's ultimate goals or objectives have been determined, they clearly cannot be achieved in a single year, or perhaps even in five years. Realistic interim goals should therefore be developed. One appropriate model to follow in the phasing of minority enrollments would be the "Philadelphia Plan" for the gradual integration of the building trades in various metropolitan areas. (The plan takes its name from the city in which it was first promulgated. Comparable plans have since been developed and applied in a number of other metropolitan areas.) This federal policy requires affirmative action to increase gradually the percentage of minority workers on federal contract projects. Four factors determine the setting of both interim and final minority employment "ranges" for each trade or craft covered by the plan: (1) the current extent of minority-group participation in the trade; (2) the availability of minority-group persons for employment in such trade; (3) the need for training programs in the area and/or the need to ensure demand for graduates of existing training programs; and (4) the impact of the program on the existing labor force.

The analogy is imperfect, to be sure. The recruitment and admission of students is a vastly different process from the training and employment of construction workers. But parallel criteria could be developed for the setting of realistic minority shares in higher education. To illustrate, these criteria would include (1) the current extent of minority enrollment on the particular campus, in the region, and nation-wide; (2) the annual numbers of minority high school graduates (or of college graduates in the case of postbaccalaureate programs) in the target region; (3) the number of applications received in the past from members of each minority group; (4) the capacity and commitment of all colleges and universities in the area to recruit and accept minority students; (5) the academic and financial needs of minority students in the area, compared with the institutional capacity to meet those needs; and (6) the effect upon the total student body of various institutional efforts to meet those academic and financial needs.

These data should be carefully reviewed as part of the general institutional process of determining admissions goals. The goals for minority students should be considered along with the optimal upper division / lower division mix, ratio of commuter to resident students, percentages of out-of-state enrollments, and the myriad other factors that make up a college or university's admissions policies. There should be extensive consultation with neighboring colleges and universities, to avoid pointless duplication or competition. Since these are goals and not quotas, the initial target should be subject to periodic reexamination and upward or downward revision should be made as circumstances demand. Drastic revisions should be avoided, however, both because minority expectations depend on such commitments, and because the setting of goals by neighboring institutions must be an interdependent process.

How Long Should Preferential Policies Continue?

Preferential policies are certainly not an end in themselves. They are at best a means to the goal of increased minority participation in American life. Preferential admissions, as necessary as they may be today to achieve that goal, should be regarded as a temporary expedient. Preference should continue only as long as it is absolutely essential to achieve equality of access and choice. When less racially oriented means will avail, they should replace racial or ethnic preference. The goal is not to put minorities in a better position than the majority, but simply to give them a fair chance of catching up after decades of deprivation and disadvantage. Thus the need for such programs should be reviewed constantly. And when the conditions that warranted the creation of a particular preference no longer exist, that preference should cease.

It may not be easy to tell when that time comes, however. Superficially it would seem that a preference should end when proportionality or parity has been achieved for the beneficiary group. That may indeed be the proper time to terminate the program. But the situation should be studied with some care. It may be, for example, that certain structural barriers or their direct effects persist and would restore former inequality if the preference were suddenly discontinued. Even if all the structural barriers have been eliminated, opportunity may not yet have so equalized as to warrant ending the preference. The achievement of anything like proportionality should provide a signal for reexamining the need for any special programs, but not necessarily the *coup de grâce*. Preferential policies should remain in force as long as—but only as long as—they are necessary to bring about equality of opportunity, access, and choice.

What Policies Should Accompany Preferential Admissions?

It is not enough for a college or university simply to adopt and apply a preferential admission policy. That was one of the mistakes the University of Washington Law School made in the early years by keeping information about the policy too much within its own confines. Not only the average Washington voter or legislator, but probably the average student or faculty member elsewhere on the campus, did not really understand what was being done by the Law School, for whom, and why. Thus the dissenting justices in the Washington Supreme Court, the Anti-Defamation League, and other local and national groups could claim they were surprised by an admission policy that diluted the university's historic commitment to merit. These charges were really quite unjustified. But the university had not adequately explained what it was doing and why. During the pendency of the *DeFunis* suit, the law faculty did refine its admission policies so as to articulate clearly the factors that would be taken into account in the special admissions program, and the rationale for doing so.

Few other colleges and universities have, however, been so open about their minority admissions programs—feeling perhaps they would risk political reprisal, or the obloquy of private donors, by "going public." Nothing less than complete candor seems warranted in this area. We have suggested earlier that the flaw in using euphemistic language like "disadvantaged" or "deprived" or even "inner city" is that it fools no one in the long run and blurs the programs in the short run. Much the same could be said here. If a university is in fact admitting minorities on a preferential basis, that information will get out eventually. It would be far better to tell people—especially governing board members, legislators, and donors—what is going on before they receive complaints from white students and think the institution is doing something nefarious or dirty. A clear statement of the policy and a full public disclosure seem far preferable to concealment.

Second, the institution that adopts preferential admission policies must approach its use of standardized test scores with caution and care. There is no need to disregard test scores for all students simply because they exclude more than a fair share of minority applicants. In fact, test scores may help to predict *among* minority applicants, so long as the basic difference between minority and majority performance is kept clearly in mind. Meanwhile, the whole educational community should support the development of new and more refined performance predictors. The time may come when test scores will again be as reliable as we always supposed they were until the critical minority underrepresentation came to haunt us.

Third, every institution which preferentially admits minority students must recognize that the obligation to these students only begins, and does not end, with the admission decision. The financial needs of disadvantaged students may far exceed those of white-Anglo students. They are far less able than their middle class fellows to incur added obligations through loans, and thus must often get a larger share of their support through grants and scholarships, supplemented by part-time employment to a degree that does not jeopardize study time. For students who come to college or even graduate school (as many do) with woefully inferior preparation in basic skills, there are educational as well as financial needs going far beyond those of the general student population. Finally, the institution must realize that the ultimate goal—more minorities in key occupations and profes-sions—requires not only producing more students with degrees, but also preparing them to perform better on the bar exams, medical licensure exams, CPA exams, etc., which determine ultimate access to the profession. Every institution which accepts minority students incurs a responsibility to get those students all the way through—either by making the professional examinations correspond more closely to the education the students receive, or by adapting or supple-menting the education to bridge the gap.

Fourth, institutions of higher learning must continue to address themselves to the basic causes of minority underrepresentation. Though colleges and universities do not create, but only inherit the effects of, the basic problems, the academic community has the capac-ity to contribute more heavily toward the solutions of such seemingly ineradicable problems as segregated housing, ghetto schools, employ-ment discrimination, and other forms of racial isolation. Ironically, the infusion of more disadvantaged minority students onto selective campuses may impress college and university professors with the urgency of the underlying problems as no amount of remote contact possibly could. Students bring the problems, and the effects, of the ghetto and the barrio into class and into the professor's office with them. Thus a potent, if unintended, catalyst for change may now be at work.

Finally, one must not lose sight of the ultimate goal. The reason for giving preference to minority groups is not to be nice to individual students or even to whole classes. Of course there may be many extraneous considerations leading to race conscious policies in higher education—guilt about the past, liberal sympathy for the disadvantaged, political pressure from minority legislators, prodding from affirmative action agencies, and a host of others. But the basic justification for taking race into account is to achieve equality for persons and groups to whom equality has long been denied—originally in obvious ways, later through subtler devices. The cure must scrupulously avoid the vices it seeks to correct. Racial quotas, for example —however "benign" they may seem to be in favoring minorities—are no less acceptable now than they were when used to keep out Jews and other minorities several decades ago. Greater equality for some must not cause a loss of equality for others. Individual whites must not be penalized on the basis of race any more than individual blacks or Puerto Ricans or chicanos can be penalized for that reason. Preference for the disadvantaged and excluded does not and should not mean a loss of opportunity for the more fortunate. What is sought is a more even distribution of burdens and benefits throughout our pluralistic society. And if expansion of opportunity for blacks from Seattle's center city means that Marco DeFunis will have to attend law school in Oregon rather than remaining at home, that seems not too heavy a price to pay for a result that can be achieved in no other way.

APPENDIX

DE FUNIS V. ODEGAARD

The Washington Supreme Court Opinion
82 Wn. 2d 11, 507 P. 2d 1169

Marco DeFunis et al., Respondents, v. *Charles Odegaard et al.,*
Appellants

Defendants, who include the members of the Board of
Regents of the University of Washington, the president of
the university, and the dean and certain members of the
Admissions Committee of the University of Washington
School of Law, appeal from a judgment ordering them to
admit plaintiff Marco DeFunis, Jr., as a first-year student to
the University of Washington School of Law, as of September 22, 1971.

Broadly phrased, the major question presented herein is
whether the law school may, in consonance with the equal
protection provisions of the state and federal constitutions,
consider the racial or ethnic background of applicants as
one factor in the selection of students.

Marco DeFunis, Jr. (hereinafter plaintiff), his wife, and
his parents commenced an action in the superior court,
alleging that plaintiff, an applicant for admission to the
University of Washington School of Law (hereinafter law
school) for the class commencing September 1971, had been
wrongfully denied admission in that no preference was
given to residents of the state of Washington in the admissions process and that persons were admitted to the law
school with lesser qualifications than those of plaintiff. The
complaint asked that the court order the defendants to
admit and enroll plaintiff in the law school in the fall of
1971 and, upon the failure of defendants to do so, that

plaintiffs recover damages in the sum of not less than $50,000.

The superior court granted a temporary restraining order and order to show cause, restraining defendants from selecting students for admission to the law school during the pendency of the action. Defendants, in turn, moved to dismiss the complaint on the grounds that the court lacked jurisdiction of the cause and that the complaint failed to state a claim upon which relief could be granted.

The superior court dismissed that portion of the plaintiff's complaint seeking monetary damages. The balance of defendants' motion to dismiss was denied, and a temporary injunction was entered enjoining the defendants from admitting students to the law school "in a number which would preclude the admission of plaintiff, Marco DeFunis, Jr., to the 1971-72 first year class, should his admission eventually be ordered by the court." After a nonjury trial, the court ruled that in denying plaintiff admission to the law school, the University of Washington had discriminated against him in violation of the equal protection of the laws guaranteed by the fourteenth amendment to the United States Constitution.

Law school admissions pose a complex problem, and require a sensitive balancing of diverse factors. To gain insight into the complicated process of selecting first-year law students, and to better appreciate the essence of plaintiff's complaint against the law school, we turn first to the circumstances and operative facts—as delineated by the record—from which this litigation arises.

Under RCW 28B.20.130(3), the Board of Regents of the University of Washington has the power and duty to establish entrance requirements for students seeking admission to the university. The dean and faculty of the law school, pursuant to the authority delegated to them by the Board of Regents and the president of the university, have established a committee on admissions and readmissions to determine who shall be admitted to the law school. For the academic year September 15, 1970, to June 15, 1971, the committee was composed of five faculty members and two student members; on June 7, 1971, the faculty of the law school expanded the membership of the committee to six faculty members and three student members. The chairman estimated that the committee spent over 1,300 hours in the selection process for the 1971-72 first-year class.

The number of qualified applicants to the law school has increased dramatically in recent years. In 1967, the law school received 618 applications; in 1968, 704; in 1969, 860; and in 1970, 1,026 applications were received. The law school received 1,601 applications for admission to the first-year class beginning September, 1971. Under the university's enrollment limitation there were only 445 positions allotted to the law school, and of these the number available for the first-year class was between 145 and 150. The chairman of the admissions committee stated that most of these applicants would be regarded as qualified by admissions standards at this and other comparable law schools in recent years. Hence, the task of selection is difficult, time-consuming and requires the exercise of careful and informed discretion, based on the evidence appearing in the application files. While many applicants are relatively easy to select for admission because of very outstanding qualifications, and others are relatively easy to reject, the middle group of candidates is much more difficult to assess. Plaintiff was in this latter category.

Applicants for admission to the law school must have earned an undergraduate degree and taken the Law School Admission Test (LSAT) administered by the Educational Testing Service of Princeton, New Jersey. They must also submit with their written application a copy of transcripts from all schools and colleges which they have attended prior to application for admission, together with statements from their undergraduate dean of students and letters of recommendation from faculty members in their major field of study. They may submit additional letters of recommendation and statements. The application for admission gives the applicant the option to indicate his "dominant" ethnic origin. The admissions process does not include personal interviews and does not reveal whether applicants are poor or affluent.

The committee's basic criteria for selecting students are expressed in the "Guide for Applicants", a copy of which plaintiff received with his 1971 application:

We below describe the process we applied to determine the class that entered the University of Washington School of Law in September 1970. We anticipate that the same process will be applied in determining membership in the class of 1971.

. . .

In assessing applications, we began by trying to identify applicants who had the potential for outstanding performance in law school. We attempted to select applicants for admission from that group on the basis of their ability to make significant contributions to law school classes and to the community at large.

For the purpose of a preliminary ranking of the applicants for the class of 1974, the junior-senior undergraduate grade point average and the Law School Admissions Test scores[1] for each applicant were combined through a formula to yield a predicted first-year of law school grade average for the applicant. This preliminary index number is called the Predicted First-Year Average (PFYA). The relative weight of grades and test scores in this formula was determined on the basis of past experience at the law school. The same formula is used for all applicants in a given year. If an applicant has taken the LSAT more than once in the past 3 years, the average score is employed rather than the latest score; this is done to offset a learning effect which statistical studies by the Educational Testing Service indicate occurs as the result of the multiple taking of the test.

Plaintiff's PFYA, as determined by the law school, was 76.23. This figure was calculated by using a formula com-

---

[1]The Law School Admissions Test yields two scores for each candidate, a general law aptitude score and a writing ability score.

bining plaintiff's junior-senior grade point average of 3.71, average LSAT score of 582 (512 plus 566 plus 668, divided by 3)[2] and average writing test score component of 61 (62 plus 58 plus 64, divided by 3).

Ranking of applicants by PFYA was used to help organize the committee's processing of the applications. On the basis of the previous year's applicant group, the committee decided that most promising applicants for the class of 1974 would be defined as applicants with predicted first-year law school averages over 77. Applicants with PFYAs above 77 were reviewed and decided by the full committee as they came in, in order to reach an early decision as to the acceptance of such students. Each of these files was assigned to a committee member for thorough review and for presentation to the committee.

Applicants with PFYAs below 74.5 were reviewed by the chairman of the committee, and were either rejected by him, or placed in a group for later review by the full committee. The decision of rejection or committee review of an application was based on the chairman's judgment derived from information in the applicant's file indicating whether the applicant had a significantly better potential for law study than the relatively low predicted first-year average tended to indicate. Cases of doubt were to be resolved in favor of deferring judgment until committee review could be undertaken.

Two exceptions were made in regard to applicants with PFYAs below 74.5. First, the law school had established a policy that persons who had been previously admitted but who were unable to enter, or forced to withdraw from, the law school because of induction into the military service, had a right to reenroll if they reapplied immediately upon honorable completion of their tour of duty. Second, all files of "minority" applicants (which the committee defined for this purpose as including Black Americans, Chicano Ameri-

---

[2]Plaintiff took the Law School Admissions Test on three different occasions: August 1969, November 1969 and December 1970.

cans, American Indians and Philippine Americans[3]) were considered by the full committee as warranting their attention, regardless of the PFYA of the individual applicant.

Applicants with predicted first-year averages between 74.5 and 76.99 were accumulated and held until the applications deadline had passed and essentially all the applications were complete and ready for review, so that the critical decisions as to the remainder of the incoming class could be made with a relatively complete view of qualified applicants not therebefore admitted. Plaintiff's application, presenting a 76.23 predicted first-year average, was placed in this third category. Included for consideration at that time, in addition to the minority group and those with PFYAs between 74.5 and 77, were some applicants with PFYAs above 77 upon whom the committee had reserved judgment, feeling that such applicants were not as promising as their PFYAs seemed to indicate.

These "close cases,"—*i.e.*, where the applicant was neither clearly outstanding nor clearly deficient—required the most effort of the committee. In selecting the applicants from this narrow range, the committee used the process described in its Guide for Applicants, a copy of which was sent to all applicants:

> We gauged the potential for outstanding performance in law school not only from the existence of high test scores and grade point averages, but also from careful analysis of recommendations, the quality of work in difficult analytical seminars, courses, and writing programs, the academic standards of the school attended by the applicant, the applicant's graduate work (if any), and the nature of the applicant's employment (if any), since graduation.
>
> An applicant's ability to make significant contributions

[3]The chairman of the admissions committee testified that Asian-Americans, *e.g.*, were not treated as "minority" applicants for admissions purposes, since a significant number could be admitted on the same basis as general applicants.

As used herein, the term "minority" refers to and includes only Black Americans, Chicano Americans, American Indians and Philippine Americans.

to law school classes and the community at large was assessed from such factors as his extracurricular and community activities, employment, and general background.

We gave no preference to, but did not discriminate against, either Washington residents or women in making our determinations. An applicant's racial or ethnic background was considered as one factor in our general attempt to convert formal credentials into realistic predictions.

Each file to be reviewed by the full committee was first assigned and read by a committee member who reported on its contents to the committee. There followed a discussion on the applicants under consideration, leading to a committee vote on the disposition of the application. Assignment of files to the committee member for initial reading was usually on a random basis. The files of Black applicants, however, were assigned to and separately read by both Professor Geoffrey Crooks and Mr. Vincent Hayes, the two committee members thought best equipped to report to the full committee on the contents of the file. Professor Crooks worked with minority applications during the summer of 1970 as director of the school's Council on Legal Education Opportunities (CLEO) program[4] and Mr. Hayes, a second-year Black law student, who previously served as director of the Governor's Multi-Service Center in Seattle, a job involving considerable personnel evaluation. Applications of Chicanos, American Indians and Filipinos were reviewed by Associate Dean Robert S. Hunt for presentation to the committee.

In considering minority applicants, the committee was guided by a university-wide policy which sought to eliminate the continued effects of past segregation and discrimination against Blacks, Chicanos, American Indians and

---

[4]A federally (OEO) funded program, sponsored by the American Bar Association, the American Association of Law Schools, the National Bar Association and the Law School Admission Council, which provides summer training programs and financial assistance to disadvantaged college students seeking admission to law school.

other disadvantaged racial and ethnic minority groups. At trial, the President of the University of Washington testified as to the origin of this policy:

> More and more it became evident to us that just an open door, as it were, at the point of entry to the University, somehow or other seemed insufficient to deal with what was emerging as the greatest internal problem of the United States of America, a problem which obviously could not be resolved without some kind of contribution being made not only by the schools, but obviously, also, by the colleges in the University and the University of Washington, in particular, given the racial distribution of this state.
>
> . . .
>
> So that was the beginning of a growing awareness that just an open-door sheer equality in view of the cultural circumstances that produced something other than equality, was not enough; that some more positive contribution had to be made to the resolution of this problem in American life, and something had to be done by the University of Washington.

Thus, the university sought to achieve a reasonable representation within the student body of persons from these groups which have been historically suppressed by encouraging their enrollment within the various programs offered at the university. Policies for admission of minorities throughout the university recognized that the conventional "mechanical" credentializing system does not always produce good indicators of the full potential of such culturally separated or deprived individuals, and that to rely solely on such formal credentials could well result in unfairly denying to qualified minority persons the chance to pursue the educational opportunities available at the university.

The law school sought to carry forward this university policy in its admission program, not only to obtain a reasonable representation from minorities within its classes, but to increase participation within the legal profession by persons from racial and ethnic groups which have been historically denied access to the profession and which, consequently, are grossly underrepresented within the legal system. In doing so, the admissions committee followed certain procedures which are the crux of plaintiff's claimed denial of equal protection of the laws.

First, in reviewing the files of minority applicants, the committee attached less weight to the PFYA in making a total judgmental evaluation as to the relative ability of the particular applicant to succeed in law school. Also, the chairman testified that although the same standard was applied to all applicants (*i.e.*, the relative probability of the individual succeeding in law school), minority applicants were directly compared to one another, but were not compared to applicants outside of the minority group. The committee sought to identify, within the minority category, those persons who had the highest probability of succeeding in law school. Thus, the law school included within its admitted group minority applicants whose PFYAs were lower than those of some other applicants, but whose entire record showed the committee that they were capable of successfully completing the law school program.[5]

As a result of this process, the committee admitted a group of minority applicants, placed a group of such applicants on a waiting list, and rejected other minority applications. The dean of the law school testified that the law school has no fixed admissions quota for minority students, but that the committee sought a reasonable representation of such groups in the law school. He added that the law school has accepted no unqualified minority applicants, but only those whose records indicated that they were capable of successfully completing the law school program.

The admissions committee sent letters of acceptance to over 200 applicants. Normal attrition among those invited was expected to reduce this group to produce a class of about 150. Against the possibility of unusually high attrition among the group of accepted applicants, the committee placed approximately 155 additional applicants on a wait-

---

[5]For example, many of the minority group applicants were first screened through special compensatory summer programs, operated primarily by CLEO.

ing list. The waiting list was ranked in approximate quartiles, with 46 applicants in the highest quartile, 38 applicants in the second quartile, 36 applicants in the third quartile, and 33 applicants in the fourth or lowest quartile. The remaining applicants—those receiving neither offers of acceptance nor waiting list assignments—received letters of denial. Plaintiff received an invitation to be placed on the waiting list and he was ranked in the fourth or lowest quartile. On July 21, 1971, the rate of attrition from the admitted applicants appearing to be within normal ranges, the committee decided to send letters of denial to those applicants in the third and fourth quartiles on the waiting list. Plaintiff was thus notified on August 2, 1971, that he was neither admitted nor any longer on the waiting list. As of August 1, 1971, 275 students were admitted to the freshman law school class and 55 students remained on the waiting list, making a total of 330 students.

Out of the 275 students given notice of admission, 127 were nonresidents of the state of Washington. Out of the 55 on the waiting list, 23 were nonresidents of the state of Washington. Thus, of the 330 applicants admitted or waiting, 180 were residents of the state of Washington. Ultimately, 32 nonresidents (21.6 percent of the entering class) actually enrolled in the first-year class.

Because of the judgmental factors in the admissions process, as outlined, the ultimate determination of applicants to whom admission was offered did not follow exactly the relative ranking of PFYAs. Of those invited, 74 had lower PFYAs than plaintiff; 36 of these were minority applicants, 22 were returning from military service, and 16 were applicants judged by the committee as deserving invitations on the basis of other information contained in their files. Twenty-nine applicants with higher PFYAs than plaintiff's were denied admission. Of the 36 minority group students invited 18 actually enrolled in the first-year class.

The trial court found that some minority applicants with college grades and LSAT scores so low that had they been of the white race their applications would have been summarily denied, were given invitations for admission; that some such students were admitted instead of plaintiff; that since no more than 150 applicants were to be admitted to the law school, the admission of less qualified students resulted in a denial of places to those better qualified; and that plaintiff had better "qualifications" than many of the students admitted by the committee. The trial court also found that plaintiff was and is fully qualified and capable of satisfactorily attending the law school.

The trial court concluded that there is no constitutional restriction upon admitting nonresidential students; and no laws or regulations provide preference to residential students over nonresidential students for admission to the University of Washington School of Law; that, in denying plaintiff admission to the law school, the University of Washington discriminated against him and did not accord to him equal protection of the laws as guaranteed by the fourteenth amendment to the United States Constitution; and therefore, that plaintiff should be admitted to the law school for the class of 1974, beginning September 22, 1971.[6]

I.

We first consider defendants' threshold contention that the record establishes the law school would not have been able to accept him even if no minority students had been admitted; and, therefore, plaintiff has no standing to question the university's minorities admissions policy. Defendants argue that the committee's evaluation of plaintiff's qualifications led it to place him in the fourth, or lowest, quartile of the waiting list. This low ranking was wholly without regard to the school's minority admissions policy, but was based on a comparison of plaintiff's qualifications with those of other nonminority applicants. Thus, contend

---

[6]At time of oral argument in this court it was stated that plaintiff had actually been admitted to the law school in September, 1971, and was still in attendance. Due to the conditions under which plaintiff was admitted and the great public interest in the continuing issues raised by this appeal, we do not consider the case to be moot.

defendants, even if the minority group students had not been admitted, all of the seats they occupied would probably have been filled by others higher than plaintiff on the waiting list.

There is no way of knowing that plaintiff would have been admitted to the law school, even had no minority student been admitted. We do not agree, however, that for this reason plaintiff lacks standing to assert the constitutional questions presented herein. As noted by the United States Supreme Court in *Flast v. Cohen,* 392 U.S. 83, 99, 20 L. Ed. 2d 947, 88 S. Ct. 1942 (1968):

> The "gist of the question of standing" is whether the party seeking relief has "alleged such a personal stake in the outcome of the controversy as to assure that concrete adverseness which sharpens the presentation of issues upon which the court so largely depends for illumination of difficult constitutional questions." *Baker v. Carr,* 369 U.S. 186, 204 (1962).

We have heretofore made similar statements. In *State ex rel. Hays v. Wilson,* 17 Wn.2d 670, 137 P.2d 105 (1943), we stated that one seeking relief must show a clear legal or equitable right and a well-grounded fear of immediate invasion of that right. Further, in *State v. Human Relations Research Foundation,* 64 Wn.2d 262, 269, 391 P.2d 513 (1964), we stated:

> A litigant who challenges the constitutionality of a statute must claim infringement of an interest peculiar and personal to himself, as distinguished from a cause of dissatisfaction with the general framework of the statute.

Plaintiff's interest in this litigation clearly constitutes the requisite "personal stake in the outcome of the controversy" necessary to request an adjudication of the merits of this case.[7]

II.

The essence of plaintiff's Fourteenth Amendment argument is that the law school violated his right to equal

---

[7]In reaching this conclusion we have also taken into consideration the university's urgent need for certainty in planning and administering its admissions policy.

protection of the laws by denying him admission, yet accepting certain minority applicants with lower PFYAs than plaintiff who, but for their minority status, would not have been admitted.[8]

To answer this contention we consider three implicit, subordinate questions: (A) whether race can ever be considered as one factor in the admissions policy of a state law school or whether racial classifications are *per se* unconstitutional because the equal protection of the laws requires that law school admissions be "color-blind"; (B) if consideration of race is not *per se* unconstitutional, what is the appropriate standard of review to be applied in determining the constitutionality of such a classification; and (C) when the appropriate standard is applied does the specific minority admissions policy employed by the law school pass constitutional muster?[9]

A.

Relying solely on *Brown v. Board of Educ.*, 347 U.S. 483, 98 L. Ed. 873, 74 S. Ct. 686, 38 A.L.R.2d 1180 (1954), the trial court held that a state law school can never consider

---

[8]Our review is specifically limited to a consideration of the alleged constitutional infirmities in the law school's admissions policy and procedures. Beyond question, it would be inappropriate for this court to determine the actual composition of the first year class through an independent evaluation of each applicant's file, substituting our criteria and judgment for those of the admissions committee. In regard to the scope of judicial review in this area, the United States Supreme Court has stated that:

In seeking to define even in broad and general terms how far this remedial power extends it is important to remember that judicial powers may be exercised only on the basis of a constitutional violation. Remedial judicial authority does not put judges automatically in the shoes of school authorities whose powers are plenary. Judicial authority enters only when local authority defaults.

Swann v. Charlotte-Mecklenburg Bd. of Educ., 402 U.S. 1, 16, 28 L. Ed. 2d 554, 91 S. Ct. 1267 (1971).

[9]Considering the statutory delegation of power to establish entrance requirements for students to the university, no serious question is raised as to whether the action of the law school here complained of constitutes "state action" within the meaning of the Fourteenth Amendment.

race as one criterion in its selection of first-year students. In holding that all such racial classifications are *per se* unconstitutional, the trial court stated in its oral opinion:

> Since no more than 150 applicants were to be admitted the admission of less qualified resulted in a denial of places to those otherwise qualified. The plaintiff and others in this group have not, in my opinion, been accorded equal protection of the laws guaranteed by the Fourteenth Amendment.
>
> In 1954 the United States Supreme Court decided that public education must be equally available to all regardless of race.
>
> After that decision the Fourteenth Amendment could no longer be stretched to accommodate the needs of any race. Policies of discrimation will inevitably lead to reprisals. In my opinion the only safe rule is to treat all races alike, and I feel that is what is required under the equal protection clause.

In *Brown v. Board of Educ., supra,* the Supreme Court addressed a question of primary importance at page 493:

> Does segregation of children in public schools solely on the basis of race, even though the physical facilities and other "tangible" factors may be equal, deprive the children of the minority group of equal educational opportunities? We believe that it does.

The court in *Brown* held the equal protection clause of the Fourteenth Amendment prohibits state law from requiring the operation of racially segregated, dual school systems of public education and requires that the system be converted into a unitary, nonracially segregated system. In so holding, the court noted that segregation inevitably stigmatizes Black children:

> To separate them from others of similar age and qualifications solely because of their race generates a feeling of inferiority as to their status in the community that may affect their hearts and minds in a way unlikely ever to be undone.

Brown v. Board of Educ., supra at 494. Moreover, "The impact is greater when it has the sanction of the law; for the policy of separating the races is usually interpreted as denoting the inferiority of the negro group." *Brown* at 494.

Brown did not hold that all racial classifications are *per se* unconstitutional; rather, it held that invidious racial classifications—*i.e.,* those that stigmatize a racial group with the stamp of inferiority—are unconstitutional. Even viewed in a light most favorable to plaintiff, the "preferential" minority admissions policy administered by the law school is clearly not a form of invidious discrimination. The goal of this policy is not to separate the races, but to bring them together. And, as has been observed,

> Preferential admissions do not represent a covert attempt to stigmatize the majority race as inferior; nor is it reasonable to expect that a possible effect of the extension of educational preferences to certain disadvantaged racial minorities will be to stigmatize whites.

O'Neil, *Preferential Admissions: Equalizing the Access of Minority Groups to Higher Education,* 80 Yale L.J. 699, 713 (1971).

While *Brown v. Board of Educ., supra,* certainly provides a starting point for our analysis of the instant case, we do not agree with the trial court that *Brown* is dispositive here. Subsequent decisions of the United States Supreme Court have made it clear that in some circumstances a racial criterion *may* be used—and indeed in some circumstances *must* be used—by public educational institutions in bringing about racial balance. School systems which were formerly segregated de jure[10] now have an affirmative duty to remedy racial imbalance.

In *Green v. County School Bd.,* 391 U.S. 430, 20 L. Ed. 2d 716, 88 S. Ct. 1689 (1968), the Supreme Court considered a

---

[10]"De jure" segregation generally refers to "segregation directly intended or mandated by law or otherwise issuing from an official racial classification," *Hobson v. Hansen,* 269 F. Supp. 401, 492 (D.D.C. 1967), *aff'd sub. nom. Smuck v. Hobson,* 408 F.2d 175 (D.C. Cir. 1969), or, in other words, to segregation which has, or had, the sanction of law. In the context of public education the United States Supreme Court has expanded the meaning of the term "de jure segregation"

> [T]o comprehend any situation in which the activities of school authorities have had a racially discriminatory impact contributing to

school board's adoption of a "freedom-of-choice" plan
which allowed a student to choose his own public school.
No student was assigned or admitted to school on the basis
of race. In holding that, on the facts presented, the plan did
not satisfy the board's duty to create a unitary, nonracial
system, the court stated at pages 437-40:

> In the context of the state-imposed segregated pattern of
> long standing, the fact that in 1965 the Board opened the
> doors of the former "white" school to Negro children and
> of the "Negro" school to white children merely begins,
> not ends, our inquiry whether the Board has taken steps
> adequate to abolish its dual, segregated system.
>
>   . . . The burden on a school board today is to come
> forward with a plan that promises realistically to work,
> and promises realistically to work *now.*
>
>   . . .

As Judge Sobeloff has put it,

> " 'Freedom of choice' is not a sacred talisman; it is only
> a means to a constitutionally required end—the abolition
> of the system of segregation and its effects. If the means
> prove effective, it is acceptable, but if it fails to undo
> segregation, other means must be used to achieve this
> end. The school officials have the continuing duty to take
> whatever action may be necessary to create a 'unitary,
> nonracial system.' " *Bowman v. County School Board,*
> 382 F.2d 326, 333 (C. A. 4th Cir. 1967) (concurring opin-
> ion).

Pursuing this principle further, the Supreme Court in
Swann v. Charlotte-Mecklenburg Bd. of Educ., 402 U.S. 1,
16, 28 L. Ed. 2d 554, 91 S. Ct. 1267 (1971), unanimously
held that school authorities, in seeking to achieve a unitary,
nonracial system of public education, need not be "color-

---

the establishment or continuation [of racial imbalance] . . .
State ex rel. Citizens Against Mandatory Bussing v. Brooks, 80 Wn.2d
121, 130, 492 P.2d 536 (1972).

Where the segregation is inadvertent and without the assistance or
collusion of school authorities, and is not caused by any "state action",
but rather by social, economic and other determinants, it will be
referred to as "de facto" herein. *See* Fiss, *Racial Imbalance in the
Public Schools: the Constitutional Concepts,* 78 Harv. L. Rev. 564,
565-66, 584, 598 (1965).

blind", but may consider race as a valid criterion when considering admissions and producing a student body:

> School authorities are traditionally charged with broad power to formulate and implement educational policy and might well conclude, for example, that in order to prepare students to live in a pluralistic society each school should have a prescribed ratio of Negro to white students reflecting the proportion for the district as a whole. To do this as an educational policy is within the broad discretionary powers of school authorities; absent a finding of a constitutional violation, however, that would not be within the authority of a federal court.

The Supreme Court then approved the district court's opinion requiring the school authorities to consider race in determining the composition of individual schools:

> As we said in *Green,* a school authority's remedial plan or a district court's remedial decree is to be judged by its effectiveness. Awareness of the racial composition of the whole school system is likely to be a useful starting point in shaping a remedy to correct past constitutional violations.

Swann v. Charlotte-Mecklenburg Bd. of Educ., supra at 25.

Thus, the constitution is color conscious to prevent the perpetuation of discrimination and to undo the effects of past segregation. In holding invalid North Carolina's anti-bussing law, which flatly forbade assignment of any student on account of race or for the purpose of creating a racial balance or ratio in the schools and which prohibited bussing for such purposes, the court stated:

> [T]he statute exploits an apparently neutral form to control school assignment plans by directing that they be "color blind"; that requirement, against the background of segregation, would render illusory the promise of *Brown v. Board of Education,* 347 U.S. 483 (1954). Just as the race of students must be considered in determining whether a constitutional violation has occurred, so also must race be considered in formulating a remedy.

North Carolina Bd. of Educ. v. Swann, 402 U.S. 43, 45, 28 L. Ed. 2d 586, 91 S. Ct. 1284 (1971). *Accord, United States v. Jefferson County Bd. of Educ.,* 372 F.2d 836 (5th Cir. 1966), *aff'd en banc,* 380 F.2d 385 (5th Cir. 1967), *cert. denied sub nom., Bd. of Educ. v. United States,* 389 U.S. 840, 19 L. Ed. 2d 104, 88 S. Ct. 77 (1967).

Clearly, consideration of race by school authorities does not violate the Fourteenth Amendment where the purpose is to bring together, rather than separate, the races. The "minority" admissions policy of the law school, aimed at insuring a reasonable representation of minority persons in the student body, is not invidious. Consideration of race is permissible to carry out the mandate of *Brown,* and, as noted, has been required in some circumstances.

However, plaintiff contends that cases such as *Green v. County School Bd., supra,* and *Swann v. Charlotte-Mecklenburg Bd. of Educ., supra,* are inapposite here since none of the students there involved were deprived of an education by the plan to achieve a unitary school system. It is questionable whether defendants deprived plaintiff of a legal education by denying him admission.[11] But even accepting this contention, arguendo, the denial of a "benefit" on the basis of race is not necessarily a *per se* violation of the Fourteenth Amendment, if the racial classification is used in a compensatory way to promote integration.

For example, in *Porcelli v. Titus,* 431 F.2d 1254 (3d Cir. 1970), *cert. denied,* 402 U.S. 944, 29 L. Ed. 2d 112, 91 S. Ct. 1612 (1971), a group of white teachers alleged that the school board had bypassed them in abolishing the regular promotion schedule and procedure for selecting principals and vice-principals, and had given priority to Black candidates in order to increase the integration of the system's faculty. In upholding the board's judgment to suspend the ordinary promotion system upon racial considerations, the court stated:

State action based partly on considerations of color, when

---

[11]Plaintiff alleged in his complaint that he had previously applied to and been accepted by the law school at each of the following universities: University of Oregon, University of Idaho, Gonzaga University and Willamette University.

color is not used per se, and in furtherance of a proper governmental objective, is not necessarily a violation of the Fourteenth Amendment.

Porcelli v. Titus, supra at 1257.

Similarly, the eighth circuit concluded that in order to eradicate the effects of past discrimination,

[I]t would be in order for the district court to mandate that one out of every three persons hired by the [Minneapolis] Fire Department would be a minority individual who qualifies until at least 20 minority persons have been so hired.

Carter v. Gallagher, 452 F.2d 315, 331 (8th Cir. 1971); *cert. denied,* 406 U.S. 950 (1972). Thus, the court ordered the department to hire minority applicants, although in doing so a more qualified nonminority applicant might be bypassed. *Cf. Contractors Ass'n v. Secretary of Labor,* 442 F.2d 159 (3d Cir. 1971), *cert. denied,* 404 U.S. 854 (1971).

We conclude that the consideration of race as a factor in the admissions policy of a state law school is not a *per se* violation of the equal protection clause of the Fourteenth Amendment. We proceed, therefore, to the question of what standard of review is appropriate to determine the constitutionality of such a classification.

B.

Generally, when reviewing a state-created classification alleged to be in violation of the equal protection clause of the Fourteenth Amendment, the question is whether the classification is reasonably related to a legitimate public purpose. And, in applying this "rational basis" test "[A] discrimination will not be set aside if any state of facts reasonably may be conceived to justify it." *McGowan v. Maryland,* 366 U.S. 420, 426, 6 L. Ed. 2d 393, 81 S. Ct. 1101 (1961).

However, where the classification is based upon race, a heavier burden of justification is imposed upon the state. In overturning Virginia's antimiscegenation law, the Supreme Court explained this stricter standard of review:

The clear and central purpose of the Fourteenth Amendment was to eliminate all official state sources of invidious racial discrimination in the States. [Citations omitted.]

. . . At the very least, the Equal Protection Clause demands that racial classifications, especially suspect in criminal statutes, be subjected to the "most rigid scrutiny," [citation omitted] and, if they are ever to be upheld, they must be shown to be necessary to the accomplishment of some permissible state objective, independent of the racial discrimination which it was the object of the Fourteenth Amendment to eliminate. . . .

There is patently no legitimate overriding purpose independent of invidious racial discrimination which justifies this classification.

Loving v. Virginia, 388 U.S. 1, 10-11, 18 L. Ed. 2d 1010, 87 S. Ct. 1817 (1967). *Accord, McLaughlin v. Florida*, 379 U.S. 184, 13 L. Ed. 2d 222, 85 S. Ct. 283 (1964); *Hunter v. Erickson*, 393 U.S. 385, 21 L. Ed. 2d 616, 89 S. Ct. 557 (1969).

It has been suggested that the less strict "rational basis" test should be applied to the consideration of race here, since the racial distinction is being used to redress the effects of past discrimination; thus, because the persons normally stigmatized by racial classifications are being benefited, the action complained of should be considered "benign" and reviewed under the more permissive standard. However, the minority admissions policy is certainly not benign with respect to nonminority students who are displaced by it. *See* O'Neil, *Preferential Admissions: Equalizing the Access of Minority Groups to Higher Education*, 80 Yale L.J. 699, 710 (1971).

The burden is upon the law school to show that its consideration of race in admitting students is necessary to the accomplishment of a compelling state interest.

C.

It can hardly be gainsaid that the minorities have been, and are, grossly underrepresented in the law schools —and consequently in the legal profession—of this state and this nation.[12] We believe the state has an overriding interest in promoting integration in public education. In light of the serious underrepresentation of minority groups in the law schools, and considering that minority groups participate on an equal basis in the tax support of the law school, we find the state interest in eliminating racial imbalance within public legal education to be compelling.

Plaintiff contends, however, that any discrimination in this case has been de facto, rather than de jure. Thus, reasons plaintiff, since the law school itself has not actively discriminated against minority applicants, it may not attempt to remedy racial imbalance in the law school student body, and, consequently, throughout the legal profession. We disagree.

In *State ex rel. Citizens Against Mandatory Bussing v. Brooks*, 80 Wn.2d 121, 128, 492 P.2d 536 (1972), we held that whether the nature of segregation is de jure or de facto is of no consequence where a voluntary plan of eliminating racial imbalance is adopted by school officials:

Reason impels the conclusion that, if the constitution supports court directed mandatory bussing to desegre-

[12]Report of Black Lawyers and Judges in the United States, 1960-70, 91st Cong., 2d Sess., 116 Cong. Rec. 30786 (1970); U.S. Dept. of Commerce, Bureau of Census, General Population Characteristics of the State of Washington, Tables 17 and 18 (1970); Office of Program Planning and Fiscal Management of the State of Washington, Pocket Data Book (1971); Rosen, *Equalizing Access to Legal Education: Special Programs for Law Students Who Are Not Admissible by Traditional Criteria*, 1970 U. Tol. L. Rev. 321 (1970); Edwards, *A New Role for the Black Law Graduates—A Reality or an Illusion?* 69 Mich. L. Rev. 1407 (1971); Gelhorn, *The Law Schools and the Negro*, 1968 Duke L.J. 1069 (1968); Reynoso, *Laraza, the Law and the Law Schools*, 1970 U. Tol. L. Rev. 809 (1970); Toles, *Black Population and Black Judges*, 17 Student Lawyer J. 20 (Feb. 1972); O'Neil, *Preferential Admissions: Equalizing Access to Legal Education*, 1970 U. Tol. L. Rev. 281 (1970); Atwood, *Survey of Black Law Student Enrollment*, 16 Student Lawyer J. 18 (June 1971); Comment, *Selected Bibliography: Minority Group Participation in the Legal Profession*, 1970 U. Tol. L. Rev. 935 (1970).

In relying on statistical evidence to establish the underrepresentation of minority groups in the legal profession, defendants are supported by ample precedent. *See, e.g., Hobson v. Hansen, supra* note 10.

gate schools in a system which is dual "de jure," then such bussing is within the appropriate exercise of the discretion of school authorities in a system which is dual "de facto."

This conclusion is supported by the reasoning of the district court in *Barksdale v. Springfield School Comm.*, 237 F. Supp. 543, 546 (D. Mass. 1965), *vacated on other grounds*, 348 F.2d 261 (1st Cir. 1965):

It is neither just nor sensible to proscribe segregation having its basis in affirmative state action while at the same time failing to provide a remedy for segregation which grows out of discrimination in housing, or other economic or social factors.

Significantly, this case does not present for review a court order imposing a program of desegregation. Rather, the minority admissions policy is a voluntary plan initiated by school authorities. Therefore, the question before us is not whether the Fourteenth Amendment *requires* the law school to take affirmative action to eliminate the continuing effects of de facto segregation; the question is whether the constitution *permits* the law school to remedy racial imbalance through its minority admissions policy. In refusing to enjoin school officials from implementing a plan to eradicate de facto school segregation by the use of explicit racial classifications, the second circuit observed: "That there may be no constitutional duty to act to undo de facto segregation, however, does not mean that such action is unconstitutional." *Offermann v. Nitkowski*, 378 F.2d 22, 24 (2d Cir. 1967).

The de jure-de facto distinction is not controlling in determining the constitutionality of the minority admissions policy voluntarily adopted by the law school.[13] Further, we see no reason why the state interest in eradicating the continuing effects of past racial discrimination is less

---

[13]We do not, therefore, reach the question of whether there is an inherent cultural bias in the Law School Admission Test, or in the methods of teaching and testing employed by the law school, which perpetuates racial imbalance to such an extent as to constitute de jure segregation.

merely because the law school itself may have previously been neutral in the matter.

The state also has an overriding interest in providing *all* law students with a legal education that will adequately prepare them to deal with the societal problems which will confront them upon graduation. As the Supreme Court has observed, this cannot be done through books alone:

> [A]lthough the law is a highly learned profession, we are well aware that it is an intensely practical one. The law school, the proving ground for legal learning and practice, cannot be effective in isolation from the individuals and institutions with which the law interacts. Few students and no one who has practiced law would choose to study in an academic vacuum, removed from the interplay of ideas and the exchange of views with which the law is concerned.

Sweatt v. Painter, 339 U.S. 629, 634, 94 L. Ed. 1114, 70 S. Ct. 848 (1950).

The legal profession plays a critical role in the policy making sector of our society, whether decisions be public or private, state or local. That lawyers, in making and influencing these decisions, should be cognizant of the views, needs and demands of all segments of society is a principle beyond dispute. The educational interest of the state in producing a racially balanced student body at the law school is compelling.

Finally, the shortage of minority attorneys—and, consequently, minority prosecutors, judges and public officials —constitutes an undeniably compelling state interest.[14] If minorities are to live within the rule of law, they must enjoy equal representation within our legal system.

Once a constitutionally valid state interest has been established, it remains for the state to show the requisite connection between the racial classification employed and that interest. The consideration of race in the law school admissions policy meets the test of necessity

---

[14]*See* O'Neil, *Preferential Admissions: Equalizing Access to Legal Education, supra* note 12.

here because racial imbalance in the law school and the legal profession is the evil to be corrected, and it can only be corrected by providing legal education to those minority groups which have been previously deprived.

It has been suggested that the minority admissions policy is not necessary, since the same objective could be accomplished by improving the elementary and secondary education of minority students to a point where they could secure equal representation in law schools through direct competition with nonminority applicants on the basis of the same academic criteria. This would be highly desirable, but 18 years have passed since the decision in *Brown v. Board of Educ.*, 347 U.S. 483, 98 L. Ed. 873, 74 S. Ct. 686, 38 A.L.R.2d 1180, and minority groups are still grossly underrepresented in law schools. If the law school is forbidden from taking affirmative action, this underrepresentation may be perpetuated indefinitely. No less restrictive means would serve the governmental interest here; we believe the minority admissions policy of the law school to be the only feasible "plan that promises realistically to work, and promises realistically to work *now*." *Green v. County School Bd.*, 391 U.S. 430, 20 L. Ed. 2d 716, 88 S. Ct. 1689 (1968) at 439.

We conclude that defendants have shown the necessity of the racial classification herein to the accomplishment of an overriding state interest, and have thus sustained the heavy burden imposed upon them under the equal protection provision of the Fourteenth Amendment.

There remains a further question as to the scope of the classification. A validly drawn classification is one "which includes all [and only those] persons who are similarly situated with respect to the purpose of the law." Tussman & tenBroek, *The Equal Protection of the Laws*, 37 Calif. L. Rev. 341, 346 (1949). The classification used by defendants does not include all racial minorities, but only four (Blacks, Chicanos, Indians and Philippine Americans). However, the purpose of the racial classification here is to give special consideration to those racial minority groups which are underrepresented in the law schools and legal profession, and which cannot secure proportionate representation if strictly subjected to the standardized mathematical criteria for admission to the law school.

In selecting minority groups for special consideration, the law school sought to identify those groups most in need of help. The chairman of the admissions committee testified that Asian Americans, *e.g.*, were not treated as minority applicants for admissions purposes since a significant number could be admitted on the same basis as general applicants. In light of the purpose of the minority admissions policy, the racial classification need not include all racial minority groups.[15] The state may identify and correct the most serious examples of racial imbalance, even though in so doing it does not provide an immediate solution to the entire problem of equal representation within the legal system.

We hold that the minority admissions policy of the law school, and the denial by the law school of admission to plaintiff, violate neither the equal protection clause of the fourteenth amendment to the United States Constitution nor article 1, section 12 of the Washington State Constitution.[16]

III.

Apart from his equal protection argument, plaintiff contends that the procedures employed by the law school in selecting first-year students constitute arbitrary and capricious administrative action, and that the law school's denial of admission to plaintiff pursuant to these procedures must be set aside.

We recently reaffirmed our long standing test of arbitrary and capricious action:

---

[15]*See* O'Neil, *Preferential Admissions: Equalizing the Access of Minority Groups to Higher Education,* 80 Yale L.J. 699, 750 (1971).

[16]As we have held, the equal protection clause of U.S. Const. amend. 14, and the privileges and immunities clause of Const. art. 1, § 12, have the same import, and we apply them as one. *Markham Adv. Co. v. State,* 73 Wn.2d 405, 427, 439 P.2d 248 (1968), *appeal dismissed,* 393 U.S. 316 (1969).

Arbitrary and capricious action of administrative bodies means willful and unreasoning action, without consideration and in disregard of facts or circumstances. Where there is room for two opinions, action is not arbitrary or capricious when exercised honestly and upon due consideration, even though it may be believed that an erroneous conclusion has been reached.

DuPont-Fort Lewis School Dist. 7 v. Bruno, 79 Wn.2d 736, 739, 489 P.2d 171 (1971). Plaintiff must carry the burden of proof on this issue. *State ex rel. Longview Fire Fighters, Local 828 v. Longview*, 65 Wn.2d 568, 572, 399 P.2d 1 (1965).

In determining whether the denial of plaintiff's application to the law school constitutes arbitrary and capricious action, we turn first to the ultimate admissions goals of the law school, pursuant to which the policy and procedures of the admissions committee have been formulated. In light of the tremendous increase in the number of qualified applicants, the law school sought to identify applicants with the potential for outstanding performance in the law school, and then "to select applicants for admission from that group on the basis of their ability to make significant contributions to law school classes and to the community at large." The guide for applicants also stated that the criteria to be applied by the law school in the selection process would not be limited to numerical indicators such as test scores and grade point averages, but would also include several other factors requiring the exercise of judgmental evaluation. Among these other factors were recommendations, the quality of work in difficult analytical seminars and writing programs, the academic standards of the applicant's undergraduate school, and the nature of the applicant's graduate work or employment (if any) since graduation. The guide added that race would be considered as one factor in the law school's attempt to convert formal credentials into realistic predictions.

Plaintiff first contends that no standards were applied by the committee in its evaluation of these criteria for admission. However, the trial court specifically refused to make a finding of fact proposed by plaintiff that:

> [T]he Admissions Committee selected and denied students for admission to the University of Washington School of Law with no set standards or procedures.

We particularly note that while race was a major factor, it was not the only factor considered by the committee in reviewing minority applications. No minority quota was established; rather, a reasonable representation of such groups in the law school was sought. Also, the dean of the law school testified (and the trial court did not find otherwise) that only "qualified" minority applicants were admitted—*i.e.*, minority persons whose entire record showed the committee that they were capable of successfully completing the law school program. Many minority applicants were denied admission. The trial court did find that some minority students admitted would have been summarily denied had they been white, since their predicted first-year averages were relatively low. Also, the court found that some minority students were admitted with "lower qualifications" than plaintiff. Thus, the record overwhelmingly indicates that the admissions committee did employ predetermined standards and procedures in selecting students.

Plaintiff further contends that the committee failed to consider all applicants on the same basis, but instead judged minority applicants by different standards. In reviewing the files of applicants, the committee did ask the same fundamental question in every case: what is the relative probability of the individual succeeding in law school and making significant contributions to law school classes and the community at large? However, minority applicants were directly compared to one another under this test, but were not compared to nonminority applicants.

The question thus raised is whether, in selecting those applicants most likely to make significant contributions to law school classes and to the community at large, it is arbitrary and capricious for the admissions committee to consider race as a factor in admitting qualified minority applicants whose strict academic credentials yield a lower PFYA than that of some nonminority applicants who are not admitted. The answer depends on whether race is relevant to the goals of the law school's admissions program as stated in the guide for applicants.

The thrust of plaintiff's objection here is that the action of the committee was arbitrary because, in admitting students, it deviated from the relative numerical ranking provided by the PFYAs. Thus, argues plaintiff, by taking subjective (*i.e.*, nonmathematical) factors into consideration, and weighting them differently for different applicants, the committee arbitrarily denied him admission. We do not agree that the exercise of judgment in evaluating an applicant's file constitutes arbitrary and capricious action. Nor do we find an abuse of that judgment here.

The president of the university testified that the decision to consider race in interpreting a minority applicant's numerical grade averages and test scores was reached because of the opinion within the university that such standardized indicators inherently exclude a disproportionate number of minority applicants.

> [We] recognize the conventional standards that have been used with regard to most students are even less reliable in dealing with students who come from culturally deprived backgrounds. I do not think this means reducing the standards. It admits that the conventional standards are not good indicators and that something more is needed.
>
> . . .
>
> . . . by paying more attention to evidence obtained by the background of the individual and from all kinds of evidence that could be adduced . . . the judgment could be made as to whether or not this particular individual seemed to have greater potential than would be indicated if they were to rely entirely on the mechanical standards.

"Basic intelligence must have the means of articulation to manifest itself fairly in a testing process." *Griggs v.*

Duke Power Co., 401 U.S. 424, 430, 28 L. Ed. 2d 158, 91 S. Ct. 849 (1971). We express no opinion as to whether the LSAT bears a cultural bias which renders the test less reliable as a predictor of law school performance for minority students than for others. But this is certainly a factor which the law school may consider in its discretion. *See Hobson v. Hansen,* 269 F. Supp. 401, 484 (D.D.C. 1967); O'Neil, *Preferential Admissions: Equalizing Access to Legal Education,* 1970 U. Tol. L. Rev. 281, 303 (1970). It would be unnecessary, of course, for the law school to consider race in interpreting the standardized numerical indicators for nonminority students, because the alleged bias operates *in favor* of those applicants.

The fallacy of plaintiff's argument is the assumption that, but for the special consideration given minority applicants, selection decisions by the committee would have been based solely upon objective, measureable mathematical projections of the academic performance of applicants. Actually, although the PFYA was a very important factor, it was not the sole determinative factor for any group of students. Rather, the committee utilized the PFYA as a starting point in making its judgment as to the fundamental criterion for admission: the applicant's potential for contributing to law school classes and to the community. That the committee considered more than the standardized numerical indicators in reviewing the files of all students is indicated by the fact that 16 *nonminority,* general applicants were admitted with lower PFYAs than plaintiff.

Moreover, we question the assumption that a minority applicant is ipso facto "less qualified" than a nonminority applicant who has a higher predicted first-year average. When judging "qualifications," the primary criterion of the law school in admitting students must be remembered. In light of the gross underrepresentation of minorities in the legal system, can it be said with such certainty as to leave no room for differing opinions that a white applicant with a higher PFYA will make a greater contribution to the law school and the community? We think not. While the probability of applicant achieving high grades in his first year of law school is an important criterion for admission, it is not the sole permissible criterion.

Where the criteria for admissions are not arbitrary and capricious, we will not vitiate the judgment of the admissions committee unless a constitutional violation is shown. Considering the debatable nature of the criteria, we do not find the consideration of race in the admission of those minority applicants who indicate competence to successfully complete the law school program to be arbitrary and capricious. Law school admissions need not become a game of numbers; the process should remain sensitive and flexible, with room for informed judgment in interpreting mechanical indicators. The committee may consider the racial or ethnic background of an applicant when interpreting his standardized grades and test scores.

As a final point, plaintiff argues that the consideration of race here was arbitrary because no inquiry was made into the background of each minority applicant to make certain that the individual was in fact educationally, economically and culturally deprived. However, the mere fact that a minority applicant comes from a relatively more affluent home does not mean that he has not been subjected to psychological harm through discrimination. *See Hobson v. Hansen, supra* at 482. Likewise, every minority lawyer is critically needed, whether he be rich or poor. A showing of actual deprivation is unnecessary for the accomplishment of the compelling state interests here.[17]

Plaintiff has failed to show that the policy and procedures of the law school in denying him admission were so unreasoned and in disregard of the facts and circumstances as to constitute arbitrary and capricious action.

IV.

Plaintiff also contends that article 9, section 1 of the Washington State Constitution[18] and certain of the statutes

---

[17]*See generally* O'Neil, *Preferential Admissions: Equalizing the Access of Minority Groups to Higher Education, supra* at 751.

[18]Art. 9 "§ 1 PREAMBLE. It is the paramount duty of the state to

governing the University of Washington[19] require preference to be given Washington residents over nonresidents in
admission to the school of law, and that in failing to give
this preference to plaintiff, the law school wrongfully denied him admission. The trial court ruled against plaintiff's
contention on this issue. We agree with the trial court.

Article 9 does not apply to the University of
Washington, *Litchman v. Shannon*, 90 Wash. 186, 155 P. 783
(1916), but is addressed only to the "common schools."
(Article 9, section 2.) *See, e.g., Edmonds School Dist. 15 v.
Mountlake Terrace*, 77 Wn.2d 609, 611, 465 P.2d 177 (1970);
Newman v. Schlarb, 184 Wash. 147, 152-54, 50 P.2d 36
(1935); *State ex rel. School Dist. 37 v. Clark County*, 177
Wash. 314, 321, 31 P.2d 897 (1934); *Litchman v. Shannon,
supra* at 191. Thus, article 9 does not call for preferential
admission treatment of residents over nonresidents at the
law school.

Nor do the statutory provisions cited by plaintiff dic-
tate the contrary. Although these provisions differentiate residents from nonresidents for various purposes
(such as qualifying for state aid, RCW 28B.10.800) they
cannot be read for the sweeping purpose desired by plaintiff. The only preferential treatment clearly stated is in
RCW 28B.15.200, in which the legislature has prescribed a
higher fee for nonresidents than residents for enrollment at
the University of Washington. This fee undoubtedly affects
the ratio of nonresidents to residents actually enrolled
within the law school.[20] However, this fee provision is the
only statutory indication of preference; any further limita-

---

make ample provision for the education of all children residing within
its borders . . ."

[19]RCW 28B.20.020, 28B.15.011, *et seq.*, and 28B.10.800.

[20]Out of the 275 students admitted to the law school's first-year class
for the 1971-72 school year, 127 were nonresidents. However, only 32
nonresidents (21.6 percent of the entering class) actually enrolled. As
the trial court noted, this high attrition rate (74.8 percent) tends to
indicate that the substantially higher fees for nonresidents significantly
affect the percentage of nonresident students in the law school.

tions upon the admission of nonresidents to the law school are controlled by the Board of Regents, who shall "Establish entrance requirements for students seeking admission to the university." RCW 28B.20.130(3). We hold that the university is not required to give admission preference to residents of the state of Washington.

The judgment of the trial court is reversed.

The foregoing opinion was prepared by Justice Marshall A. Neill while a member of this court. It is adopted by the undersigned as the opinion of the court.

FINLEY, HAMILTON, STAFFORD, WRIGHT, and UTTER, JJ., and TUTTLE, J. Pro Tem.

WRIGHT, J. (concurring)—I have signed the majority opinion because I agree with the result. A law school admissions program should not and need not be based upon purely mathematical factors.

In many human activities and particularly in the activities of every branch and level of government there must be a careful balancing to insure on the one hand impartiality, honesty and integrity and on the other hand reasonable exercise of discretion and judgment.

In the case of law school admissions, the problem is highly complex for several reasons. We are here concerned with the academic year starting in the fall of 1971. For that year, it was possible to admit into the first-year class of the law school not more than 150 students. There were 1,601 applicants, most of whom were qualified and could have been admitted except for the need to limit the size of the class.

Of course, the easy way would be to devise a purely mathematical formula for admissions and then apply it inflexibly. That, however, might not produce the best results. It is a matter in which the administration of the university and of the law school should exercise some discretion. Certainly there is enough intelligence, experience and common sense within the admissions committee to properly exercise its discretion.

My primary reason for writing this brief concurring opinion is to point out the desirability of more complete published standards for admission. The publication of such standards would insure not only the complete fairness of the process, but also the appearance of fairness.

FINLEY and STAFFORD, JJ., concur with WRIGHT, J.

HALE, C.J. (dissenting)—Racial bigotry, prejudice and intolerance will never be ended by exalting the political rights of one group or class over those of another. The circle of inequality cannot be broken by shifting the inequities from one man to his neighbor. To aggrandize the first will, to the extent of the aggrandizement, diminish the latter. There is no remedy at law except to abolish all class distinctions heretofore existing in law. For that reason, the constitutions are, and ever ought to be, color blind. Now the court says it would hold the constitutions color conscious that they may stay color blind. I do not see how they can be both color blind and color conscious at the same time toward the same persons and on the same issues, so I dissent.

The court, as I see it, upholds palpably discriminatory law school admission practices of the state university mainly because they were initiated for the laudable purpose of enhancing the opportunities of members of what are described as "ethnic minorities." It thus suggests a new rule of constitutional interpretation to be applied here that, if the administrative intentions are adequately noble in purpose, Mr. DeFunis may be deprived of equal protection of the laws and certain special immunities and privileges may be granted to others which, on the same terms, are denied to him. One should keep in mind the wisdom of the old saying that the road to perdition is paved with good intentions.

The court holds that the university law school may give preferential treatment to persons who come from groups "which have been historically suppressed by encouraging their enrollment within the various programs offered at the

University." But what seems to me to be a flagrant departure from the constitutions, ignored by the court, is epitomized in the statement that the admission policy was adopted by the law school "to increase participation within the legal profession by persons from racial and ethnic groups which have been historically denied access to the profession and which, consequently, are grossly underrepresented within the legal system." This assertion confesses to prior racial discrimination which I doubt existed, and fails to recognize, in a case where the demand for seats in the law school is much greater than the school's capacity, that the increased minority participation assured by such admission procedures inevitably produces a correlative denial of access to nonminority applicants.

Thus, in keeping with what may be described as the expanding horizons of latter-day constitutional principles in perpetual processes of invention and assertion, the court discovers in an administrative agency of the state the power to determine, first, who, among the applicants, shall be classified as Black Americans, Chicano Americans, American Indians and Philippine Americans and, then, a concomitant power to exclude all other ethnic minorities, including Asian Americans, from the preferred classification. It lets the agency grant preferences—or as they more accurately should be described, indulgences—accordingly. For reasons not clear in the record, Asian Americans and all others of different ethnic derivation than those enumerated are not included among those to receive such preferences or indulgences.

Parenthetically, the record reveals, to me at least, another invidious form of discrimination—that against the residents of this state. According to some members of the admissions committee, the school has a goal to become a "national" law school, that is, one of nationally recognized prestige and purpose. In pursuance of this goal, the committee declines to discriminate against residents of other states and foreign countries. It is something of a mystery, however, how that goal can be achieved by the substantial lowering of academic standards for admission. In trying to create a national law school by means of procedures now in vogue, the law school must inevitably indulge in what might be deemed an inverse form of discrimination against bona fide residents of the state because the policies of admission operate to deny to residents of the state those preferences which are due them. The admissions committee gives little or no heed to whether the applicant comes from within the state or out of the state and declines to observe an overt policy of affording preference to residents of the state of Washington as required by law and public policy. Although not so intended, the failure to honor that peculiar but logical preference which the university should accord to the people who live here ipso facto generates an inverse discrimination against them.

When one considers the numerical ratio of nonresidents to state residents in a nation as large as ours, this practice, if maintained over a period of years, while conceivably operating to transform the law school into a national law school, may, except for purposes of providing the tax money to keep it operating, keep it from functioning as a state university. Nowhere, constitutional principles aside, can I find that the legislature has ever conferred such sweeping powers upon the administration or faculty of the university. Thus, in admitting out-of-state students with low academic credentials at the expense of residents of this state with high academic records, the law school not only has violated the constitutions but at the same time has both discriminated against the youth of this state and repudiated a fundamental idea that a great university, if it stands for anything at all, must stand for academic excellence.

Mr. DeFunis supported his application for admission with every conceivable evidence of competence except possibly an astrological horoscope. The record shows that his parents had been residents of and taxpayers to the state for about 50 years, and that he had lived here all of his life, graduating from Franklin High School in Seattle. His admission files showed, and the court found as a specific fact, that he had been graduated from the University of Washington with an overall grade average of 3.62 out of a possible 4, and a junior-senior grade point average as calculated by the law school of 3.71, which would be 3.8 if 9 hours of straight A (4) in Latin earned in the first quarter of his junior year during the summer quarter, 1968, were included. Although a straight A in Latin may speak for little in the current techniques for evaluating law school applicants, one can be sure that John Marshall, Oliver Wendell Holmes, John Storey, Benjamin N. Cardozo and John Harlan, along with Thomas Jefferson, Abraham Lincoln and Franklin Delano Roosevelt, would have found it impressive.

Mr. DeFunis was refused enrollment not once but twice by the school of law. He first applied for and was denied admission by the entering law class in the fall of 1970, but was informed that he had a better chance of being admitted to the beginning law class the next year, in the fall of 1971. During that interval, while waiting for the latter class, he worked nearly 40 hours per week for the Seattle Park Department and at the same time earned 21 hours of straight A in graduate school, receiving also 3 hours of incomplete. His LSAT, or law school aptitude test scores, for tests taken on three separate occasions, were 512 and 566 in 1969, and a quite remarkable 668 in December, 1970. The 668 score placed in the top 7 percent of all law school applicants nationally computed during a 3-year test period. Even if the scores were averaged, as the testing service suggests should be done, that average of 582, along with his grade average, placed him in the category of those marked for admission. His predicted first-year average (PFYA)— calculated by formula applied to his junior-senior grade point average of 3.71 and his averaged three LSAT scores along with his average writing test score of 61—gave him a predicted score of 76.23. By all standards and requirements of the admission policies openly announced by the law school, he should have been admitted.

The way things worked out, however, the law school failed to apply even its own vague, loose and whimsical admission standards. Of the approximately 155 enrolled in the entering law class in the fall of 1971, 29 had higher PFYAs than Mr. DeFunis, but there were 74, including minority students, with lower PFYAs. Excluding Asians, 18 of the 36 minority students with lower PFYAs than Mr. DeFunis actually did enroll; the other 18 notified of their admission, also with lower PFYAs than plaintiff, for reasons not discernible in the record did not enroll.

Altogether, 275 applicants were given formal notice of acceptance into the class entering in the fall of 1971 and another 55 were put on a waiting list making a total of 330 students who were formally accepted or notified that they probably would be. The reason for giving notice of acceptance to 275 for a class which was limited to 155 is that usually many applicants apply to several schools; others, for one reason or another, are unable or disinclined to enroll. Plaintiff Marc DeFunis, Jr., was neither among the 275 notified of acceptance nor among those added to the waiting list of 55.

The discriminatory action in refusing his admission becomes even more glaring when an overall view is taken of the admission practices. Of the 275 students who were explicitly told they had been accepted to the entering 1971 fall class, 180 had lower junior-senior grade point averages than plaintiff DeFunis and only 95 had higher. Of 330 accepted for admission, which included those notified of admission and the additional 55 placed on a waiting list, 224 had lower junior-senior grade point averages and only 106 had a better average—and this without allowing for the 9 hours of A in Latin he had received in his junior year. Among the 275 admitted, 44 were minority, *i.e.*, Afro-American, Philippine American, Chicano or American Indian, and of these 44 minority admitted, only 6 had higher academic qualifications than Mr. DeFunis and 38 had lower qualifications. Among these latter admitted students with lower qualifications were some whose college grades and aptitude scores were so low that, had they not been minority students, their applications would have been summarily denied.

Although preference was shown students from the so-called minority groups, no preference whatever was shown on the basis of Washington residency. Of the 275 admitted (excluding the waiting list of 55), 127 were nonresidents— a curious departure from the obvious public policy for which the university was established and has been primarily maintained for over a century, the education of the people of this state. To ignore bona fide state residence appears to be incompatible with the declared policy expressed in Const. art. 9, § 1, that it is the paramount duty of the state to educate children within its borders, as implemented by early legislation (preceding RCW 28B.20.020), that, with limited exceptions, *tuition* at the university *shall be free to all bona fide residents of the state.* (Formerly RCW 28.77.020.) Although now by statute the university must charge tuition to state residents (RCW 28B.15.200), this does not alter the obvious long-existing policy of affording preference to residents of this state. This existing statute recognizes this preference in the assessment of higher tuition charges to nonresidents than to residents. Although the statutes authorize certain discretionary powers in the Board of Regents to admit nonresidents and require disparate tuition fees from both state residents and out-of-state residents, the traditional policy of preference to bona fide residents for admission to the state's institutions of higher learning remains intact. The one idea clearly emerging from the constitution and statutes affecting higher education in the state's own colleges is that the people of the territory and state founded and have since maintained and supported a state university primarily for the benefit of those who live here.

Mr. DeFunis' case presents the curious situation of a state university school of law founded, maintained and operated by the people of this state and deriving most of its subsistence from their taxes and good will, designed to enable them and their children to obtain a professional education which a substantial number of them could not afford were they studying in a private school, inviting the nation at large to compete for seats in the law school, and then not awarding the seats to the winners of the competition. I think it not a narrow provincialism to say that, by and large, the major resources of the state university should be devoted to the purpose for which it was created and has been maintained—service not only to mankind at large but additionally and primarily to the people of the commonwealth who founded and perpetually have supported it. Nonresident students should, of course, be admitted, but their numbers ought to be limited and their admission selective and probably based on reciprocal policies of the other states and foreign countries. Admission of out-of-state residents should be in consonance with the principle that a state university exists primarily for the people of the state and secondarily for residents of other states and foreign countries.

The law faculty was, as the court observes, motivated by a laudable purpose—to increase the number of minority students studying law and with the avowed purpose of equalizing opportunities among applicants who come from the lower income and economic groups with those who come from the higher. This policy of ethnic minority selection apparently was not to apply to faculty positions for the record does not show that any qualified nonminority applicant for the teaching staff was refused nor any faculty member ousted to make room for law teachers with questionable credentials from a minority ethnic group.

In deciding which particular groups should be classified as ethnic minorities, the committee on admissions first made an assumption supported by no evidence whatever, *i.e.,* that all of the accepted minority students except Asian Americans were of a lower economic status than Mr. De-Funis. No comparative investigation or study as to the financial condition or economic background was made to establish the relative economic and cultural condition of the students applying. It was thus categorically assumed that the ethnic minority applicants were, to use the descriptive term current in academic circles, culturally deprived—meaning, one must suppose, that the environmental factors surrounding a minority student and tending to affect his academic achievements were of a lower order than those surrounding white or majority students. This sweeping and unsupported assumption, derived from no real evidence whatever, that all of the admitted minority students were both poor and culturally deprived, supplied the modus vivendi for the scheme of preferences. It ignored the correlative assumption which inevitably had to be made that neither Mr. DeFunis nor any of the nonminority applicants had been equally culturally or economically deprived.

Aside from the questions of equal protection and the granting of special privileges and immunities, there arises from this record a compelling but subsidiary question as to how such bizarre results came about. How, under any rational admissions policy, could an outstanding student, one of superb academic achievement, be denied admission to his state university law school while others, some of them nonresidents and of mediocre academic standing, were admitted? Did the legislative or the executive branches of government ever delegate authority to handle admission of a state university law school in this fashion? Following is a brief description of the admission procedures as shown by this record.

The admissions practices which operated to deny Mr. DeFunis' application were developed by the law faculty under the claimed authority of the Board of Regents and the president of the university. An admissions and readmissions committee consisting of five members of the faculty and, for reasons not made clear in the record, two law students, had been established by the dean and a majority of the law faculty to decide who would be admitted. Although each of the two law student members possessed full voting powers and served with exactly the same authority as each of the five faculty members, the record is devoid of any standards applied as basis for their appointment to the committee on admissions.

For example, Tama Zorn, one of the student members who testified, said that she had become a member during her first year in law school. Although actually a resident of Washington, D.C., she had been accorded what she described as resident status for tuition purposes on entering law school. She had not been selected for appointment to the committee on admissions or readmissions by the faculty, the regents or the president of the university, but, rather, had been delegated to it by an entity called the Student Bar Association. Her appointment to the committee on admissions and readmissions was based on little more than her application to that organization. In this fashion, the Student Bar Association appointed the two student members to the committee largely upon their request with little or no thought to their qualifications and less as to their purpose, and with no indication in this record that the Student Bar Association itself possessed any particular talents or qualifications to pass in turn upon the qualifications of its incoming fellow students.

Mrs. Zorn said that the admission committee members had no personal acquaintance with the applicants; that her knowledge of the applicants' aptitudes and qualifications had to be derived exclusively from their application files and the decisions reached from a "policy that intends to encourage minority students to come to law school and practice law in the community." Minority students could readily be identified from the files of the applicants but one could not tell whether they were economically underprivileged or, as the term is used, culturally deprived. She did acknowledge, however, that Asian Americans, although a minority, were given no preferential treatment.

In devising the modus operandi for carrying out the policy of preferential treatment, little thought was given to the possibility that, in addition to being suspect constitutionally, the practice might well be ultra vires for it placed a controlling power over the careers and even the lives of many potential students in the hands of their fellow students.

The two law student members of the committee each exercised an initial and virtually controlling vote in the screening of about 60 or 70 applicants. Each member of the committee, including student members, was given approximately 70 files upon which to make recommendation for admission or rejection, with instructions that only about 10 were to be approved for admission and the remaining 60 rejected. Thus, of over 1,500 files to be examined, 490 files were distributed among the committee members. Each member would arrive at what was determined to be a cutoff point below which the files would be summarily rejected, and in the usual course of events those files received no further consideration.

Of the approximately 70 files given to each member, both student and faculty accordingly would return to the whole committee a recommendation of 10 for admission. Since the 70 files per committee member represented only 490 of some 1,500 plus, Mrs. Zorn testified she assumed that several hundred applicants had been summarily rejected before distribution of the 70 files to each member, and quite possibly some had been summarily admitted. In general, it is a fair summary of the record, I think, that of the approximately 70 files distributed to each committee member, an applicant neither included in the 10 recommended nor in some 20 more carried as secondary possibilities had little or no chance for admission.

Thus, some 40 student applicants were categorically rejected, another 20 given only secondary or uncertain chances, and 10 applicants put in a categorically positive position for admission upon nothing more than the recommendation of a first- or second-year law student. Mrs. Zorn testified that of the 40 files marked by her for rejection, she had no subsequent knowledge or further contact. As far as she knew, they were consigned thenceforth to bureaucratic oblivion.

After reviewing Mr. DeFunis' file prior to trial, Mrs. Zorn said that it indicated nothing derogatory, but, as she expressed it, showed something perhaps negative. This vague or perhaps negative feeling she derived, as she testified, from the following comment contained in his file, appearing in one of the recommendations supplied on Mr. DeFunis' behalf:

"This guy is a person I would refer to as the planner. He sets his goal and steadily works toward it, come Hell or high water. I admire him in his persistence, but there seems to be the slight tendency of not caring upon whom he might step in the process. I have known him for four years and as an adviser for three quarters, and as a student in one of my classes. His major is in political science but with strong—". Well, I can't read that next word, "in history and sociology. His hobbies are sports, classical music collection and classical guitar. He has helped finance his education by sales work, book store and Seattle Park Department laborer. His activities are campers—" THE COURT: Campus. MR. DIAMOND: "—on campus have been largely political oriented, mobile, model congress and mock political convention. He wishes to practice law. I recommend."

The negative qualities of these file comments are, indeed, hard to identify, but for some reason or other Mrs. Zorn thought them to be unfavorable and said that they contributed to warranting a rejection. She conceded, however, that Mr. DeFunis' LSAT score was higher than the scores of many she recommended for acceptance.

There is also a curious aura of civil, political or community "activism," as it is sometimes called, surrounding the recommendations for admission or rejection. One student applicant recommended by Mrs. Zorn had an LSAT of 562, substantially lower than the average of Mr. DeFunis, but was recommended for the waiting list because of being very active on campus and in his community. The activity which impressed her the most was that he was a founding member of Isla Vista Branch of the American Civil Liberties Union and president of its student chapter at the University of California, Santa Barbara. He had participated in the John Tunney for Senate campaign in California and in the operation of a student owned and operated radio station in Santa Barbara. Also, the applicant had been a campus news reporter and a member of several other campus organizations. Mrs. Zorn had concluded that these activities, despite the low LSAT. established sound basis for admission to the law school. She recommended, however, against the admission of another student with a 3.9 junior-senior grade average because she did not think that his area of study, the field of finance, adequately significant. Finance, as she put it, was a program without rigor. She was apparently unaware of the rigorous nature of courses in accountancy, statistics, economics and banking as taught at the University of Washington.

Another student member of the admissions committee, Mr. Hayes, testified he had been put on the committee during his first year of law school but left it because of poor grades. As he explained his departure, "I just barely made it to the second year." Like Mrs. Zorn, Mr. Hayes was given a stack of files to review, but, because of his part-time work, he reviewed substantially fewer files than did the other members of the committee. He said he had had no special training with respect to judging or passing upon applicants to the university law school and had been put on the committee simply by adding his name to a sign-up sheet from which the Student Bar Association had then picked him. Testifying concerning one applicant whose junior-senior grade point average was only 2.89, a comparatively low grade, he acknowledged, that applicant's file cover contained the statement entered by a committee member, "We seem to have bungled this one pretty conclusively. He's got us." The committee, having mistakenly accepted that applicant, he said, did not rectify the error and the particular applicant remained admitted.

The committee, he said, was trying to achieve what he described as a class balance based on an estimated potential for getting through school. He said most of the files given him for review were those of minority students. Another applicant he recommended for admission had a junior-senior grade point average of only 2.63 with the notation, "Excellent recommendations, sound record. Divorced with five kids. Could make it if her personal situation could be worked out, lightened load possibility? Admit."

Another student member, Mrs. Rochelle Kleinberg, was put on the admissions committee during her second year of law school. She was appointed, she said, by the Student Bar Association as was Mrs. Zorn simply by putting her name on a posted sign-up sheet. When asked why she had sought the appointment, she said that she thought it had an important role in the law school and wished to participate. As it turned out, the role was in fact extremely important for the future of many highly qualified student applicants.

Mrs. Kleinberg, as did most of the others, initially received about 70 files for review and eliminated 50 or 60 of them below what she deemed an appropriate cutoff point. Thus, the rejected applicants had no way of knowing that their opportunities for admission had been summarily curtailed by the simple act of rejection done by a law student engaged in the initial review of some 70 files.

A random examination of the records of various students accepted by the law school in the entering classes for which Mr. DeFunis had applied shows extraordinary and inexplicable variations in their qualifications. One admitted applicant showed an almost vertical academic climb. He had a junior-senior grade point average of 3.64, but an overall grade point average of 2.85. The admission committee notes in his file read as follows: "Overall GPA 2.85. strange recommend. 'arrogant, conceited' but apparently bright . . . [not readable] Take a chance on his screwy personality & admit." His PFYA was 78.35 with a writing score of 71. One cannot discern from the files whether a height-

ened community or campus activity, or whatever, constituted the determining factor for admission. One young
woman with a junior-senior GPA of 3, an LSAT of 702, and
a writing score of 66, was admitted by a letter from the
dean dated September 14, 1971, with no comment, remark
or recommendation whatever from the admissions council.

An applicant with a junior-senior GPA of 2.37 and an
LSAT score of 475, was admitted by letter from the associate dean dated July 29, 1971, despite the remarks of the
admissions committee that he be rejected. Another applicant with a junior-senior GPA of 3.32, an LSAT of 759, and
a writing score of 60 was admitted by letter of July 23,
1971, from the associate dean of the law school despite the
admissions committee's remarks set forth in his file that his
"recommendations are equivocal and his academic career
unimpressive." The admissions council deemed unimpressive a 3.32 junior-senior average earned in chemistry,
physics, analytical geometry, calculus and general physics
laboratory. This particular applicant with the so-called unimpressive academic record had also earned 6 hours of A in
advanced calculus, 6 hours of A in mechanics and an A in
introduction to digital computers.

Another young woman, earlier alluded to, was admitted
to the law school with a junior-senior grade point average
of 2.63, an LSAT of 481, and a writing score of 55. The file
shows that she was 35 years of age at the time of admission
and would thus be 38 upon graduation, if indeed able to
complete the program on schedule. The remarks entered by
the admissions council in her file note that she was "Divorced with five kids. Could make it if her personal situation could be worked out." It added, "Excellent recommendations; sound record," and upon these conclusions recommended admission to the law school.

By letter of March 2, 1971, an applicant with a junior-
senior grade point average of 2.89, an LSAT of 663 and a
writing score of 58 was accepted. Other than pointing out
that the applicant was a member of a minority, the admissions council was noncommittal.

Another applicant admitted with a junior-senior grade point average of 3.56 had an LSAT of 625. Despite these high qualifications, the determining factor for admission here as revealed in the file is the remark on the admissions council list: "Enthusiastic recommendation. Abundant community action projects."

Another applicant earned a remarkably high junior-senior GPA of 3.90 and scored 599 in the LSAT, but achieved a writing score of only 46. He was notified of his acceptance by letter September 14, 1971, by the dean of the law school. There is apparently very slight correlation in many cases among the GPA, the LSAT, and the writing scores.

An applicant with a GPA of 3.55 was notified of his acceptance by the law school by letter of May 21, 1971, from the associate dean after achieving an LSAT of 625 and a writing score of 61. For some reason or other, the admissions committee recommended against outright admission but that he be placed on the waiting list. Despite this, however, the applicant was categorically admitted.

Of the approximately 150 students actually enrolled in the class for which petitioner DeFunis made his application, only some 42 admission files were placed in evidence. But an inspection of these files, in my judgment, fails to show any consistent policy on admissions at which a prelaw student could aim his career. If he is intelligent, works hard, and achieves high grades, his place in the law school class may be preempted by someone with lesser grades but who is engaged in what is described as "community activities," or is otherwise described as a student activist. Or, if he is engaged in community activities and still attains high grades through diligence and intelligence and long hours at the books, his position may be taken in the entering class by one who has neither engaged in "community activity" nor achieved high grades but, nevertheless, has made a high LSAT score. Or, even if he studied hard, is intelligent, and placed high in grades, LSAT and PFYA, and engaged in what are called community activities, his place might still be awarded to a minority student who has done none of these. All of these inequities are, I fear, bound to foster a spirit of anti-intellectualism in the heart of what should be an intellectual center.

The discriminatory character of the admissions policy is, I think, well epitomized by the trial court in its oral decision:

> The applications of the black students were separated from all others and assigned for review to a black student and a professor who had worked closely with the CLEO Program.
>
> Some minority students were admitted whose college grades and aptitude test scores were so low that had they been whites their applications would have been summarily denied. Excluding the Asians, only one minority student out of 31 admitted among the applicants had a predicted first year average above the plaintiff's.
>
> Since no more than 150 applicants were to be admitted the admission of less qualified resulted in a denial of places to those otherwise qualified.

This method of selection operated to deprive Mr. De-Funis of his position in the entering law classes both in 1970 and again in 1971. Not being a member of a preferred ethnic minority, he found his place taken by others who not only possessed far lower credentials and qualifications but among whom were some who on the face of their records were unqualified. He was the victim of what in current parlance has come to be described as "affirmative action," which includes preferential treatment for the sake of creating a more equitable racial balance—a process which the court now finds constitutional.

If this be constitutional, then, of course, the constitutions are not color blind; one racial group may be given political or economic preferment over another solely because of race or ethnic origin. Yet, this was the very thing that the Fourteenth Amendment was designed to prevent. All races, and all individuals, are entitled to equal opportunity to enter the law school. To admit some solely because of race or ethnic origin is to deny others that privilege solely for the same reasons, which in law amounts to a denial of equal protection to the one while granting special privileges and immunities to the other.

The United States District Court, Northern District of California, recently stated what I perceive to be the controlling principle here when it said in its findings of fact in *Anderson v. San Francisco Unified School Dist.,* 357 F. Supp. 248   (N.D. Cal. 1972):

> No one race or ethnic group should ever be accorded preferential treatment over another. No race or ethnic group should ever be granted privileges or prerogatives not given to every other race. There is no place for race or ethnic groupings in America. Only in individual accomplishment can equality be achieved.

With the possible exception of administering justice, I accept the dicta in *Brown v. Board of Educ.,* 347 U.S. 483, 98 L. Ed. 873, 74 S. Ct. 686, 38 A.L.R.2d 1180 (1954), that education is probably the most important function of state and local government. It should not be forgotten, however, that in striking down decisively the separate but equal concept of segregated schools, the rationale of that decision rested on equality of opportunity and the premise that segregation based on race or color amounted categorically to an unconstitutional denial of that equality. In speaking of equality of educational opportunity, the court there said, "Such an opportunity, where the state has undertaken to provide it, is a right which must be made available to all on equal terms." 347 U.S. at 493.

The mainstream of current constitutional law runs forthrightly against the discriminatory practice of preferential treatment based on race, color, or ethnic origin. In *McLaughlin v. Florida,* 379 U.S. 184, 13 L. Ed. 2d 222, 85 S. Ct. 283 (1964), an adultery statute imposing greater penalties when the participants were of different races was held unconstitutional under the Fourteenth Amendment. Despite the wide legislative judgment to be sustained in determining whether an act is reasonably designed to attack the evil aimed at, any classification based upon race must, it was held, be suspect at the outset on the general rule that the constitution and amendments were intended to eliminate all racial discrimination arising from official actions. *Bolling v. Sharpe*, 347 U.S. 497, 98 L. Ed. 884, 74 S. Ct. 693 (1954).

As pointed out in *McLaughlin v. Florida, supra*, racial classification has been held invalid in many cases: race was required to be designated in voting and property records (*Virginia State Bd. of Elections v. Hamm*, 379 U.S. 19, 13 L. Ed. 2d 91, 85 S. Ct. 157 (1964)); designation of race on nomination papers and ballots (*Anderson v. Martin*, 375 U.S. 399, 11 L. Ed. 2d 430, 84 S. Ct. 454 (1964)); racial segregation in public parks and playgrounds (*Watson v. Memphis*, 373 U.S. 526, 10 L. Ed. 2d 529, 83 S. Ct. 1314 (1963)); segregation in the public schools (*Brown v. Board of Educ.*, 349 U.S. 294, 99 L. Ed. 1083, 75 S. Ct. 753 and 347 U.S. 483, 98 L. Ed. 873, 74 S. Ct. 686, 38 A.L.R.2d 1180 (1954)); segregation of the races in public transportation (*Gayle v. Browder*, 352 U.S. 903, 1 L. Ed. 2d 114, 77 S. Ct. 145 (1956)); and as a social practice even without sanction of ordinance or statute in public restaurants (*Lombard v. Louisiana*, 373 U.S. 267, 10 L. Ed. 2d 338, 83 S. Ct. 1122 (1963)); and in public swimming areas. *Baltimore v. Dawson*, 350 U.S. 877, 100 L. Ed. 774, 76 S. Ct. 133 (1955). All were held repugnant to the constitution. If the Fourteenth Amendment stands for anything at all, it should be clear from these decisions that it stands for the principle that all discrimination based on race, religion, creed, color or ethnic background by any state, its constitutions, its subdivisions, or its agencies, is prohibited.

The majority concedes and the record is indisputable that petitioner DeFunis was ousted from the list of acceptable students solely because of preference accorded others, and that this preference was granted to many solely because of race and ethnic origin. Even though there are many areas of public endeavor where it would be deemed a valid and constitutional exercise of the police power to provide special assistance for those segments of our population described as disadvantaged or poor, or culturally deprived, such special assistance could not constitutionally deprive Mr. DeFunis of a seat in the law school and award it to a member of a group whose existence is defined or controlled by considerations of race or ethnic origin. When the seat in the law school is awarded on the basis of race or ethnic origin, the procedure necessarily falls within the constitutional principles prohibiting racial segregation or preference.

In referring to special aid and assistance, the fact remains that the committee on admissions and readmissions made no investigation whatever as to whether any of the minority students admitted were poorer, more disadvantaged or more culturally deprived than some of the students of higher educational and aptitude qualifications who had been turned down. The committee simply applied a theory and ipso facto assumed that every Black American, Indian American or Chicano, or Philippine American, because of his ethnic origin of necessity had to be more disadvantaged, poorer and more culturally deprived than those of Asian, Caucasian, or other ethnic origin.

The case of *Jones* v. *Alfred H. Mayer Co.*, 392 U.S. 409, 20 L. Ed. 2d 1189, 88 S. Ct. 2186 (1968), sustaining an act of Congress which prohibited racial discrimination against Blacks in occupying or purchasing federally aided housing, in my view, supports rather than disparages DeFunis' position and does not, I think, purport to find the constitution color conscious. There the court held that the Congress had constitutional power to prevent the expenditure of public funds for the enhancement of one racial group to the detriment of other racial groups. It held that, where state law affords preference on the basis of race so that it works a detriment to others on the basis of race, the law and regulation pursuant to it are inevitably repugnant to the Fourteenth Amendment.

This means that this court's decision in *State ex rel. Citizens Against Mandatory Bussing* v. *Brooks*, 80 Wn.2d

121, 492 P.2d 536 (1972), would tend to sustain DeFunis'
position in the present case. There is no more than a coinci-
dental parallel between the *Mandatory Bussing* case and
Mr. DeFunis' case. There we sustained a modest program of
compulsory bussing initiated by the Seattle school district
for the stated purpose of assuring higher quality of education for all students of whatever racial, religious or ethnic
background. The policy of required bussing has been
adopted because the school board was of the opinion that
racially segregated schools, even those where the segregation is de facto and not de jure, are inferior to integrated
schools, and that a racially segregated student body will
receive an education inferior to that of a racially integrated
student body. This court held that the school board was
acting within its lawful powers in reaching this conclusion
and in implementing its views by a program of mandatory
bussing. In the *Mandatory Bussing* case, the Seattle school
board did no more than act officially upon conclusions it
had the authority to reach, and provide for racially integrated education while curtailing de facto segregation.

There is no genuine parallel between Mr. DeFunis' case
and the case of the children required to ride the busses.
There, we were dealing with a procedurally sound administrative determination that every child, under the plan and
the constitution, would gain an integrated and thereby superior education at the expense of no other child. Providing
one child with a better, *i.e.*, integrated, education did not
operate to deprive another of an equal, integrated education. Benefit to one would not be at the expense of another.
Putting one child on a bus to ride to school did not operate
to take away another's seat in the classroom. Ordering
bussing to eliminate segregated schools was no less compatible with the constitutions than the idea that children need-
ing or requesting specialized training may have to ride
busses to special schools because every department and
facility of a school system, in the nature of things, cannot
be equidistant from all children. In the *Mandatory Bussing*
case, the Seattle school board was attempting to discharge

its constitutional duty of providing equality of educational opportunity for all children within the district at the expense of no child or children.

Here we have precisely the opposite. Putting some applicants into the classroom deprived a qualified applicant of his seat there. It operated to deprive him thereby of the equal protection of the laws and at the same time granted to others privileges and immunities not available to him on equal terms. Thus, aside from the patently arbitrary and capricious method earlier delineated, by which Mr. DeFunis' position was given to a less qualified applicant, his ouster fell explicitly within the constitutional principle that education must be provided to all students on equal terms and all public education programs must be conducted without regard to race, color or national origin. *Kemp v. Beasley*, 352 F.2d 14 (8th Cir. 1965).

Are there methods by which a state owned and operated law school may be fairly and constitutionally administered so as to comport with the constitutions? Although the courts have neither the power nor the aptitude to operate a university and should be without the inclination to do so, several possible methods come to mind which prima facie, at least, meet the fairness and equal protection standards of the constitutions. One would be a system of comprehensive competitive examinations in predesignated courses such as English, history, basic science, mathematics, economics and sociology, and with optional courses in other fields selected by the student.

Another method would be to work out a reasonably accurate mathematical correlation between grade values from different colleges or universities in preannounced prelaw courses and to compute those equivalent grades with admission granted the 150 students with the highest grades. This gives every student a fair chance to achieve his ambition.

Another possible solution—in case the faculty believes that high prelaw grades should not be the main criterion—prescribe a sound but not extraordinarily high prelaw grade standard and make a random selection by lot and chance of the 275 applicants to be admitted from among those qualifying. And the fairest way of all—but I doubt its efficacy—admit all applicants possessing a minimum prerequisite grade point in prescribed courses; conduct the law classes in the field house or stadium, if necessary; give frequent examinations; and let the better qualified few survive on the basis of their grades in law school. There are, of course, other methods equally fair and impartial which may be readily developed, all of which will meet the constitutional tests of fair and impartial application. But whatever scheme is developed, one thing is certain: Keep it within the principles of the constitutions, no one can be preferred and no one can be disparaged because of race, color, creed, ethnic origin or domestic environment.

If it is the state policy—and I think it should be—to afford special training, guidance and coaching to those students whose domestic environment has deprived them of a fair chance to compete, or to provide financial assistance to students in economic straits, it is within the state's constitutional powers to do so, but once these students have reached the point of seeking admission to a professional or graduate school, no preference or partiality can or should, under the constitutions, be shown them.

The rationale of *Anderson v. San Francisco Unified School Dist.*, 357 F. Supp. 248 (N.D. Cal. 1972), an opinion dated October 30, 1972, filed in the United States District Court, Northern District of California, I think, expresses the principles which should govern the *DeFunis* case. That court held unconstitutional a school district's plan to give preference in employment and promotions to members of ethnic minorities in administrative and supervisory positions, such as principals, assistant principals, deans and heads of departments—a plan designed to increase the numerical representation of ethnic minorities in the administration of the schools. That court, in holding the scheme unconstitutional, said that "The key issue in this case is whether or not a classification which is based on race is valid," and answered it with a statement of principles which ought to control here:

Preferential treatment under the guise of "affirmative action" is the imposition of one form of racial discrimination in place of another. The questions that must be asked in this regard are: must an individual sacrifice his right to be judged on his own merit by accepting discrimination based solely on the color of his skin? How can we achieve the goal of equal opportunity for all if, in the process, we deny equal opportunity to some?

Mr. DeFunis came before the bar of the Superior Court much as did petitioners, parents of school children, in *Brown v. Board of Educ.*, 347 U.S. 483, 98 L. Ed. 873, 74 S. Ct. 686 (1954), asking that he not be denied admission to the university law school because of race or ethnic origin. The trial court properly ordered his admission. So, too, would I, and, therefore, I would affirm.

HUNTER, J., concurs with HALE, C.J.

HUNTER, J. (dissenting)—The majority supports a laudable purpose—to enable students of certain minority races to enter the University of Washington School of Law in order that ultimately there will be a greater representation of practicing lawyers of those races in the legal profession— with which purpose I do not disagree. This must not be accomplished, however, by clear and willful discrimination against students of other races as the Admissions Committee of the University of Washington School of Law has done in this case by denying admission to the respondent, Marco DeFunis, Jr., to this school, as found by the trial court and amply supported by the record.

This action by the admissions committee of the school of law constitutes arbitrary and capricious action, flaunting the guarantees of the equal protection provisions to all citizens as provided in our state and federal constitutions.

The line of federal cases cited by the majority are not in point. They stand for the proposition that full opportunity for education be afforded to students of all races; whereas, the present case denies the opportunity of education to students of one race to make room for students of other races and with lesser qualifications.

I would affirm the trial court, directing the admissions committee to admit the respondent, Marco DeFunis, Jr., to the University of Washington School of Law.

HALE, C.J., concurs with HUNTER, J.

The United States Supreme Court Opinion
416 U.S. 312, 40 L. Ed. 2d 164, 94 S. Ct. 1704 (1974)

Marco DeFunis et al., Petitioners, v. *Charles Odegaard,*
President of the University of Washington, et al.

PER CURIAM.

In 1971 the petitioner Marco DeFunis, Jr.,[1] applied for
admission as a first-year student at the University of
Washington Law School, a state-operated institution.
The size of the incoming first-year class was to be limited
to 150 persons, and the Law School received some 1,600
applications for these 150 places. DeFunis was eventually notified that he had been denied admission. He
thereupon commenced this suit in a Washington trial
court, contending that the procedures and criteria employed by the Law School Admissions Committee invidiously discriminated against him on account of his
race in violation of the Equal Protection Clause
of the Fourteenth Amendment to the United States
Constitution.

DeFunis brought the suit on behalf of himself alone,
and not as the representative of any class, against the
various respondents, who are officers, faculty members,
and members of the Board of Regents of the University
of Washington. He asked the trial court to issue a
mandatory injunction commanding the respondents to
admit him as a member of the first-year class entering
in September 1971, on the ground that the Law School
admissions policy had resulted in the unconstitutional
denial of his application for admission. The trial court
agreed with his claim and granted the requested relief.

---

[1] Also included as petitioners are DeFunis' parents and his wife.
Hereafter, the singular form "petitioner" is used.

DeFunis was, accordingly, admitted to the Law School and began his legal studies there in the fall of 1971. On appeal, the Washington Supreme Court reversed the judgment of the trial court and held that the Law School admissions policy did not violate the Constitution. By this time DeFunis was in his second year at the Law School.

He then petitioned this Court for a writ of certiorari, and MR. JUSTICE DOUGLAS, as Circuit Justice, stayed the judgment of the Washington Supreme Court pending the "final disposition of the case by this Court." By virtue of this stay, DeFunis has remained in law school, and was in the first term of his third and final year when this Court first considered his certiorari petition in the fall of 1973. Because of our concern that DeFunis' third-year standing in the Law School might have rendered this case moot, we requested the parties to brief the question of mootness before we acted on the petition. In response, both sides contended that the case was not moot. The respondents indicated that, if the decision of the Washington Supreme Court were permitted to stand, the petitioner could complete the term for which he was then enrolled but would have to apply to the faculty for permission to continue in the school before he could register for another term.[2]

We granted the petition for certiorari on November 19, 1973.   414 U. S. 1038.   The case was in due course orally argued on February 26, 1974.

In response to questions raised from the bench during the oral argument, counsel for the petitioner has informed the Court that DeFunis has now registered "for his final

---

[2] By contrast, in their response to the petition for certiorari, the respondents had stated that DeFunis "will complete his third year [of law school] and be awarded his J. D. degree at the end of the 1973–74 academic year regardless of the outcome of this appeal."

quarter in law school." Counsel for the respondents have made clear that the Law School will not in any way seek to abrogate this registration.[3] In light of DeFunis' recent registration for the last quarter of his final law school year, and the Law School's assurance that his registration is fully effective, the insistent question again arises whether this case is not moot, and to that question we now turn.

The starting point for analysis is the familiar proposition that "federal courts are without power to decide questions that cannot affect the rights of litigants in the case before them." *North Carolina* v. *Rice,* 404 U. S. 244 246 (1971). The inability of the federal judiciary "to review moot cases derives from the requirement of Article III of the Constitution under which the exercise of judicial power depends upon the existence of a case or controversy." *Liner* v. *Jafco, Inc.,* 375 U. S. 301, 306 n. 3 (1964); see also *Powell* v. *McCormack,* 395 U. S. 486, 496 n. 7 (1969); *Sibron* v. *New York,* 392 U. S. 40, 50 n. 8 (1968). Although as a matter of Washington state law it appears that this case would be saved from mootness by "the great public interest in the continuing issues raised by this appeal," 82 Wash. 2d 11, 23 n. 6, 507 P. 2d 1169, 1177 n. 6 (1973), the fact remains that under Art. III "[e]ven in cases arising in the state courts, the question of mootness is a federal one which a federal court must resolve before it assumes jurisdiction." *North Carolina* v. *Rice, supra,* at 246.

The respondents have represented that, without regard to the ultimate resolution of the issues in this case,

---

[3] In their memorandum on the question of mootness, counsel for the respondents unequivocally stated: "If Mr. DeFunis registers for the spring quarter under the existing order of this court during the registration period from February 20, 1974, to March 1, 1974, that registration would not be canceled unilaterally by the university regardless of the outcome of this litigation."

DeFunis will remain a student in the Law School for the duration of any term in which he has already enrolled. Since he has now registered for his final term, it is evident that he will be given an opportunity to complete all academic and other requirements for graduation, and, if he does so, will receive his diploma regardless of any decision this Court might reach on the merits of this case. In short, all parties agree that DeFunis is now entitled to complete his legal studies at the University of Washington and to receive his degree from that institution. A determination by this Court of the legal issues tendered by the parties is no longer necessary to compel that result, and could not serve to prevent it. DeFunis did not cast his suit as a class action, and the only remedy he requested was an injunction commanding his admission to the Law School. He was not only accorded that remedy, but he now has also been irrevocably admitted to the final term of the final year of the Law School course. The controversy between the parties has thus clearly ceased to be "definite and concrete" and no longer "touch[es] the legal relations of parties having adverse legal interests." *Aetna Life Ins. Co.* v. *Haworth,* 300 U. S. 227, 240–241 (1937).

It matters not that these circumstances partially stem from a policy decision on the part of the respondent Law School authorities. The respondents, through their counsel, the Attorney General of the State, have professionally represented that in no event will the status of DeFunis now be affected by any view this Court might express on the merits of this controversy. And it has been the settled practice of the Court, in contexts no less significant, fully to accept representations such as these as parameters for decision. See *Gerende* v. *Election Board,* 341 U. S. 56 (1951); *Whitehill* v. *Elkins,* 389 U. S. 54, 57–58 (1967); *Ehlert* v. *United States,* 402 U. S. 99,

107 (1971); cf. *Law Students Research Council* v. *Wadmond,* 401 U. S. 154, 162–163 (1971).

There is a line of decisions in this Court standing for the proposition that the "voluntary cessation of allegedly illegal conduct does not deprive the tribunal of power to hear and determine the case, *i. e.,* does not make the case moot." *United States* v. *W. T. Grant Co.,* 345 U. S. 629, 632 (1953); *United States* v. *Trans-Missouri Freight Assn.,* 166 U. S. 290, 308–310 (1897); *Walling* v. *Helmerich & Payne, Inc.,* 323 U. S. 37, 43 (1944); *Gray* v. *Sanders,* 372 U. S. 368, 376 (1963); *United States* v. *Phosphate Export Assn.,* 393 U. S. 199, 202–203 (1968). These decisions and the doctrine they reflect would be quite relevant if the question of mootness here had arisen by reason of a unilateral change in the *admissions procedures* of the Law School. For it was the admissions procedures that were the target of this litigation, and a voluntary cessation of the admissions practices complained of could make this case moot only if it could be said with assurance "that 'there is no reasonable expectation that the wrong will be repeated.'" *United States* v. *W. T. Grant Co., supra,* at 633. Otherwise, "[t]he defendant is free to return to his old ways," *id.,* at 632, and this fact would be enough to prevent mootness because of the "public interest in having the legality of the practices settled." *Ibid.* But mootness in the present case depends not at all upon a "voluntary cessation" of the admissions practices that were the subject of this litigation. It depends, instead, upon the simple fact that DeFunis is now in the final quarter of the final year of his course of study, and the settled and unchallenged policy of the Law School to permit him to complete the term for which he is now enrolled.

It might also be suggested that this case presents a question that is "capable of repetition, yet evading review," *Southern Pacific Terminal Co.* v. *ICC*, 219 U. S. 498, 515 (1911); *Roe* v. *Wade*, 410 U. S. 113, 125 (1973), and is thus amenable to federal adjudication even though it might otherwise be considered moot. But DeFunis will never again be required to run the gantlet of the Law School's admission process, and so the question is certainly not "capable of repetition" so far as he is concerned. Moreover, just because this particular case did not reach the Court until the eve of the petitioner's graduation from law school, it hardly follows that the issue he raises will in the future evade review. If the admissions procedures of the Law School remain unchanged,[4] there is no reason to suppose that a subsequent case attacking those procedures will not come with relative speed to this Court, now that the Supreme Court of Washington has spoken. This case, therefore, in no way presents the exceptional situation in which the *Southern Pacific Terminal* doctrine might permit a departure from "[t]he usual rule in federal cases . . . that an actual controversy must exist at stages of appellate or certiorari review, and not simply at the date the action is initiated." *Roe* v. *Wade*, *supra*, at 125; *United States* v. *Munsingwear, Inc.*, 340 U. S. 36 (1950).

Because the petitioner will complete his law school studies at the end of the term for which he has now registered regardless of any decision this Court might reach on the merits of this litigation, we conclude that the Court cannot, consistently with the limitations of

---

[4] In response to an inquiry from the Court, counsel for the respondents has advised that some changes have been made in the admissions procedures "for the applicants seeking admission to the University of Washington law school for the academic year commencing September, 1974." The respondents' counsel states, however, that "[these] changes do not affect the policy challenged by the petitioners . . . in that . . . special consideration still is given to applicants from 'certain ethnic groups.'"

Art. III of the Constitution, consider the substantive constitutional issues tendered by the parties.[5] Accordingly, the judgment of the Supreme Court of Washington is vacated, and the cause is remanded for such proceedings as by that Court may be deemed appropriate.

It is so ordered.

MR. JUSTICE DOUGLAS, dissenting.

I agree with MR. JUSTICE BRENNAN that this case is not moot, and because of the significance of the issues raised I think it is important to reach the merits.

I

The University of Washington Law School received 1,601 applications for admission to its first-year class beginning in September 1971. There were spaces available for only about 150 students, but in order to enroll this number the school eventually offered admission to 275 applicants. All applicants were put into two groups, one of which was considered under the minority admissions program. Thirty-seven of those offered admission had indicated on an optional question on their application that their "dominant" ethnic origin was either Black, Chicano, American Indian, or Filipino, the four groups included in the minority admissions program. Answers to this optional question were apparently the sole basis

---

[5] It is suggested in dissent that "[a]ny number of unexpected events—illness, economic necessity, even academic failure—might prevent his graduation at the end of the term." *Post*, at 348. "But such speculative contingencies afford no basis for our passing on the substantive issues [the petitioner] would have us decide," *Hall* v. *Beals*, 396 U. S. 45, 49 (1969), in the absence of "evidence that this is a prospect of 'immediacy and reality.'" *Golden* v. *Zwickler*, 394 U. S. 103, 109 (1969); *Maryland Casualty Co.* v. *Pacific Coal & Oil Co.*, 312 U. S. 270, 273 (1941).

upon which eligibility for the program was determined. Eighteen of these 37 actually enrolled in the Law School.

In general, the admissions process proceeded as follows: An index called the Predicted First Year Average (Average) was calculated for each applicant on the basis of a formula combining the applicant's score on the Law School Admission Test (LSAT) and his grades in his last two years in college.[1]   On the basis of its experience with previous years' applications, the admissions committee, consisting of faculty, administration, and students, concluded that the most outstanding applicants were those with averages above 77; the highest average of any applicant was 81.   Applicants with averages above 77 were considered as their applications arrived by random distribution of their files to the members of the committee who would read them and report their recommendations back to the committee.   As a result of the first three committee meetings in February, March, and April 1971, 78 applicants from this group were admitted, although virtually no other applicants were offered admission this early.[2]   By the final conclusion of

---

[1] The grades are calculated on a conventional 4.0 scale, and the LSAT is scored on a scale ranging from 200 to 800.   A Writing Test given on the same day as the LSAT and administered with it is also included in the formula; it is scored on a scale of 20 to 80.   The Admissions Committee combines these scores into the Average by calculating the sum of 51.3, 3.4751 × the grade-point average, .0159 × LSAT score, and .0456 × the Writing Test score. App. 24. For a brief discussion of the use of the LSAT in combination with undergraduate grades to predict law school success, see Winterbottom, Comments on "A Study of the Criteria for Legal Education and Admission to the Bar," An Article by Dr. Thomas M. Goolsby, Jr., 21 J. Legal Ed. 75 (1968).

[2] The only other substantial group admitted at this point were 19 "military" applicants.   These were students who had previously been admitted to the school but who had either been unable to come, or forced to leave during their tenure, because of the draft.   They were

the admissions process in August 1971, 147 applicants with averages above 77 had been admitted, including all applicants with averages above 78, and 93 of 105 applicants with averages between 77 and 78.

Also beginning early in the admissions process was the culling out of applicants with averages below 74.5. These were reviewed by the Chairman of the Admissions Committee, who had the authority to reject them summarily without further consideration by the rest of the Committee. A small number of these applications were saved by the Chairman for committee consideration on the basis of information in the file indicating greater promise than suggested by the Average. Finally during the early months the Committee accumulated the applications of those with averages between 74.5 and 77 to be considered at a later time when most of the applications had been received and thus could be compared with one another. Since DeFunis' average was 76.23, he was in this middle group.

Beginning in their May meeting the Committee considered this middle group of applicants, whose folders had been randomly distributed to Committee members for their recommendations to the Committee. Also considered at this time were remaining applicants with averages below 74.5 who had not been summarily rejected, and some of those with averages above 77 who had not been summarily admitted, but instead held for further consideration. Each Committee member would consider the applications competitively, following rough guide-

given preferential treatment upon reapplication after completing their military obligation. Since neither party has raised any issue concerning this group of applicants, the remaining consideration of the admissions procedure will not discuss them. Four minority applicants were also admitted at this time, although none apparently had scores above 77. App. 31. Their admission was presumably pursuant to the procedure for minority applicants described below.

lines as to the proportion who could be offered admission. After the Committee had extended offers of admission to somewhat over 200 applicants, a waiting list was constructed in the same fashion, and was divided into four groups ranked by the Committee's assessment of their applications. DeFunis was on this waiting list, but was ranked in the lowest quarter. He was ultimately told in August 1971 that there would be no room for him.

Applicants who had indicated on their application forms that they were either Black, Chicano, American Indian, or Filipino were treated differently in several respects. Whatever their averages, none were given to the Committee Chairman for consideration of summary rejection, nor were they distributed randomly among committee members for consideration along with the other applications. Instead, all applications of Black students were assigned separately to two particular Committee members: a first-year Black law student on the Committee, and a professor on the Committee who had worked the previous summer in a special program for disadvantaged college students considering application to Law School.[3] Applications from among the other three minority groups were assigned to an assistant dean who was on the Committee. The minority applications, while considered competitively with one another, were never directly compared to the remaining applications, either by the subcommittee or by the full Committee. As in the admissions process generally, the Committee sought to find "within the minority category, those persons who we thought had the highest probability of

---

[3] This was a Council on Legal Education Opportunities program, federally funded by the Office of Economic Opportunity and sponsored by the American Bar Association, the Association of American Law Schools, the National Bar Association, and the Law School Admissions Council.

succeeding in Law School." [4]   In reviewing the minority applications, the Committee attached less weight to the Average "in making a total judgmental evaluation as to the relative ability of the particular applicant to succeed in law school." 82 Wash. 2d 11, 21, 507 P. 2d 1169, 1175. In its publicly distributed Guide to Applicants, the Committee explained that "[a]n applicant's racial or ethnic background was considered as one factor in our general attempt to convert formal credentials into realistic predictions." [5]

Thirty-seven minority applicants were admitted under this procedure. Of these, 36 had Averages below De-Funis' 76.23, and 30 had averages below 74.5, and thus would ordinarily have been summarily rejected by the Chairman. There were also 48 nonminority applicants admitted who had Averages below DeFunis. Twenty-three of these were returning veterans, see n. 2, *supra,* and 25 others presumably admitted because of other factors in

---

[4] Testimony of the Chairman of the Admissions Committee, Statement of Facts 353.

[5] The Guide to Applicants explained:

"We gauged the potential for outstanding performance in law school not only from the existence of high test scores and grade point averages, but also from careful analysis of recommendations, the quality of work in difficult analytical seminars, courses, and writing programs, the academic standards of the school attended by the applicant, the applicant's graduate work (if any), and the nature of the applicant's employment (if any), since graduation.

"An applicant's ability to make significant contributions to law school classes and the community at large was assessed from such factors as his extracurricular and community activities, employment, and general background.

"We gave no preference to, but did not discriminate against, either Washington residents or women in making our determinations. An applicant's racial or ethnic background was considered as one factor in our general attempt to convert formal credentials into realistic predictions." 82 Wash. 2d 11, 18–19, 507 P. 2d 1169, 1174.

their applications making them attractive candidates despite their relatively low averages.

It is reasonable to conclude from the above facts that while other factors were considered by the Committee, and were on occasion crucial, the Average was for most applicants a heavily weighted factor, and was at the extremes virtually dispositive.[6] A different balance was apparently struck, however, with regard to the minority applicants. Indeed, at oral argument, the Law School advised us that were the minority applicants considered under the same procedure as was generally used, none of those who eventually enrolled at the Law School would have been admitted.

The educational policy choices confronting a university admissions committee are not ordinarily a subject for judicial oversight; clearly it is not for us but for the law school to decide which tests to employ, how heavily to weigh recommendations from professors or undergraduate grades, and what level of achievement on the chosen criteria are sufficient to demonstrate that the candidate is qualified for admission. What places this case in a special category is the fact that the school did not choose one set of criteria but two, and then determined which to apply to a given applicant on the basis of his race. The

---

[6] The respondents provided the following table in response to an interrogatory during the proceedings in the state court:

First Year Averages	Number of Applications Received	Number Accepted
81	1	1
80	2	2
79	11	11
78	42	42
77	105	93
76	169	53
75	210	22

App. 34.

Committee adopted this policy in order to achieve "a reasonable representation" of minority groups in the Law School. 82 Wash. 2d, at 20, 507 P. 2d, at 1175. Although it may be speculated that the Committee sought to rectify what it perceived to be cultural or racial biases in the LSAT or in the candidates' undergraduate records, the record in this case is devoid of any evidence of such bias, and the school has not sought to justify its procedures on this basis.

Although testifying that "[w]e do not have a quota ..." the Law School dean explained that "[w]e want a reasonable representation. We will go down to reach it if we can," without "taking people who are unqualified in an absolute sense . . . ." (Statement of Facts 420.) By "unqualified in an absolute sense" the dean meant candidates who "have no reasonable probable likelihood of having a chance of succeeding in the study of law . . . ." (*Ibid.*) But the dean conceded that in "reaching," the school does take "some minority students who at least, viewed as a group, have a less such likelihood than the majority student group taken as a whole." (*Id.*, at 423.)

> "Q. Of those who have made application to go to the law school, I am saying you are not taking the best qualified?
> "A. In total?
> "Q. In total.
> "A. In using that definition, yes." (*Id.*, at 423–424.)

It thus appears that by the Committee's own assessment, it admitted minority students who, by the tests given, seemed less qualified than some white students who were not accepted, in order to achieve a "reasonable representation." In this regard it may be pointed out that for the year 1969–1970—the year before the class to which DeFunis was seeking admission—the Law School reported an enrollment of eight Black students out of a total of 356.[7] (Defendants' Ex. 7.) That percentage, approximately 2.2%, compares to a percentage of Blacks in the population of Washington of approximately 2.1%.[8]

II

There was a time when law schools could follow the advice of Wigmore, who believed that "the way to find out whether a boy has the makings of a competent lawyer is to see what he can do in a first year of law studies." Wigmore, Juristic Psychopoyemetrology—Or, How to Find Out Whether a Boy Has the Makings of a Lawyer, 24 Ill. L. Rev. 454, 463–464 (1929). In those days there were enough spaces to admit every applicant who met minimal credentials, and they all could be given the opportunity to prove themselves at law school. But by the 1920's many law schools found that they could not admit all minimally qualified applicants, and some selection process began.[9] The pressure to use some kind of admissions test mounted, and a number of schools instituted them. One early precursor to the modern day LSAT was the Ferson-Stoddard Law Aptitude examination. Wigmore conducted his own study of that test with 50 student volunteers, and concluded that it "had no substantial practical value." *Id.*, at 463. But his conclusions were not accepted, and the harried law

---

[7] Although there is apparently no evidence in point in the record, respondents suggest that at least some of these eight students were also admitted on a preferential basis. Brief for Respondents 40 n. 27.

[8] United States Bureau of the Census, Census of Population: 1970, General Population Characteristics, Washington, Final Report PC (1)—B49, Table 18.

[9] For a history of gradual acceptance among law schools of standardized tests as an admission tool, see Ramsey, Law School Admissions: Science, Art, or Hunch?, 12 J. Legal Ed. 503 (1960).

schools still sought some kind of admissions test which
would simplify the process of judging applicants, and in
1948 the LSAT was born. It has been with us ever
since.[10]

The test purports to predict how successful the applicant will be in his first year of law school, and consists of
a few hours' worth of multiple-choice questions. But the
answers the student can give to a multiple-choice question are limited by the creativity and intelligence of the
test-maker; the student with a better or more original
understanding of the problem than the test-maker may
realize that none of the alternative answers are any good,
but there is no way for him to demonstrate his understanding. "It is obvious from the nature of the tests
that they do not give the candidate a significant opportunity to express himself. If he is subtle in his choice
of answers it will go against him; and yet there is no
other way for him to show any individuality. If he is
strong-minded, nonconformist, unusual, original, or creative—as so many of the truly important people are—he
must stifle his impulses and conform as best he can to
the norms that the multiple-choice testers set up in their
unimaginative, scientific way. The more profoundly
gifted the candidate is, the more his resentment will rise
against the mental strait jacket into which the testers
would force his mind." B. Hoffmann, The Tyranny of
Testing 91–92 (1962).

Those who make the tests and the law schools which
use them point, of course, to the high correlations between the test scores and the grades at law school the
first year. *E. g.,* Winterbottom, Comments on "A Study
of the Criteria for Legal Education and Admission to the

---

[10] For a survey of the use of the LSAT by American law schools
as of 1965, see Lunneborg & Radford, The LSAT: A Survey of
Actual Practice, 18 J. Legal Ed. 313 (1966).

Bar," An Article by Dr. Thomas M. Goolsby, Jr., 21 J. Legal Ed. 75 (1968). Certainly the tests do seem to do better than chance. But they do not have the value that their deceptively precise scoring system suggests. The proponents' own data show that, for example, most of those scoring in the bottom 20% on the test do better than that in law school—indeed six of every 100 of them will be in the *top* 20% of their law school class. *Id.*, at 79. And no one knows how many of those who were not admitted because of their test scores would in fact have done well were they given the chance. There are many relevant factors, such as motivation, cultural backgrounds of specific minorities that the test cannot measure, and they inevitably must impair its value as a predictor.[11] Of course, the law school that admits only those with the highest test scores finds that on the average they do much better, and thus the test is a convenient tool for the admissions committee. The price is paid by the able student who for unknown reasons did not achieve that high score—perhaps even the minority with a different cultural background. Some tests, at least in the past, have been aimed at eliminating Jews.

The school can safely conclude that the applicant with a score of 750 should be admitted before one with a score of 500. The problem is that in many cases the choice will be between 643 and 602 or 574 and 528. The numbers create an illusion of difference tending to overwhelm other factors. "The wiser testers are well aware of the defects of the multiple-choice format and the danger of placing reliance on any one method of assessment to the exclusion of all others. What is distressing is how little their caveats have impressed the people who succumb to the propaganda of the test-

---

[11] Rock, Motivation, Moderators, and Test Bias, 1970 U. Tol. L. Rev. 527, 535.

makers and use these tests mechanically as though they were a valid substitute for judgment." Hoffmann, *supra,* at 215.

Of course, the tests are not the only thing considered; here they were combined with the prelaw grades to produce a new number called the Average. The grades have their own problems; one school's A is another school's C. And even to the extent that this formula predicts law school grades, its value is limited. The law student with lower grades may in the long pull of a legal career surpass those at the top of the class. "[L]aw school admissions criteria have operated within a hermetically sealed system; it is now beginning to leak. The traditional combination of LSAT and GPA [undergraduate grade point average] may have provided acceptable predictors of likely performance in law school in the past. . . . [But] [t]here is no clear evidence that the LSAT and GPA provide particularly good evaluators of the intrinsic or enriched ability of an individual to perform as a law student or lawyer in a functioning society undergoing change. Nor is there any clear evidence that grades and other evaluators of law school performance, and the bar examination, are particularly good predicators of competence or success as a lawyer." Rosen, Equalizing Access to Legal Education: Special Programs for Law Students Who Are Not Admissible by Traditional Criteria, 1970 U. Tol. L. Rev. 321, 332–333.

But, by whatever techniques, the law school must make choices. Neither party has challenged the validity of the Average employed here as an admissions tool, and therefore consideration of its possible deficiencies is not presented as an issue. The Law School presented no evidence to show that adjustments in the process employed were used in order validly to compare applicants of different races; instead, it chose to avoid making such comparisons. Finally, although the Committee did consider other information in the files of all applicants, the Law School has made no effort to show that it was because of these additional factors that it admitted minority applicants who would otherwise have been rejected. To the contrary, the school appears to have conceded that by its own assessment—taking all factors into account—it admitted minority applicants who would have been rejected had they been white. We have no choice but to evaluate the Law School's case as it has been made.

III

The Equal Protection Clause did not enact a requirement that Law Schools employ as the sole criterion for admissions a formula based upon the LSAT and undergraduate grades, nor does it prohibit law schools from evaluating an applicant's prior achievements in light of the barriers that he had to overcome. A Black applicant who pulled himself out of the ghetto into a junior college may thereby demonstrate a level of motivation, perseverance and ability that would lead a fairminded admissions committee to conclude that he shows more promise for law study than the son of a rich alumnus who achieved better grades at Harvard. That applicant would not be offered admission because he is Black, but because as an individual he has shown he has the potential, while the Harvard man may have taken less advantage of the vastly superior opportunities offered him. Because of the weight of the prior handicaps, that Black applicant may not realize his full potential in the first year of law school, or even in the full three years, but in the long pull of a legal career his achievements may far outstrip those of his classmates whose earlier records appeared superior by conventional criteria. There is currently no test available to the Admissions

Committee that can predict such possibilities with assurance, but the Committee may nevertheless seek to gauge it as best it can, and weigh this factor in its decisions. Such a policy would not be limited to Blacks, or Chicanos or Filipinos, or American Indians, although undoubtedly groups such as these may in practice be the principal beneficiaries of it. But a poor Appalachian white, or a second generation Chinese in San Francisco, or some other American whose lineage is so diverse as to defy ethnic labels, may demonstrate similar potential and thus be accorded favorable consideration by the committee.

The difference between such a policy and the one presented by this case is that the Committee would be making decisions on the basis of individual attributes, rather than according a preference solely on the basis of race. To be sure, the racial preference here was not absolute—the Committee did not admit all applicants from the four favored groups. But it did accord all such applicants a preference by applying, to an extent not precisely ascertainable from the record, different standards by which to judge their applications, with the result that the Committee admitted minority applicants who, in the school's own judgment, were less promising than other applicants who were rejected. Furthermore, it is apparent that because the Admissions Committee compared minority applicants only with one another, it was necessary to reserve some proportion of the class for them, even if at the outset a precise number of places were not set aside.[12] That proportion, apparently 15% to

---

[12] At the outset the Committee may have chosen only a range, with the precise number to be determined later in the process as the total number of minority applicants, and some tentative assessment of their quality, could be determined. This appears to be the current articulated policy, see Appendix § 6, and we are advised by the respondents that § 6 "represents a more formal statement of the policy which was in effect in 1971 . . . but does not represent

20%, was chosen because the school determined it to be "reasonable," [13] although no explanation is provided as to how that number rather than some other was found appropriate. Without becoming embroiled in a semantic debate over whether this practice constitutes a "quota," it is clear that, given the limitation on the total number of applicants who could be accepted, this policy did reduce the total number of places for which DeFunis could compete—solely on account of his race. Thus, as the Washington Supreme Court concluded, whatever label one wishes to apply to it, "the minority admissions policy is certainly not benign with respect to nonminority students who are displaced by it." 82 Wash. 2d, at 32, 507 P. 2d, at 1182. A finding that the state school employed a racial classification in selecting its students subjects it to the strictest scrutiny under the Equal Protection Clause.

The consideration of race as a measure of an applicant's qualification normally introduces a capricious and irrelevant factor working an invidious discrimination, *Anderson* v. *Martin*, 375 U. S. 399, 402; *Loving* v. *Virginia*, 388 U. S. 1, 10; *Harper* v. *Virginia Board of Elections*, 383 U. S. 663, 668. Once race is a starting point educators and courts are immediately embroiled in competing claims of different racial and ethnic groups that would make difficult, manageable standards consistent

---

any change in policy." Letter to the Court dated March 19, 1974, p. 1. The fact that the Committee did not set a precise number in advance is obviously irrelevant to the legal analysis. Nor does it matter that there is some minimal level of achievement below which the Committee would not reach in order to achieve its stated goal as to the proportion of the class reserved for minority groups, so long as the Committee was willing, in order to achieve that goal, to admit minority applicants who, in the Committee's own judgment, were less qualified than other rejected applicants and who would not otherwise have been admitted.

[13] See n. 12, *supra,* and Appendix § 6.

with the Equal Protection Clause. "The clear and central purpose of the Fourteenth Amendment was to eliminate all official state sources of invidious racial discrimination in the States." *Loving, supra,* at 10. The Law School's admissions policy cannot be reconciled with that purpose, unless cultural standards of a diverse rather than a homogeneous society are taken into account. The reason is that professional persons, particularly lawyers, are not selected for life in a computerized society. The Indian who walks to the beat of Chief Seattle of the Muckleshoot Tribe in Washington [14] has a different culture from examiners at law schools.

The key to the problem is the consideration of each application *in a racially neutral way.* Since LSAT reflects questions touching on cultural backgrounds, the Admissions Committee acted properly in my view in setting minority applications apart for separate processing. These minorities have cultural backgrounds that are vastly different from the dominant Caucasian. Many Eskimos, American Indians, Filipinos, Chicanos, Asian Indians, Burmese, and Africans come from such disparate backgrounds that a test sensitively tuned for most applicants would be wide of the mark for many minorities.

The melting pot is not designed to homogenize people, making them uniform in consistency. The melting pot as I understand it is a figure of speech that depicts the wide diversities tolerated by the First Amendment under one flag. See 2 S. Morison & H. Commager, The Growth of the American Republic, c. VIII (4th ed. 1950). Minorities in our midst who are to serve actively in our public affairs should be chosen on talent and character alone, not on cultural orientation or leanings.

---

[14] Uncommon Controversy, Report Prepared for American Friends Service Committee 29–30 (1970).

I do know, coming as I do from Indian country in Washington, that many of the young Indians know little about Adam Smith or Karl Marx but are deeply imbued with the spirit and philosophy of Chief Robert B. Jim of the Yakimas, Chief Seattle of the Muckleshoots, and Chief Joseph of the Nez Perce which offer competitive attitudes towards life, fellow man, and nature.[15]

I do not know the extent to which Blacks in this country are imbued with ideas of African Socialism.[16] Leopold Senghor and Sékou Touré, most articulate of African leaders, have held that modern African political philosophy is not oriented either to Marxism or to capitalism.[17] How far the reintroduction into educational curricula of ancient African art and history has reached the minds of young Afro-Americans I do not know. But at least as respects Indians, Blacks, and Chicanos—as well as those from Asian cultures—I think a separate classification of these applicants is warranted, lest race be a subtle force in eliminating minority members because of cultural differences.

Insofar as LSAT tests reflect the dimensions and orientation of the Organization Man they do a disservice to minorities. I personally know that admissions tests were once used to eliminate Jews. How many other minorities they aim at I do not know. My reaction is that the presence of an LSAT test is sufficient warrant for a school to put racial minorities into a separate class in order better to probe their capacities and potentials.

The merits of the present controversy cannot in my view be resolved on this record. A trial would

---

[15] See C. Fee, Chief Joseph, The Biography of a Great Indian (1936).

[16] See F. Brockway, African Socialism (1963); African Socialism (W. Friedland & C. Rosberg ed. 1964).

[17] See L. Senghor, On African Socialism (M. Cook ed. 1964).

involve the disclosure of hidden prejudices, if any, against certain minorities and the manner in which substitute measurements of one's talents and character were employed in the conventional tests. I could agree with the majority of the Washington Supreme Court only if, on the record, it could be said that the Law School's selection was racially neutral. The case, in my view, should be remanded for a new trial to consider, *inter alia*, whether the established LSAT tests should be eliminated so far as racial minorities are concerned.

This does not mean that a separate LSAT test must be designed for minority racial groups, although that might be a possibility. The reason for the separate treatment of minorities as a class is to make more certain that racial factors do not militate *against an applicant or on his behalf*.[18]

There is no constitutional right for any race to be preferred. The years of slavery did more than retard the progress of Blacks. Even a greater wrong was done the whites by creating arrogance instead of humility and by encouraging the growth of the fiction of a superior race.

---

[18] We are not faced here with a situation where barriers are overtly or covertly put in the path of members of one racial group which are not required by others. There was also no showing that the purpose of the school's policy was to eliminate arbitrary and irrelevant barriers to entry by certain racial groups into the legal profession groups. *Griggs* v. *Duke Power Co.*, 401 U. S. 424. In *Swann* v. *Charlotte-Mecklenburg Board of Education*, 402 U. S. 1, 16, we stated that as a matter of educational policy school authorities could, within their broad discretion, specify that each school within its district have a prescribed ratio of Negro to white students reflecting the proportion for the district as a whole, in order to disestablish a dual school system. But there is a crucial difference between the policy suggested in *Swann* and that under consideration here: the *Swann* policy would impinge on no person's constitutional rights, because no one would be excluded from a public school and no one has a right to attend a segregated public school.

There is no superior person by constitutional standards. A DeFunis who is white is entitled to no advantage by reason of that fact; nor is he subject to any disability, no matter what his race or color. Whatever his race, he had a constitutional right to have his application considered on its individual merits in a racially neutral manner.

The slate is not entirely clean. First, we have held that *pro rata* representation of the races is not required either on juries, see *Cassell* v. *Texas,* 339 U. S. 282, 286–287, or in public schools, *Swann* v. *Charlotte-Mecklenburg Board of Education,* 402 U. S. 1, 24. Moreover, in *Hughes* v. *Superior Court,* 339 U. S. 460, we reviewed the contempt convictions of pickets who sought by their demonstration to force an employer to prefer Negroes to whites in his hiring of clerks, in order to ensure that 50% of the employees were Negro. In finding that California could constitutionally enjoin the picketing there involved we quoted from the opinion of the California Supreme Court, which noted that the pickets would " 'make the right to work for Lucky dependent not on fitness for the work nor on an equal right of all, regardless of race, to compete in an open market, but, rather, on membership in a particular race. If petitioners were upheld in their demand then other races, white, yellow, brown and red, would have equal rights to demand discriminatory hiring on a racial basis.' " *Id.,* at 463–464. We then noted that

> "[t]o deny to California the right to ban picketing in the circumstances of this case would mean that there could be no prohibition of the pressure of picketing to secure proportional employment on ancestral grounds of Hungarians in Cleveland, of Poles in Buffalo, of Germans in Milwaukee, of Portuguese in New Bedford, of Mexicans in San Antonio, of the

numerous minority groups in New York, and so on through the whole gamut of racial and religious concentrations in various cities." *Id.,* at 464.

The reservation of a proportion of the law school class for members of selected minority groups is fraught with similar dangers, for one must immediately determine which groups are to receive such favored treatment and which are to be excluded, the proportions of the class that are to be allocated to each, and even the criteria by which to determine whether an individual is a member of a favored group. There is no assurance that a common agreement can be reached, and first the schools, and then the courts, will be buffeted with the competing claims. The University of Washington included Filipinos, but excluded Chinese and Japanese; another school may limit its program to Blacks, or to Blacks and Chicanos. Once the Court sanctioned racial preferences such as these, it could not then wash its hands of the matter, leaving it entirely in the discretion of the school, for then we would have effectively overruled *Sweatt* v. *Painter,* 339 U. S. 629, and allowed imposition of a "zero" allocation.[19] But what standard is the Court to apply when a rejected applicant of Japanese ancestry brings suit to require the University of Washington to extend the same privileges to his group? The Committee might conclude that the population of Washington is now 2% Japanese, and that Japanese also constitute 2% of the

---

[19] *Sweatt* held that a State could not justify denying a black admission to its regular law school by creating a new law school for blacks. We held that the new law school did not meet the requirements of "equality" set forth in *Plessy* v. *Ferguson,* 163 U. S. 537.

The student, we said, was entitled to "legal education equivalent to that offered by the State to students of other races. Such education is not available to him in a separate law school as offered by the State." 339 U. S. 629, 635.

Bar, but that had they not been handicapped by a history of discrimination, Japanese would now constitute 5% of the Bar, or 20%. Or, alternatively, the Court could attempt to assess how grievously each group has suffered from discrimination, and allocate proportions accordingly; if that were the standard the current University of Washington policy would almost surely fall, for there is no Western State which can claim that it has always treated Japanese and Chinese in a fair and evenhanded manner. See, *e. g., Yick Wo* v. *Hopkins,* 118 U. S. 356; *Terrace* v. *Thompson,* 263 U. S. 197; *Oyama* v. *California,* 332 U. S. 633. This Court has not sustained a racial classification since the wartime cases of *Korematsu* v. *United States,* 323 U. S. 214 (1944), and *Hirabayashi* v. *United States,* 320 U. S. 81 (1943), involving curfews and relocations imposed upon Japanese-Americans.[20]

---

[20] Those cases involved an exercise of the war power, a great leveler of other rights. Our Navy was sunk at Pearl Harbor and no one knew where the Japanese fleet was. We were advised on oral argument that if the Japanese landed troops on our west coast nothing could stop them west of the Rockies. The military judgment was that, to aid in the prospective defense of the west coast, the enclaves of Americans of Japanese ancestry should be moved inland, lest the invaders by donning civilian clothes would wreak even more serious havoc on our western ports. The decisions were extreme and went to the verge of wartime power; and they have been severely criticized. It is, however, easy in retrospect to denounce what was done, as there actually was no attempted Japanese invasion of our country. While our Joint Chiefs of Staff were worrying about Japanese soldiers landing on the west coast, they actually were landing in Burma and at Kota Bharu in Malaya. But those making plans for defense of the Nation had no such knowledge and were planning for the worst. Moreover, the day we decided *Korematsu* we also decided *Ex parte Endo,* 323 U. S. 283, holding that while evacuation of the Americans of Japanese ancestry was allowable under extreme war conditions, their detention after evacuation was not. We said:

"A citizen who is concededly loyal presents no problem of espio-

Nor obviously will the problem be solved if next year the Law School included only Japanese and Chinese, for then Norwegians and Swedes, Poles and Italians, Puerto Ricans and Hungarians, and all other groups which form this diverse Nation would have just complaints.

The key to the problem is consideration of such applications *in a racially neutral way*. Abolition of the LSAT would be a start. The invention of substitute tests might be made to get a measure of an applicant's cultural background, perception, ability to analyze, and his or her relation to groups. They are highly subjective, but unlike the LSAT they are not concealed, but in the open. A law school is not bound by any legal principle to admit students by mechanical criteria which are insensitive to the potential of such an applicant which may be realized in a more hospitable environment. It will be necessary under such an approach to put more effort into assessing each individual than is required when LSAT scores and undergraduate grades dominate the selection process. Interviews with the applicant and others who know him is a time-honored test. Some schools currently run summer programs in which potential students who likely would be bypassed under conventional admissions criteria are given the opportunity to try their hand at law courses,[21] and certainly their performance in such programs could be weighed heavily. There is, moreover, no bar to considering an individual's prior achievements in

_____

nage or sabotage. Loyalty is a matter of the heart and mind, not of race, creed, or color. He who is loyal is by definition not a spy or a saboteur. When the power to detain is derived from the power to protect the war effort against espionage and sabotage, detention which has no relationship to that objective is unauthorized." *Id.*, at 302.

[21] See n. 3, *supra*.

light of the racial discrimination that barred his way, as a factor in attempting to assess his true potential for a successful legal career. Nor is there any bar to considering on an individual basis, rather than according to racial classifications, the likelihood that a particular candidate will more likely employ his legal skills to service communities that are not now adequately represented than will competing candidates. Not every student benefited by such an expanded admissions program would fall into one of the four racial groups involved here, but it is no drawback that other deserving applicants will also get an opportunity they would otherwise have been denied. Certainly such a program would substantially fulfill the Law School's interest in giving a more diverse group access to the legal profession. Such a program might be less convenient administratively than simply sorting students by race, but we have never held administrative convenience to justify racial discrimination.

The argument is that a "compelling" state interest can easily justify the racial discrimination that is practiced here. To many, "compelling" would give members of one race even more than *pro rata* representation. The public payrolls might then be deluged say with Chicanos because they are as a group the poorest of the poor and need work more than others, leaving desperately poor individual Blacks and whites without employment. By the same token large quotas of blacks or browns could be added to the Bar, waiving examinations required of other groups, so that it would be better racially balanced.[22]

---

[22] In *Johnson* v. *Committee on Examinations*, 407 U. S. 915, we denied certiorari in a case presenting a similar issue. There the petitioner claimed that the bar examiners reconsidered the papers submitted by failing minority applicants whose scores were close to the cutoff point, with the result that some minority appli-

The State, however, may not proceed by racial classification to force strict population equivalencies for every group in every occupation, overriding individual preferences. The Equal Protection Clause commands the elimination of racial barriers, not their creation in order to satisfy our theory as to how society ought to be organized. The purpose of the University of Washington cannot be to produce Black lawyers for Blacks, Polish lawyers for Poles, Jewish lawyers for Jews, Irish lawyers for Irish. It should be to produce good lawyers for Americans and not to place First Amendment barriers against anyone.²³ That is the point at the heart of all our

---

cants were admitted to the Bar although they initially had examination scores lower than those of white applicants who failed.

As the Arizona Supreme Court denied Johnson admission summarily, in an original proceeding, there were no judicial findings either sustaining or rejecting his factual claims of racial bias, putting the case in an awkward posture for review here. Johnson subsequently brought a civil rights action in Federal District Court, seeking both damages and injunctive relief. The District Court dismissed the action and the Court of Appeals affirmed, holding that the lower federal courts did not have jurisdiction to review the decisions of the Arizona Supreme Court on admissions to the state bar. Johnson then sought review here and we denied his motion for leave to file a petition for mandamus, prohibition and/or certiorari on February 19, 1974. *Johnson* v. *Wilmer*, 415 U. S. 911. Thus in the entire history of the case no court had ever actually sustained Johnson's factual contentions concerning racial bias in the bar examiners' procedures. *DeFunis* thus appears to be the first case here squarely presenting the problem.

²³ Underlying all cultural background tests are potential ideological issues that have plagued bar associations and the courts. *In re Summers*, 325 U. S. 561, involved the denial of the practice of law to a man who could not conscientiously bear arms. The vote against him was five to four. *Konigsberg* v. *State Bar*, 353 U. S. 252, followed, after remand, by *Konigsberg* v. *State Bar*, 366 U. S. 36, resulted in barring one from admission to a state bar because of his refusal to answer questions concerning Communist Party member-

school desegregation cases, from *Brown* v. *Board of Education*, 347 U. S. 483, through *Swann* v. *Charlotte-Mecklenburg Board of Education*, 402 U. S. 1. A segregated admissions process creates suggestions of stigma and caste no less than a segregated classroom, and in the end it may produce that result despite its contrary intentions. One other assumption must be clearly disapproved, that Blacks or Browns cannot make it on their individual merit. That is a stamp of inferiority that a State is not permitted to place on any lawyer.

If discrimination based on race is constitutionally permissible when those who hold the reins can come up with "compelling" reasons to justify it, then constitutional guarantees acquire an accordionlike quality. Speech is closely brigaded with action when it triggers a fight, *Chaplinsky* v. *New Hampshire*, 315 U. S. 568, as shouting "fire" in a crowded theater triggers a riot. It may well be that racial strains, racial susceptibility to certain diseases, racial sensitiveness to environmental conditions that other races do not experience, may in an extreme situation justify differences in racial treatment that no fairminded person would call "invidious" discrimination. Mental ability is not in that category. All races can compete fairly at all professional levels. So

---

ship. He, too, was excluded five to four. The petitioner in *Schware* v. *Board of Bar Examiners*, 353 U. S. 232, was, however, admitted to practice even though he had about 10 years earlier been a member of the Communist Party. But in *In re Anastaplo*, 366 U. S. 82, a five-to-four decision, barred a man from admission to a state bar not because he invoked the Fifth Amendment when asked about membership in the Communist Party, but because he asserted that the First Amendment protected him from that inquiry. *Baird* v. *State Bar of Arizona*, 401 U. S. 1, held by a divided vote that a person could not be kept out of the state bar for refusing to answer whether he had ever been a member of the Communist Party; and see *In re Stolar*, 401 U. S. 23.

far as race is concerned, any state-sponsored preference to one race over another in that competition is in my view "invidious" and violative of the Equal Protection Clause.

The problem tendered by this case is important and crucial to the operation of our constitutional system; and educators must be given leeway. It may well be that a whole congeries of applicants in the marginal group defy known methods of selection. Conceivably, an admissions committee might conclude that a selection by lot of, say, the last 20 seats is the only fair solution. Courts are not educators; their expertise is limited; and our task ends with the inquiry whether, judged by the main purpose of the Equal Protection Clause—the protection against racial discrimination [24]—there has been an "invidious" discrimination.

We would have a different case if the suit were one to displace the applicant who was chosen in lieu of DeFunis. What the record would show concerning his potentials would have to be considered and weighed. The educational decision, provided proper guidelines were used, would reflect an expertise that courts should honor. The problem is not tendered here because the physical facilities were apparently adequate to take DeFunis in addition to the others. My view is only that I cannot say by the tests used and applied he was invidiously discriminated against because of his race.

I cannot conclude that the admissions procedure of the Law School of the University of Washington that excluded DeFunis is violative of the Equal Protection Clause of the Fourteenth Amendment. The judgment of the Washington Supreme Court should be vacated and the case remanded for a new trial.

---

[24] See *Slaughter House Cases*, 16 Wall. 36, 81.

APPENDIX TO OPINION OF DOUGLAS, J.,
DISSENTING

The following are excerpts from the Law School's current admissions policy, as provided to the Court by counsel for the respondents.

ADMISSIONS

A. Policy Statement Regarding Admission to Entering Classes of Juris Doctor Program—Adopted by the Law Faculty December 4, 1973.

§ 1. The objectives of the admissions program are to select and admit those applicants who have the best prospect of high quality academic work at the law school and, in the minority admissions program described below, the further objective there stated.

§ 2. In measuring academic potential the law school relies primarily on the undergraduate grade-point average and the performance on the Law School Admission Test (LSAT). The weighting of these two indicators is determined statistically by reference to past experience at this school. For most applicants the resulting applicant ranking is the most nearly accurate of all available measures of relative academic potential. In truly exceptional cases, *i. e.,* those in which the numerical indicators clearly appear to be an inaccurate measure of academic potential, the admission decision indicated by them alone may be altered by a consideration of the factors listed below. The number of these truly exceptional cases in any particular year should fall somewhere from zero to approximately forty. These factors are used, however, only as an aid in assessing the applicant's academic potential in its totality, without undue emphasis or reliance upon one or a few and without an attempt to quantify in advance the strength of their application, singly or as a whole, in a particular case. They are:

a) the difficulty or ease of the undergraduate curriculum track pursued;

b) the demanding or non-demanding quality of the undergraduate school or department;

c) the attainment of an advanced degree, the nature thereof, and difficulty or ease of its attainment;

d) the applicant's pursuits subsequent to attainment of the undergraduate degree and the degree of success therein, as bearing on the applicant's academic potential;

e) the possibility that an applicant many years away from academic work may do less well on the LSAT than his or her counterpart presently or recently in academic work;

f) substantial change in mental or physical health that indicates prospect for either higher or lower quality of academic work;

g) substantial change in economic pressures or other circumstances that indicates prospect for either higher or lower quality of academic work;

h) exceptionally good or bad performance upon the writing test ingredient of the LSAT, if the current year's weighting of the numerical indicators does not otherwise take the writing score into account;

i) the quality and strength of recommendations bearing upon the applicant's academic potential;

j) objective indicators of motivation to succeed at the academic study of law;

k) variations in the level of academic achievement over time; and

l) any other indicators that serve the objective stated above.

§ 6. Because certain ethnic groups in our society

have historically been limited in their access to the legal profession and because the resulting underrepresentation can affect the quality of legal services available to members of such groups, as well as limit their opportunity for full participation in the governance of our communities, the faculty recognizes a special obligation in its admissions policy to contribute to the solution of the problem.

Qualified minority applicants are therefore admitted under the minority admissions program in such number that the entering class will have a reasonable proportion of minority persons, in view of the obligation stated above and of the overall objective of the law school to provide legal education for qualified persons generally. For the purpose of determining the number to be specially admitted under the program, and not as a ceiling on minority admissions generally, the faculty currently believes that approximately 15 to 20 percent is such a reasonable proportion if there are sufficient qualified applicants available. Under the minority admissions program, admission is offered to those applicants who have a reasonable prospect of academic success at the law school, determined in each case by considering the numerical indicators along with the listed factors in Section 2, above, but without regard to the restriction upon number contained in that section.

No particular internal percentage or proportion among various minority groups in the entering class is specified; rather, the law school strives for a reasonable internal balance given the particular makeup of each year's applicant population.

As to some or all ethnic groups within the scope of the minority admissions program, it may be appropriate to give a preference in some degree to residents of the state; that determination is made each year in view of all the particulars of that year's situation, and the preference is given when necessary to meet some substantial local need for minority representation.

MR. JUSTICE BRENNAN, with whom MR. JUSTICE DOUG-LAS, MR. JUSTICE WHITE, and MR. JUSTICE MARSHALL concur, dissenting.

I respectfully dissent. Many weeks of the school term remain, and petitioner may not receive his degree despite respondents' assurances that petitioner will be allowed to complete this term's schooling regardless of our decision. Any number of unexpected events—illness, economic necessity, even academic failure—might prevent his graduation at the end of the term. Were that misfortune to befall, and were petitioner required to register for yet another term, the prospect that he would again face the hurdle of the admissions policy is real, not fanciful; for respondents warn that "Mr. DeFunis would have to take some appropriate action to request continued admission for the remainder of his law school education, and *some discretionary action by the University on such request would have to be taken.*" Respondents' Memorandum on the Question of Mootness 3–4 (emphasis supplied). Thus, respondents' assurances have not dissipated the possibility that petitioner might once again have to run the gantlet of the University's allegedly unlawful admissions policy. The Court therefore proceeds on an erroneous premise in resting its mootness holding on a supposed inability to render any judgment that may affect one way or the other petitioner's completion of his law studies. For surely if we were to reverse the Washington Supreme Court, we could insure that, if for some reason petitioner did not graduate this spring, he would be entitled to re-enrollment at a later time on the same basis as others who have not faced the hurdle of the University's allegedly unlawful admissions policy.

In these circumstances, and because the University's position implies no concession that its admissions policy is unlawful, this controversy falls squarely within the Court's long line of decisions holding that the "[m]ere voluntary cessation of allegedly illegal conduct does not moot a case." *United States* v. *Phosphate Export Assn.*, 393 U. S. 199, 203 (1968); see *Gray* v. *Sanders*, 372 U. S. 368 (1963); *United States* v. *W. T. Grant Co.*, 345 U. S. 629 (1953); *Walling* v. *Helmerich & Payne, Inc.*, 323 U. S. 37 (1944); *FTC* v. *Goodyear Tire & Rubber Co.*, 304 U. S. 257 (1938); *United States* v. *Trans-Missouri Freight Assn.*, 166 U. S. 290 (1897). Since respondents' voluntary representation to this Court is only that they will permit petitioner to complete this term's studies, respondents have not borne the "heavy burden," *United States* v. *Phosphate Export Assn., supra,* at 203, of demonstrating that there was not even a "mere possibility" that petitioner would once again be subject to the challenged admissions policy. *United States* v. *W. T. Grant Co., supra,* at 633. On the contrary, respondents have positioned themselves so as to be "free to return to [their] old ways." *Id.,* at 632.

I can thus find no justification for the Court's straining to rid itself of this dispute. While we must be vigilant to require that litigants maintain a personal stake in the outcome of a controversy to assure that "the questions will be framed with the necessary specificity, that the issues will be contested with the necessary adverseness and that the litigation will be pursued with the necessary vigor to assure that the constitutional challenge will be made in a form traditionally thought to be capable of judicial resolution," *Flast* v. *Cohen*, 392 U. S. 83, 106 (1968), there is no want of an adversary contest in this case. Indeed, the Court concedes that, if petitioner has lost his stake in this controversy, he did so only when he registered for the spring term. But petitioner took that action only after the case had been fully litigated in the state courts, briefs had been filed in this Court, and oral argument had been heard. The case is thus ripe for decision on a fully developed factual record with sharply defined and fully canvassed legal issues. Cf. *Sibron* v. *New York,* 392 U. S. 40, 57 (1968).

Moreover, in endeavoring to dispose of this case as moot, the Court clearly disserves the public interest. The constitutional issues which are avoided today concern vast numbers of people, organizations, and colleges and universities, as evidenced by the filing of twenty-six *amicus curiae* briefs. Few constitutional questions in recent history have stirred as much debate, and they will not disappear. They must inevitably return to the federal courts and ultimately again to this Court. Cf. *Richardson* v. *Wright,* 405 U. S. 208, 212 (1972) (dissenting opinion). Because avoidance of repetitious litigation serves the public interest, that inevitability counsels against mootness determinations, as here, not compelled by the record. Cf. *United States* v. *W. T. Grant Co., supra,* at 632; *Parker* v. *Ellis,* 362 U. S. 574, 594 (1960) (dissenting opinion). Although the Court should, of course, avoid unnecessary decisions of constitutional questions, we should not transform principles of avoidance of constitutional decisions into devices for sidestepping resolution of difficult cases. Cf. *Cohens* v. *Virginia,* 6 Wheat. 264, 404–405 (1821) (Marshall, C. J.).

On what appears in this case, I would find that there is an extant controversy and decide the merits of the very important constitutional questions presented.

BIBLIOGRAPHY

This book has been written primarily for the general reader who is unfamiliar with legal materials. There may, however, be some interest in further inquiry or study of particular topics. Moreover, a lawyer must always be conscious of sources and authorities, even when writing without case citations or detailed footnotes. Thus it has seemed most suitable to include a brief essay on sources and legal materials, to which the interested or legally trained reader might turn for additional references. This essay is organized by chapters, and contains references both to cases and works cited in the text and to others that are pertinent although not specifically mentioned earlier.

There are several general reference sources that deserve mention at the outset. The entire set of briefs filed by the parties and all amici curiae in the *DeFunis* case (at least in the U.S. Supreme Court) has been collected and published in a three-volume edition. It appears under the title *DeFunis* Versus *Odegaard and the University of Washington* (Oceana Publications, 1974), edited by Ann Fagan Ginger. In addition to the briefs, these volumes contain the pleadings in the trial court, excerpts from the transcript of the trial, and the text of all the state court opinions as well as the U.S. Supreme Court opinions. One other general source on both legal and nonlegal aspects of minority group legal education should be mentioned. In 1970 the editors of the *Toledo Law Review* devoted two issues to a symposium entitled, "Disadvantaged Students and Legal Education—Programs for Affirmative Action," which comprises pages 277–986 of the 1970 volume.

Much of the legal material in this book has been adapted from the author's earlier articles on the subject of preferential admissions. One appears in the Toledo symposium at pages 281–320. A longer and more general discussion of both legal and policy issues is "Preferential Admissions: Equalizing the Access of Minority Groups to Higher Education," 80 *Yale Law Journal* 699–767 (1971). Two articles appeared shortly after the *DeFunis* decision, one in a *Virginia Law Review* symposium, *"DeFunis:* The Road Not Taken," 60 *Virginia Law Review* 917–1011 (1974); the other, "After *DeFunis:* Filling the Constitutional Vacuum," in 27 *University of Florida Law Review* 315–42 (1975). Some of the legal theories summarized in this book are more fully (and technically) articulated in the articles just cited.

Chapter 1

The pleadings and lower court decisions in the *DeFunis* case will, as noted above, be found in the first volume of the Ginger compilation. None of the trial court orders or findings have been officially reported.

The Washington Supreme Court decision is *DeFunis* v. *Odegaard,* 82 Wash. 2d 11, 507 P.2d 1169 (1973). (A brief word about legal case citations may be helpful to the general reader. The *DeFunis* opinion appears in the Washington state reports, which is the official series published by the state supreme court, and also in the *Pacific Reporter,* published by the West Publishing Company and including cases from a number of other states as well. Both reports are now in their second series, as the numbers indicate. The *Pacific Reporter* can be found at nearly every law library; the state court reports are available at large law school and major bar association libraries. State supreme court decisions always receive parallel citations to both the official and the unofficial reports. Later we will encounter federal court decisions for which only one reference is given. For U.S. Supreme Court decisions only one citation—to the United States Reports—will be given here.)

Much of the personal background on Marco DeFunis and the evolution of the case is found in Nina Totenberg, "Discriminating to End Discrimination," *New York Times Magazine,* April 14, 1974, p. 9. Also helpful is Mark Drucker, "Reverse Discrimination?" *College,* April 1974, p. 17. Attorney Wilson's comments on the impact of the Washington state decision are found in his article, "Admissions and Preferences: Sequel to *DeFunis,*" 1 *Journal of College and University Law* 38–45 (1973). Vice President Agnew's caustic comments about minority preference in higher education were reported in the *Chronicle of Higher Education,* April 20, 1970, p. 1.

Basic materials on the growth of demand for and on enrollment in legal education comes from the American Bar Association's *Report of the Task Force on Professional Utilization,* which appeared early in 1973. Detailed data, broken down by law schools and by trends over time, is found in *Law Schools and Bar Admission Requirements,* published periodically by the American Bar Association's Section of Legal Education and Admissions to the Bar. The fall 1973 version of this booklet contains (p. 44) a summary table on enrollments for each of the principal minority groups in all approved law schools for the academic years 1969–70 through 1973–74.

Chapter 2

Most of the material for this chapter comes, of course, from the briefs of the parties and of the many amici curiae, all reprinted in the Ginger volumes. Additional material on the tortuous course of the case through the courts is found in the March 1, 1974 issue of the *Harvard Law Record* (which dispatched a student editor to Seattle to do the story shortly before the oral argument). An excellent summary of the oral argument is found in 42 *United States Law Week*, 3496–3498 (March 5, 1974). The long vigil of the Harvard student is recounted in a spring 1974 issue of the *Harvard Law School Bulletin*, pp. 6–9. Fred Hechinger's comments on Justice Douglas's dissent are found in the *Saturday Review*, July 27, 1974, pp. 51–52.

Critical comments made after the Supreme Court decision are found in a broad range of media—*Equal Justice*, Spring 1974, p. 7; a *New York Times* editorial on April 24, 1974 (p. 36); a *Christian Science Monitor* editorial on April 25, 1974; a *Washington Post* editorial, April 26, 1974, and a number of other sources.

Several court decisions are cited in this chapter. The earlier decision on mootness, involving challenges to the New Jersey school aid program, is *Doremus* v. *Board of Education*, 342 U.S. 429 (1952). The case which immediately preceded *DeFunis*, involving a claim of mootness because the strike had ended, is *Super Tire Engineering Co.* v. *McCorkle*, 416 U.S. 115 (1974). The citation for *DeFunis* itself in the Supreme Court is 416 U.S. 312 (1974).

Many legal commentaries on the *DeFunis* case were written following the Supreme Court's disposition. In addition to the *Virginia Law Review* Symposium noted above, one might consult Professor John Ely's perceptive article, "The Constitutionality of Reverse Racial Discrimination," 41 *University of Chicago Law Review* 723–741 (1974), and that of Professor Richard Posner, in the 1974 *Supreme Court Review* (pp. 1–32), both of which are substantially at variance with the position espoused in this book. For a law student's comment on the case, see Robert Cohen, "A Postmortem on the *DeFunis* Case," *Student Lawyer*, September 1974, pp. 42–44.

Chapter 3

For general background on the admissions process, one might consult B. Alden Thresher, *College Admissions and the Public Interest* (1966); Earl McGrath, ed., *Selected Issues in College Administration* (1967); or the more practical guide by Benjamin Fine, *How to be Accepted by the College of Your Choice* (1971).

In terms of special minority group programs, an excellent study is Helen Astin et al., *Higher Education and the Disadvantaged Student* (1972). On the background of the Council on Legal Education Opportunity, see the article by Professor Sanford Rosen (then associate director of the program), in the 1970 *Toledo Law Review* at pp. 321–76. More detailed information about minority enrollments at the graduate level is found in Elaine El-Khawas, *Enrollment of Minority Graduate Students at Ph.D. Granting Institutions* (Higher Education Panel Report No. 19, August 1974); and *Minority Groups*

Among United States Doctorate Level Scientists, Engineers and Scholars, 1973 (Prepared by the Commission on Human Resources of the National Research Council, 1974). The Educational Testing Service annually publishes *Graduate and Professional Opportunities for Minority Students,* a survey listing available programs.

Data about undergraduate minority enrollments come from the annual American Council on Education surveys of entering freshmen, from the biennial HEW surveys of enrollments by race at all colleges and universities receiving federal funds (reported in detail in the *Chronicle of Higher Education*), and in special surveys by various higher education groups of their respective constituencies. These surveys have noted downturns in the matriculation of black freshmen in the fall of 1973 and 1974. Early and extremely useful studies were John Egerton, *State Universities and Black Americans* (1969); and Alan Bayer and Robert Boruch, *The Black Student in American Colleges* (1969).

The case involving the requirement of bilingual instruction for Chinese-speaking students in the San Francisco public schools is *Lau* v. *Nichols,* 414 U.S. 563 (1974).

Chapter 4

For the classic study of the origins and objectives of the equal protection clause, see Joseph Tussman and Jacobus ten Broek, *The Equal Protection of the Laws,* 37 *California Law Review* 341 (1949). The earliest decision involving individual discrimination claims was *Yick Wo.* v. *Hopkins,* 118 U.S. 356 (1886). Justice Harlan's "color blind" dictum appeared in his dissenting opinion in *Plessy* v. *Ferguson,* 163 U.S. 537, 554, 559 (1896). The central premise of *Plessy* was of course overruled and the modern concept of equality set by the Supreme Court in *Brown* v. *Board of Education,* 347 U.S. 483 (1954). The Supreme Court's casual comment about the inclusion/exclusion of Negroes from juries came in *Cassell* v. *Texas,* 339 U.S. 282 (1950).

The two cases involving (and striking down) state miscegenation and interracial cohabitation laws on equal protection grounds are *Loving* v. *Virginia,* 388 U.S. 1 (1967); and *McLaughlin* v. *Florida,* 379 U.S. 184 (1964). The district court decision allowing the use of race for certain incident record-keeping purposes is *Hamm* v. *Virginia State Board of Elections,* 230 F. Supp. 156 (E.D. Va. 1964), affirmed under the name of *Tancil* v. *Woolls,* 379 U.S. 19 (1964).

The major Supreme Court case suggesting the propriety of using race as a criterion in school desegregation is *North Carolina State Board of Education* v. *Swann,* 402 U.S. 43 (1971). There is no clear holding on this issue with regard to northern and western school imbalance, although lower federal and state courts have simply assumed that race may play a role there as well. The Supreme Court has so implied, but not squarely held, in its Denver and Detroit decisions *Milliken* v. *Bradley,* 418 U.S. 717 (1974), and *Keyes* v. *School District No. 1,* 413 U.S. 189 (1973).

In the area of employment, several federal circuits have upheld clear quota-hiring orders based explicitly on race: *Bridgeport Guardians, Inc.* v. *Members of Bridgeport Civil Service Commission,* 482 F.2d 1333 (2d Cir. 1973); *Castro* v. *Beecher,* 459 F.2d 725 (1st Cir. 1972); *Pennsylvania* v. *O'Neill,* 473 F.2d 1029 (3d Cir. 1973); *Carter* v. *Gallagher,* 452 F.2d 315 (8th Cir. 1972); *Morrow* v. *Crisler,* 491 F.2d 1053 (5th Cir. 1974). While the Supreme Court has not passed on the merits of this issue, it has declined to review a number of lower federal court quota-hiring decisions brought before it. There is at least an implication of constitutional approval in the consistent refusal to disturb these orders.

Several additional cases are mentioned in this chapter. The Norwalk, Conn., relocation decision is *Norwalk CORE* v. *Norwalk Redevelopment Agency,* 395 F.2d 920 (2d Cir. 1968). The Supreme Court's decision on school financing is *San Antonio Independent School District* v. *Rodriguez,* 411 U.S. 1 (1973); the welfare maximum grant case, which also applied the "rational basis" test of equal protection despite the presence of important human concerns, is *Dandridge* v. *Williams,* 397 U.S. 471 (1970). The recent decision involving the Bureau of Indian Affairs preference for Indians is *Morton* v. *Mancari,* 417 U.S. 535 (1974). The Japanese relocation case (one of a number during World War II) is *Hirabayashi* v. *United States,* 320 U.S. 81 (1943). The case involving residence restrictions on welfare is *Shapiro* v. *Thompson,* 394 U.S. 618 (1969). The decision upholding nonresident tuition differentials for state college and university students is *Vlandis* v. *Kline,* 412 U.S. 441 (1973).

In addition to the various articles cited earlier, such as those of Professors Ely and Posner, two earlier discussions should be noted. They are John Kaplan, "Equal Justice in an Unequal World," 61 *Northwestern University Law Review* 363 (1966); and Alfred Vieira, "Racial Imbalance, Black Separatism, and Permissible Classification by Race," 67 *Michigan Law Review* 1553 (1969).

Chapter 5

The cited work, one of the best in recent years on trends and problems in American higher education, is Christopher Jencks and David Riesman, *The Academic Revolution* (1969). For more specific comments on the extent of minority involvement in legal education and in the legal profession, reference is made to Ernest Gellhorn, "The Law Schools and the Negro," 1968 *Duke Law Journal* 1069, an early and seminal work on the whole question;

and to Walter Leonard, "The Development of the Black Bar," *Annals of the American Academy of Political and Social Science,* May 1973, pp. 134–143. There are various detailed studies of the status of blacks in the bars of particular states, e.g., "Negro Members of the Alabama Bar," 21 *Alabama Law Review* 306 (1969).

The comments of Mr. Justice Brennan were made at the dedication of the new Rutgers Law school building and are quoted in the brief amicus curiae of the Board of Governors of Rutgers in the *DeFunis* case, at p. 17. Lieutenant Governor Mondragon's eloquent statement about the need for lawyers from and of minority groups comes from his article in the *Student Lawyer,* Feb. 1973, pp. 41–44. The David Kirp–Mark Yudoff article appeared in *Change Magazine,* November 1974, pp. 22–26, under the title *"DeFunis* and Beyond." Dr. Kenneth Clark's comments about the value of ethnic studies for nonminority students appeared in the *New York Times,* May 23, 1969, p. 29. The perceptive comments of James A. McPherson about the experiences of a black law student at the Harvard Law School, shortly following his own graduation from that institution, appear in the *Atlantic Monthly,* April 1970, p. 98, under the title "The Black Law Student: A Problem of Fidelities."

There is much material concerning the fairness of standardized testing for minority applicants and students. See, for example, the comments of the then executive director of the Law School Admission Council, Charles Consalus, in "The Law School Admission Test and the Minority Student," 1970 *Toledo Law Review* 501. Later comments from a prominent member of the Council, Professor Walter Raushenbush, appear in the Newsletter of the AALS Section on Minority Groups, May 1974, p. 1. Two recent papers prepared for the Law School Admission Council shed additional light: Hunter Breland, *"DeFunis* Revisited: A Psychometric View," (1974); and Robert Linn, "Test Bias and the Prediction of Grades in Law School," (1974). For an earlier and more general study, see Alexander Astin, "Racial Considerations in Admissions," in *The Campus and the Racial Crisis,* (1970), p. 113. These references comprise only a small portion of the substantial and swelling literature on the fairness of standardized tests—a theme which is approached in the text from a lay point of view.

The two cases cited in this chapter are *Griggs* v. *Duke Power Co.,* 401 U.S. 424 (1971), holding that tests and other employment criteria which have a racially exclusionary effect must be proved to be job-related or may not be used; and *Berkelman* v. *San Francisco Unified School District,* 501 F.2d 1264 (9th Cir. 1974), striking down the two-tiered admission system at Lowell High School because of its discriminatory effect upon female students. There are numerous cases involving the dual higher education systems in the southern states, notably *Adams* v. *Richardson*, 351 F. Supp. 636 (D.D.C. 1972), which is still pending on the issue of the federal government's obligation to bring about a quicker end to the racially segregated postsecondary systems.

Chapter 6

On the subject of black colleges as a possible alternative to more vigorous integration efforts, see Frank Bowles and Frank DeCosta, *Between Two Worlds: A Profile of Negro Higher Education* (1971), a study prepared for the Carnegie Commission on Higher Education; and the controversial, less sympathetic, article by Christopher Jencks and David Riesman, "The American Negro College," 37 *Harvard Education Review* 3 (1967). The data concerning the preferences of black high school graduates in North Carolina are found in *New York Times*, December 31, 1973, p. 8, col. 1–3. (The tenor of the article is generally quite pessimistic, as evidenced by the title, "Future Dim for Black Colleges as Students and Funds Decline.")

Much has been written about the subject of open admissions in the City University of New York. A recent comprehensive survey of the effects is found in *New York Times*, June 7, 1974, p. 1, col. 2–3. Frequent stories and letters to the editor of the *New York Times* have kept the controversy very much alive there, although it has rather limited interest for the rest of the country.

The two cases discussed in the chapter involved the use of a general criterion of "disadvantage" as an alternative to or euphemism for race and ethnic status. One is *Ray Baillie Trash Hauling, Inc.* v. *Kleppe*, 477 F.2d 696 (5th Cir. 1973), upholding a heavy minority concentration in the award of contracts from the Small Business Association. The other case, which sustained the admissions policies of the Milwaukee Inner City Library Institute, is *Bergeron* v. *Board of Regents*, 363 F. Supp. 346 (E.D. Wis., 1973).

The initially successful use of alternative criteria for evaluation of New York City high school principals and supervisors is reported in *New York Times*, July 21, 1974, p. 52, col. 1.

Chapter 7

The most vigorous voice of opposition has been that of the Anti-Defamation League of B'nai B'rith, set forth in Benjamin Epstein and Arnold Forster, *Preferential Treatment and Quotas* (1974). Around the same time the Carnegie Commission published a study highly critical of affirmative action programs in higher education and, incidentally, of preferential admission policies. Richard Lester, *Antibias Regulation of Universities* (1974) deals critically with a number of issues and practices in this field. For another highly critical view from a conservative academic leader, see Sidney Hook's guest column, "A Quota Is a Quota is a Quota", *New York Times,* November 12, 1974, p. 39. The emergence of the Italian-American antipreferential groups is recounted in *New York Times,* June 28, 1974, p. 29, col. 1–6. For a general survey of such opposition from white ethnic groups, see "Reverse Discrimination Means . . . Scram, White Man," *National Observer,* July 13, 1974, p. 1, col. 1–2.

Even within the Jewish community, opinion is clearly not monolithic. The views of former Justice and Ambassador Goldberg are found in Nina Totenberg, "Discriminating to end Discrimination," *New York Times Magazine,* April 14, 1974, p. 9. The extremely important comments of John M. Lavine, a leader in the Anti-Defamation League and a University of Wisconsin regent, are contained in consecutive issues of the *Jewish Post,* May 31 and June 7, 1974. See also the sympathetic views of the National Jewish Community Relations Council, *New York Times,* June 30, 1974, p. 43, col. 3.

Several other critical comments are quoted in the chapter. Professor John Roche's trenchant observations appear in the *Chronicle of Higher Education,* April 20, 1970, p. 2, col. 1. Professor Thomas Sowell's critique appeared in an article, "Colleges Are Skipping Over Competent Blacks to Admit Authentic Ghetto Types," *New York Times Magazine,* December 13, 1970, p. 49. Dr. Kenneth Clark's warning against double standards as a result of preferential or special minority programs appeared in the *Chicago Tribune,* June 29, 1971.

Chapter 8

In the final chapter I mention several pending post-*DeFunis* cases; none has yet been reported. The case with which the chapter opens is *Stewart* v. *New York University,* 74 Civ. 4126, Southern District of New York, filed September 23, 1974. The case against the University of California (Davis) Medical School was decided by the Superior Court in March, 1975, and may go either to the intermediate appellate court or directly to the California Supreme Court. The plaintiff is one Alan Bakke. Also pending is a pair of cases brought against the City University of New York, challenging the admissions policies of the new biomedical program. One suit, speaking for Italian-American groups, is *Scognamilio* v. *Board of Higher Education,* 75 Civ. 178, Southern District of New York. The other case has the backing of the Anti-Defamation League and involves a Jewish applicant; it is *Hupart* v. *Board of Higher Education,* pending in the Eastern District (Brooklyn). Several other cases of similar sort appear to be pending in other states, although there is no central roster of litigation on this issue.

INDEX